Green Ink

Green

AN INTRODUCTION

TO ENVIRONMENTAL

JOURNALISM

Ink

BY MICHAEL FROME

UNIVERSITY OF UTAH PRESS
SALT LAKE CITY

Printed on acid-free paper

5   4   3   2   1
2001   2000   1999   1998

Designed by Linda Mae Tratechaud, LiMiTeD Edition Book Design

Library of Congress Cataloging-in-Publication Data

Frome, Michael.
    Green ink : an introduction to environmental journalism / by
Michael Frome.
        p.   cm.
    Includes bibliographical references.
    ISBN 0-87480-582-1 (alk. paper)
    1. Environmental protection—Press coverage.   I. Title
PN4888.E65F76   1998
070.4'493637—dc21   98-38062

To the memory of Gary Gray,
Student, friend, and a good companion on the trail

Contents

Preface

As a journalist and teacher of journalism, I believe in thorough investigation, analysis, documentation, and a strong conclusion clearly expressed. I do teach a different kind of journalism, advocacy journalism in behalf of the environment, yet hewing to basic principles of literacy, accuracy, fairness, and meeting the deadline. I ask students to heed the words of the late Rachel Carson: "Do your homework. Speak good English. And care a lot." That is what it takes, and what it is about.

Advocacy is a word we have been taught to avoid. It marks a bias, something most journalists are convinced should not be acknowledged, despite the fact that it is inescapable. But my point is that we ought to be advocates for the health and safety of the planet, professionally and personally concerned with global warming, acid rain, destruction of tropical and temperate forests, loss of wilderness and wildlife, toxic wastes, pollution of air and water, and population pressures that degrade the quality of life.

It will be helpful at the outset to face and resolve the question of "objectivity." In 1988, one year after coming to Western Washington University, I received a grant to consult various experts on how best to structure a program of study in environmental journalism. I recall a particularly choice interview with Ben Bagdikian, who had retired as dean of the graduate journalism program at the University of California, Berkeley, and is probably best known as author of *The Media Monopoly,* one of the great journalism books of our time. He said it well: "Objectivity is in the eye of the beholder. Every journalist must decide personally what's important and less important to humanity. In making these choices, you're selective, no longer objective. Journalists who don't think they do that are fooling themselves." Or as George Laycock, who has written many books and articles about the outdoors and the environment, told me in 1998, "If there is such an animal [as writing with objectivity], the result can only be dull writing."[1]

I define environmental journalism as writing with a purpose, designed to present the public with sound, accurate data as the basis of informed participation in the process of decision making on environmental issues. It requires an understanding of the nature and purpose of mass communication, an ability to research and to report findings with accuracy, and a love of language that facilitates expression with clarity. It requires more than learning "how to write," but learning the power of emotion and imagery, to think not simply of Who, What, When, Where, and Why—but to think Whole, with breadth and perspective.

"Journalism," Joseph Pulitzer declared in 1902 (when he announced his plan to underwrite a school of journalism at Columbia University), "is, or ought to be, one of the great and intellectual professions." I love journalism as a great and intellectual profession, affording a sense of self and opportunity for self-expression in helping to shape society's view of community and the natural world.

That is not the way it works in "mainstream" or "conventional" journalism. As practiced by most dailies and other outlets, established journalism continues to suffer under the delusion that objectivity is being maintained. Not only is this a sham, but it does not promote as much digging into contrary views as the alternative of advocacy. Digging deep on both sides and using the strongest reasoning employed by each party is crucial to both the truth of the story and the drama therein. Objectivity, the genuine article at its best, is a means of gathering information, a foundation of reality that justifies feeling.

The level to which television and so many papers, daily and otherwise, have sunk is disgraceful. I offer this article on the front page of the *Miami Herald* that opens as follows:

> It's not enough to be one of the premier shopping malls in the country and the second-largest tourist destination in Florida.
>
> Sawgrass Mills broke ground Wednesday on a $30 million expansion that will make it a destination for evening revelers as well as shoppers. The move is in keeping with trends in the retail industry that combine shopping and entertainment at one location.
>
> The 300,000-square-foot expansion will bring to Sawgrass an Everglades-oriented wildlife theme park and the first South Florida outpost for the Wolfgang Puck Cafe. Steven Spielberg's Game-Works will also open a high-tech video arcade and Regal Cinemas will expand its existing movie theater from 18 screens to 24, including some theaters with stadium seating.[2]

That article could easily have been written by the head of public relations of Sawgrass Mills, conveniently ignoring the degradation and uglification of Florida's natural environment by mall developments like

Sawgrass Mills catering to unrestrained population growth. The mall is imaged as the destination in itself, its "Everglades-oriented theme park" a contrived substitute for the real and endangered Everglades.[3]

Then, in the same edition, "Wheels and Waves" covers sixteen pages, mostly of retail automotive advertising. The first page of the section provides the editorial sizzle for the advertising sell. In the main story, about the "the auto world's show of shows," the hot news is about the new Volkswagen Beetle: "When the car starts arriving in U.S. showrooms from the VW factory in Mexico, there will be a buying frenzy. . . ." And another article reports that "Ford's popular F-series full-size pickup truck celebrated its 50th birthday by claiming the title of best-selling vehicle in America for the 16th year in a row."

Elsewhere in the *Herald* of the same day, columnist Carl Hiaasen notes that around Miami "pretty much everything and everybody has been up for sale at one time or another." He was referring to votes-for-cash in the latest election, but he might have had his own newspaper in mind as well.

Journalists want to do better. They want to practice their profession and be proud of it. James L. Aucoin in his doctoral dissertation, completed at the University of Missouri School of Journalism in 1993, reviewed the history of investigative journalism and of the organization of Investigative Reporters and Editors (IRE). In a book based on his Ph.D. studies, Aucoin wrote that IRE was founded in 1978 because many editors and reporters saw investigative reporting as a responsibility. They wanted to investigate and expose corruption and misuse of power, and felt pressed to do more after the murder of investigative reporter Don Bolles of Phoenix, Arizona, who was tracking political slush funds, bribery, and land fraud. Aucoin discovered, however, that "the institutions supporting investigative journalism—newspapers, magazines, book publishers, and broadcast news divisions—are always susceptible to the pressures of profits. Hence, unlike the practice itself, they cannot be depended on to maintain, nurture, and expand the practice [of investigative reporting]. . . . Substantial pressures are applied by management for cost-effective results and to hold an audience that is all-too-often attracted by sensationalism than by serious, solid reporting."[4]

Yes, verily, the pressures for profits and for cost-effective results override the desire of journalists for professional fulfillment. This point is further substantiated in the headline and excerpt from an article in the *Eugene (Oreg.) Register-Guard* summing up the purchase of eight Oregon newspapers (dailies, weeklies, and shoppers) by Lee Enterprises for a reported $185 million. The article was written by Jackman Wilson, associate editor of the *Register-Guard,* formerly of Lee's *Corvallis (Oreg.) Gazette-Times,* where, he explained, he had enrolled in the employee stock-purchase plan and in twelve years turned a $520 investment into stock worth $2700:

> "Chain Papers' Mission: Profits"
>
> "Lee Enterprises Won't Meddle Much with Its New Oregon Newspapers—So Long as They Make Money"

> Lee Enterprises prints news as a means to an end—making money—rather than as a worthwhile endeavor in its own right. The company exists above all to serve shareholders like me, and service to the communities in which its "franchises" are located is provided with that goal constantly in mind. The stockholders get the better of this arrangement, at the expense of readers and employees.[5]

In the quarterly *Treasure State Review,* the publisher and editor, Nathaniel Blumberg, former dean of the University of Montana School of Journalism, warned that publishers untrained in journalism "regard their newsroom employees as little more than cogs in a money machine." Blumberg wrote that publishers make no effort to hide their antilabor biases, help to promote the political agenda of corporations extracting profit at the expense of the environment, and, by limiting investigative reporting, "keep the public from getting too aroused by what is going on behind closed doors."[6]

Advocacy journalism is open, honest journalism, without closed doors. It serves the interest of God-given nature and humanity rather than of those who exploit and profit from them. It centers on the integrity and creativity of the writer.

In the *Planet,* the student environmental quarterly at Western Washington University, the editors wrote: "Environmental journalism students have listened to their instructor (and *Planet* advisor), Michael Frome, talk about interviewing long enough to decide to turn the tables and interview him." They asked first about interviews I had conducted.

P. In class you've emphasized preparation—

F. Correct; if you go in cold, you'll come out with a pretty poor story, at best what the subject of the interview wants you to have. The more you know in advance, the more you'll learn. That's what environmental journalism is all about.

P. Exactly how do you mean?

F. In our free society the role of the media should be to provide Americans with sound data as the basis of intelligent decision-making. The 1990s clearly present a decade of decision-making in the field of the environment. Yet news people report superficially, scratching the surface. Tragedies like Valdez, Chernobyl, Bhopal, Love Canal, and Three Mile Island are covered as "stories" for the morning edition or the nightly newscast by reporters with little background. Consequently the public is poorly served.

Few newspeople dig through files or penetrate the doublespeak of politicians and polluters. But the public needs to understand the ramifications of a degraded environment and the options for coping with it. Environmental journalists can and will make the difference. . . .

P. What have you learned as a writer turned to teacher?

F. Two points come to mind. First, I'm still working to be patient—to keep standards high, but allow students time and space to learn and develop. Second, and maybe more important, students with whom I come in contact are caring and sharing people, who want to give to society more than they take from it.

P. Any last words for the interview?

F. Tell it like it is, without fear or favor.[7]

Acknowledgments

I HAVE PROBABLY BEEN preparing to write this book for most of my life, but the idea to go ahead and do it came from my wife, June Eastvold, whom I married in Seattle on December 31, 1994. On several occasions before and after that date she said to me, "When people ask what my husband does and I tell them, they say: 'Environmental journalism? What is it?' You should write a book that explains it."

That was the beginning, thanks to June. In addition, I have had invaluable help from many people, principally friends and colleagues who have given input from their own experience and reviewed and critiqued drafts of the manuscript. Among journalists and authors, I include Knute Berger, editor of *Seattle Weekly;* Jim Fisher, editorial writer and columnist at the *Lewiston (Idaho) Morning Tribune;* Margaret Foster, editor-in-chief of The Mountaineers; David Helvarg, author of *The War against the Greens;* George Laycock, author of many books and articles on the outdoors and the environment; Ben Long, reporter and columnist at the *Kalispell (Mont.) Daily Interlake;* Gregory McNamee, author and former editor-in-chief of the University of Arizona Press; Richard Manning, author of *The Last Stand;* Karen Anspacher Meyer, partner and producer at Green Fire Productions; John Mitchell, senior assistant editor of the *National Geographic Magazine;* Dan Oko, editor of the *Missoula (Mont.) Independent;* Philip Shabecoff, author and former environmental reporter of the *New York Times;* Steve Stuebner, author and former environmental reporter of the *Boise (Idaho) Statesman;* Patricia Tummons, editor of "Environment Hawaii"; Tom Turner, editor at the EarthJustice Legal Defense Fund; and Ted Williams, editor-at-large of *Audubon* and conservation editor of *Fly Rod and Reel.*

I am indebted to these friends in education: James R. Fazio, of the University of Idaho; Michael Kirkhorn, Gonzaga University; T. H. Watkins, Montana State University; Carl Reidel, University of Vermont; and W. Scott Olsen of Concordia College and SueEllen Campbell of Colorado State University, both of whom reviewed the manuscript for the University of Utah Press. At this point I express particular thanks to Dawn Marano, acquisitions editor of the University of Utah Press, for her considerable and constructive involvement, far beyond what most editors do anymore; and Jeffrey L. Grathwohl, director of the press; plus all their colleagues in the offices at Salt Lake City. Former students now making their way in the world of communications have helped with this work: Scott Brennan, Traci Edge, Lisa Friend (with both her critique and her indexing), Richard Navas, Sara Olason Noland, Neils Nokkendtved, and DeAnna Woolston.

I appreciate also the review and input of Brock Evans, director of the Endangered Species Coalition, and his wife, Linda Garcia; Denis Hayes, president of the Bullitt Foundation; Mitch Friedman, executive director of the Northwest Ecoystem Alliance; Audrie Krause, executive director of NetAction; Ted Pankowski, former executive director of the Washington Environmental Council; and Mack Prichard, state naturalist of Tennessee.

Part I

A Calling of Conscience and Advocacy

Facing the Downside in the Media's Message

DAILY NEWSPAPERS AROUND THE COUNTRY have been going out of business, or merging, or "downsizing," which means keeping the profits high by reducing staff to the barest minimum, and cheating the reader with a second-rate or third-rate product. I read a speech by the managing editor of the *New York Times,* Gene Roberts, delivered early in 1996 at the University of California, Riverside. He was critical of his own industry, calculating that 75 percent of America's 1,548 dailies were controlled by a handful of corporate chains, which, said Roberts, have mandated increasingly shallow and niggardly coverage, "managing their newspapers like chain shoe stores," without any sense of community responsibility.

I am not so sure about the *New York Times* either. In 1990 it dumped its veteran environmental correspondent, Philip Shabecoff, a pacesetter in his profession, widely respected and admired, because it considered him biased, "too close to environmentalists," only to send forth a replacement plainly motivated by antienvironmental bias. It was not a convincing case of community responsibility.[1]

More recently, *EXTRA!* (the magazine of Fairness and Accuracy in Reporting, or FAIR)[2] featured an article titled "Clean-Up Job—The *New York Times* Glosses over Hudson River's Toxic Problem," charging that the *Times* had "greenwashed" the Hudson River, "removing the toxic legacy left by decades of General Electric's using the river as a dump for poisonous waste."[3]

In two lengthy front-page articles, the *Times* reported ecological gains in the 315-mile Hudson River, which runs past New York City into the

Atlantic Ocean. The Hudson, lifeless a quarter century ago, plainly is considerably cleaner. State and federal laws have reduced dumping raw sewage and industrial chemicals, so now people can swim and the fish have come back.

The series examined the gains. Both installments jumped from the front page to extensive "spreads" across two interior facing pages with maps, photos, and related pieces, or "sidebars." The first article, headlined "Shaking Off Man's Taint, Hudson Pulses with Life," was accompanied by a front-page photo of a fisherman happily holding up his catch, a striped bass caught near 125th Street, "one of many signs that efforts to clean up the Hudson are finally bearing fruit." The second article, headlined "Life's Hubbub Returns to Oft-Shunned Hudson," focused on growing recreational use.[4]

But Jim Gordon, the author of the article in *EXTRA!* noted that the *Times* pieces never mentioned that, due to heavy contamination from polychlorinated biphenyls, or PCBs, the entire Hudson River below Albany is a federal Superfund site. "Unpleasant facts about PCBs—and about GE's role in polluting the river—are either glossed over or entirely ignored," wrote Gordon.[5]

A sidebar headlined "Years After a Plant Closed, Its Chemical Stain Lingers" mentioned the GE plant at Hudson Falls, from which much of the PCBs—persistent carcinogenic chemicals that rise through the food chain—were dumped into the Hudson for decades. However, it did not give figures on how much was dumped (estimated between 500,000 and 1.5 million pounds) or make clear that PCBs can still be found along the river bottom reaching New York Harbor and into the Atlantic Ocean. There was not much about it until the seventeenth paragraph with the first mention of PCBs: "These are the chemicals that make eating more than an occasional striped bass unwise."[6] Better yet, throw that bass back!

Yes, able reporters and editors have done great work for the environment, but nowhere near enough to be representative. Yes, many editors and writers are well informed and disciplined to ideas of professional ethics about evidence, balance, truthfulness, and the public's right to know. They try to be fair, but the odds are against them, and against the environment getting a fair shake, in the mainstream, for-profit media, as we now know them.

For one thing, media personnel work from their own limited backgrounds on tight deadlines—daily for newspapers, maybe hourly for TV or radio—that prohibit thorough research and reflection. They deal with tight space in print and tight time on the air: a reporter is lucky to get anything more than the average 1:40 minutes on a television newscast.

At a conference on Northwest Media and the Environment, in 1994, Dan Evans, former governor and former senator, made this point regarding the timber controversy in the region:

> Most of us recognize the spotted owl as merely an indicator species for something fundamentally broader, the forest ecosystem. But the focus has been virtually entirely on the owl, its fate and future. I'm amazed that intelligent environmental reporters failed to alert the public early on that the forest ecosystem was the basic issue of concern. Recent reports find more and more spotted owls in second growth in northern California. If that happens in this part of the country, what then? We'll find another indicator species. Because it isn't the spotted owl alone, but the forest that counts, hopefully reporters will get it right the second time and will focus correctly on the forest, rather than on owls, or any single species.[7]

Evans also said that "every journalist reporting environmental affairs at least ought to be able to read *Scientific American* without moving his or her lips." But the media in the Northwest focused on the forest crisis in shallow terms of "owls versus jobs" and contributed more to public misunderstanding than to clarity. In 1990 the headline over an Associated Press report read: "Survey: Owl Set-Asides May Claim 48,000 Timber, 63,000 Related Jobs." The ensuing article charged that the total was more than 110,000 jobs, an economic catastrophe for the Northwest, if it were so. The text of the article made plain that the survey was conducted by a regional accounting firm in the hire of the timber industry. Nevertheless, it was dispatched by the supposedly trustworthy, unbiased, objective Associated Press and therefore assumed to be accurate. But the public would be better informed if the Associated Press had conducted its own survey, with figures it was prepared to defend.[8]

Denis Hayes, president of the Bullitt Foundation in Seattle, a longtime environmental leader, who began his career as a student activist in the first Earth Day in 1970, offers this thoughtful critique:

> Modern editing seems obsessed with getting "balance" and accurate quotations. But it doesn't help to quote someone accurately if he or she is lying. Balancing quotations doesn't help at all. If the

same Associated Press article had quoted the Sierra Club or Audubon to the effect that "Owl set-asides will create more jobs than they destroy," that wouldn't help distill the truth. Two lies are no better than one.

In this case, there was no way in 1990 to know how many jobs would be lost. Even years later, there is still no way to count how many jobs actually have been lost. There is a place for reasonable calculations, based on clear fact and explicit assumption, but the media ought to distinguish these from baseless propaganda.

A better example would be more fact-based. The charge that forest companies have stolen large quantities of logs from national forests is verifiable, but every story merely quotes the Association of Forest Service Employees for Environmental Ethics (AFSEE), Weyerhaeuser and the Forest Service disagreeing with one another. I don't need a newspaper for that; I can guess what all three will say and be right ninety-nine percent of the time. I want to know what's true. I want the reporter to drive out to the national forest, photograph the stumps, read and review the sales record, and be prepared to vouch for the thoroughness of his or her research.

When a journalist writes a story that purports to report on facts, he or she should prepare to vouch for the accuracy of the facts—not merely the accuracy of quotations alleging facts. Better do more reporting before rushing to print.[9]

Unfortunately they do not do more, or better, reporting. But, of course, the mission of the mass media collectively is not public service. The "bottom line," of profit over loss, counts most, making it difficult for any periodical or radio or television station to restrict itself to either dispassionate or in-depth reporting.

Advertising pays the bills. Advertising powers the media engines, determining the number of pages in the newspaper, the extent of color pages in the magazine, the character and quality of television and radio, the dividends to investors, and the salaries of publishers and broadcasters. With daily papers, circulation also pays the bills—at least to the extent that it brings in the advertising. But fear of losing readers cripples journalistic creativity and daring.

In one-newspaper cities, steadily increasing in number across America, monopoly allows the media to cover as much or as little of the news, in whatever depth it chooses.[10] Without competition there is more profit in fewer employees covering less of the news.

Many articles are based on press releases—many *are* press releases verbatim. "We can't check on everything," local editors will say in their defense; or, "I admit we're spread thin." In 1970, Samuel Day wrote in the *Intermountain Observer:* "To say that Idahoans are on the whole rather poorly served by the press—which means radio and television as well as daily and weekly newspapers—is to put it mildly." One sad aspect, he continued, was that most of the news media in Idaho does not even bother to cover the meetings of major state boards, including those concerned with natural resources. They are under the impression the job is being done for them; but this is an illusion, for the wire-service reports on which they rely are based mostly on material prepared by publicity men of the agencies themselves, reflecting the official point of view. "The inadequacy of news coverage in Idaho actually goes deeper than that," Day wrote. "Too often the reporter goes no further than official news sources, or sources where the news has been packaged neatly for him."[11]

Inadequacy of coverage has not changed from that time. It prevails in larger and many more places than Idaho. Public relations, promoting the interests of those who can afford it, has become more a source of news than the public itself. Government and industry spin doctors flood the media with press releases, briefings, background papers, leaks, and staged events. Outsiders and poor people rarely make the news or talk shows on radio and television. In an article called "The Fame Game," Joshua Wolf Shenk wrote that talk shows thrive by rotating stars eager to promote their latest projects: "Dozens of magazines are filled with celebrity profiles, in which the terms of the deal are either carefully negotiated or underlined by an unspoken deal: 'We'll assign our best writers to tease, flatter, and aggrandize you.' "[12]

In 1980 the *Columbia Journalism Review (CJR)* did a critical review of the *Wall Street Journal.* The *CJR* found a full-page ad the *Journal* had bought in the *New York Times,* proclaiming, "We enter the Eighties determined to improve and expand the *Journal's* news coverage and space." Improve and expand from what? The *CJR* examined the front page of the *Journal* and turned through the inside pages: many articles read like rewritten press releases. Were they? The *CJR* checked with companies referred to in 111 of the articles. Seventy firms responded to the query. In 53 cases—or 72 percent of responses—news stories were based solely on press releases. In 32 cases, the releases were printed almost verbatim or in paraphrase, while in 21 other cases, only perfunctory additional reporting was evident. Most troublesome, 20 stories (29 percent) carried the slug "By a *Wall Street Journal* Reporter." Based on survey returns, the *CJR* estimated that 45 percent of the day's 188 news items were based on press releases.[13]

The best journalism carries authority and a sense of purpose. Literate writing, advocacy writing, contributes to a view of the world that is more rather than less complicated. Most journalism, the mainstream variety, however, focuses on events, "stories," actual happenings, "photo ops," black-and-white conflict, with scant treatment of meaning, cause, or solution. I do not mean only in reference to the environment. Linda Fairstein, chief of the Sex Crimes Prosecution Unit in the district attorney's office of New York County (and author of the novels *Final Jeopardy* and *Likely to Die*), vents her own complaints:

> There's very little effort at either understanding or explaining to the public the different issues in, for example, stranger rape and acquaintance rape—that more than 70 percent of people who report rapes have been sexually assaulted by someone known to them, whether or not these cases are difficult to prosecute, whether or not victims are supported by the legal and medical communities and mental health communities, what resources are available, what the likely outcome is.
>
> A lot of the issues involved in these trials, cases and investigations have not been reported or even understood by reporters, who tend to focus on aspects that make headlines. The overwhelming coverage that the public sees is tabloid coverage, which still tends to sensationalize and emphasize the tawdrier side of the cases.[14]

In August 1996, while President Clinton was politicking around the country for reelection, he generated a story from Yellowstone National Park that covered over his mixed and mushy environmental record and made him a hero in nearly every paper and on nearly every broadcast. It concerned a deal with Noranda, a Canadian-based mining company that agreed to abandon plans to reopen an old gold and silver mine just outside the Yellowstone Park boundary in return for $65 million in federal property elsewhere. Noranda agreed to spend a third of the amount to clean up existing pollution at the site. The president announced the deal to the coterie of reporters covering the campaign, presenting himself as the savior of Yellowstone and all that it symbolizes.

The trouble was that the news reports omitted one key fact. Negotiations that led to the deal were the result of a Clean Water Act lawsuit brought by environmental organizations. In fact, a federal judge had found Noranda liable for thousands of violations of the law, and penalties could have run as high as $135 million. The company decided it would rather deal than fight. That part of it was unreported except by *High Country News* and the publications of environmental groups.

Toxic waste, polluted beaches, Earth Day, oil spills, and forest fires may make the nightly news, but for the most part ecological disturbances are poorly reported, while poisons in the soil and water, vanishing open space, disappearance of species, and overpopulation are simply not sufficiently dramatic to make much of a story.

Media accounts of the Exxon oil spill in 1989, for example, underplayed long-term damage; few reporters went after lax government shipping regulations or Exxon's cost cutting. I interviewed Joseph L. Sax, a well-known professor of environmental law at the University of Michigan and later at the University of California, Berkeley, who made this observation: "Writers showed no background, no history, no awareness of the setting. As a result, media coverage was extremely poor and the public ill-served. My sense, as a consumer of journalism, is that most journalists are at a disadvantage when required to cover something they know little about. I would spend six months researching a subject on which they would spend two hours, or two days. If they can't bring some appreciation, or background, they become victims of people who say the most flamboyant, self-serving things."[15]

Dan Sholley, the chief ranger of Yellowstone National Park, in his book *Guardians of Yellowstone* decried the coverage of the 1988 Yellowstone fires, when the park was invaded by "headline-hungry journalists who came in droves and demanded answers to mindless questions and then sped away to cover in six inches of print, or one minute of television a subject that had taken a whole day to explain properly."[16]

Officials and technical experts almost always feel that way about the media, fairly or unfairly. Television reporters at Yellowstone consistently asked one question: "Where can I find reliable flames?" Television and print reporters used loaded words and phrases, such as "acres destroyed" and "acres consumed." Yellowstone National Park was "the disaster," reduced to ashes, although scientific studies have shown that periodic fire is virtually inevitable, and ecologically beneficial.

Conrad Smith, then a journalism professor at Ohio State University (before moving to the University of Wyoming), conducted a systematic study of media treatment of the fires that started in June and early July 1988 and then of new fires in the ensuing dry weather and high winds of August and early September, burning through as much as 160,000 acres of vegetation in a single day.

Smith examined hundreds of newspaper stories and videos of television coverage and interviewed many participants. He found that while three major fires started outside the park and burned into it, news accounts generally treated all fires as though they had started in the park under the jurisdiction of Yellowstone fire managers. He defined and tested a basic premise: that by simplifying complex issues and focusing on dramatic images, network-television reporters misrepresented the effects of the fires, distorted the issues, and omitted important information needed by viewers to make their own intelligent judgment. He quoted Roger O'Neill, Denver bureau chief of NBC, that mistakes in coverage were due in some degree to "a mostly inept public information system," but that the network's desire to "have the best stuff on the air . . . is a constant in the back of any national reporter's mind. . . . Please don't take this out of context, but let's face it, even television at the network level has, to my chagrin, become 'entertainment-ized.' " Smith concluded, "As with other stories about natural catastrophes, the networks covered the 1988 Yellowstone fires in a stylized and stereotyped way: as fables about brave firefighters, powerful natural forces, bumbling bureaucrats, and anthropomorphized fires and forest creatures, all represented in symbolized terms by Old Faithful as a national icon and by fire as a largely evil threat to Yellowstone as a natural wonder. The findings here reinforce other studies suggesting the media do a better job of describing events than interpreting them, and that news accounts are social constructs rather than objective accounts of reality."[17]

The media want life, whether battle, war, forest fire, or bombing of a federal building, to conform to "the story." Harmony is boring: there is no story in it. When reporters cover environmental issues, they go mostly to accepted authorities and official sources, accessible and respectable. The independent-minded, irreverent reporter who digs through files and interviews dissenters is apt to pay the price of a complaint to the editor for that unforgivable sin, "losing objectivity." Consequently, the modern media, comprising the one institution of society presumed to watchdog all the others and keep them honest, are themselves disempowering, of their own talented journalists as well as their audiences.

All across America media executives attend businessmen's luncheons and serve on booster committees of Rotary clubs and chambers of commerce with their fellow pillars of the community. Real estate and land-zoning scams and toxic dumping may be widespread, and environmental crimes every bit as serious as armed robberies and drug deals, but newspapers and local radio and television that expose them are few and far between.

In Memphis, Tennessee, citizens in the late 1960s into the 1970s faced a challenge to protect Overton Park, one of the finest urban forests in the world, from an interstate highway aimed through the heart of the park. Because federal highway funds were involved, their heroic effort ultimately was debated before Congress and the Supreme Court. In their own city, however, the media chose to ridicule or at best ignore the citizens. The editors of *Architecture Memphis*, published by the Memphis chapter of the American Institute of Architects, reviewed the case in 1970:

> Why is it that Overton Park, an acknowledged civic treasure, is about to be despoiled by the legalized vandalism of the highway-man? The answer is complex, but in part it is the hope of pumping dollars into a moribund downtown that has created an establishment hysteria eager to damn the park and build the expressway.
>
> At the forefront of this drive for self-destruction, anxious to protect the advertising revenues derived from downtown mercantile sources, is the Scripps-Howard controlled news media. Scripps-Howard in Memphis, with its two newspapers, and a radio and television station, has effectively censored and blacked out the pro-conservation sentiment that exists in the community. It has aligned itself with regressive political leadership to stifle and ridicule those who would protect our natural heritage. It has painted the cause of preservation as a hopeless waste of time, and the leaders of Citizens to Preserve Overton Park as anti-progress, bleeding hearted do-gooders.
>
> The result is that the bulldozers are at the gates of the park and the earth moving machines are waiting to cut a swath of destruction through the virgin forest. Memphis has been told by the *Press*

Scimitar that "the loss is nothing as bad as it's been painted. Some large trees will be felled, but mostly the areas to be used for the expressway bear scrubby trees and bushes." To this we can only ask, what happened to the ideals of the late Edward J. Meeman [pioneering conservationist in the Scripps-Howard chain]?[18]

Fortunately, the citizens prevailed. Overton Park has remained secure. Ironically, the *Memphis Press Scimitar,* however, has disappeared into oblivion.

With an overpowering mission in mass marketing, the mainstream media spread the gospel of a consumer society, supported by economics of infinite growth. Television has become our primary window on the world, the central nervous system of modern society. The average person watches twenty-five thousand commercials a year, but commercials do more than push particular products: they promote values and lifestyles that surround consumption of the product. Television distorts reality. It keeps people indoors, validates noise over quiet, entertainment over dialogue. Pornography, violence, gossip, and trivia are common denominators on network television. Most of it, whether comedy, drama, or documentary, is mediocre and mind numbing. Sometimes I wonder about the writers and what they really wanted to do at the start of their careers.

The main purpose of television is neither to educate—if it were there would be no need for educational television—nor to stimulate consumer concern, but to sell automobiles, detergents, beer, and deodorants, superfluities that mark an overconsumptive, wasteful age. Newscasters are like actors, lighting up the sizzle in advance of the sell. The few shows of value, truly enlightening and entertaining, would not exist without public broadcast. If the private sector were interested in high-quality programs, it could easily have produced or outbid public broadcasting for any of them. But the emphasis is on creating an environment conducive to selling the products of corporate advertisers.

In the field of motion pictures, blockbusters with overpowering technology have become the moviemakers' goal. Following the spectacular success of *Star Wars* and like films early in the 1980s, producers have focused on big names, big budgets, big action, and dazzling disasters like *Titanic.* A film seems to be judged on how much money it grosses, not the quality of its art, with little room for meaningful environmental stories such as *The China Syndrome, The Milagro Beanfields War,* and *Never Cry*

Wolf. Fantasies connect to the twenty-first century or beyond with super-technology and violence, but not to the heart.

Automobile manufacturers and their dealers love the world of illusion. They want reports about the economy, car safety, pollution, anything bearing on automobiles to be upbeat; they and other advertisers do not want to support media transmitting editorial messages contrary to their own interests.[19] The *Wall Street Journal* in a front-page story by G. Bruce Knecht described how major advertisers, including Chrysler, Ford, Ameritech, and Bell South, demand warnings about controversial articles and the option of removing advertising from offensive issues. Knecht cited a letter sent to publishers by Chrysler's advertising agency, requiring that the company "be alerted in advance of any and all editorial content that encompasses sexual, political, or social issues or any editorial that might be construed as provocative or offensive." This stirred the American Society of Magazine Editors to issue a statement of concern, but editors know too well who pays the bills. In a follow-up article, the *Journal* quoted various distraught editors, but gave the last word to a Chrysler spokesman, who said, "We don't try to influence editorial content, but we don't want our ads in places where they polarize our customers by suggesting that we have a stance on some kind of issue."[20]

Perhaps the worst of it is that a handful of mammoth private organizations (such as Disney, Gannett, Time Warner, Bertelsmann, Rupert Murdoch, Hachette, and Viacom) dominate the mass media. They control information and entertainment that define social and cultural attitudes. They shape the public images of political leaders and political debate. Ben Bagdikian in *The Media Monopoly* gives fair warning: "Each year it is more likely that the American citizen who turns to any medium—newspapers, magazines, radio or television, books, movies, cable, recordings, video cassettes—will receive information, ideas, or entertainment controlled by the same handful of corporations, whether it is daily news, a cable entertainment program, or a textbook."[21]

Nor does this go for only the American reader or viewer. *Top Fifty European Media Owners 1996*, published by Zenith Media of London, shows that the long arms of Reed Elsevier, Europe's giant among giants, stretch from conventional paper and new electronic-information publications for scientific, medical, business, and professional worlds to twenty-eight of the United Kingdom's top one hundred consumer magazines. Bertelsmann, which started as a publisher of serious books in Germany, has grown into the world's leading book-club operator; it owns imprints in the United States and much of the world's music business. A subsidiary, Gruner and Jahr, publishes forty magazines in Germany and forty in other countries.

The global media system is dominated by a first tier of nine giant firms. The five largest, in order of 1997 sales, are Time Warner ($24 billion); Disney ($22 billion); Bertelsmann ($15 billion); Viacom ($13 billion); and News Corporation (Rupert Murdoch, $11 billion). Each is integrated to encompass film, books, magazines, newspapers, television, music, retail stores, big-league sports teams, and amusement parks. The second four are TCI, General Electric, Sony, and Seagram.[22] Book publishers absorb one another and then are swallowed by bigger businesses. For example, Macmillan, Prentice Hall, and Scribners, once substantial in their own right, are mere subsidiaries of Simon & Schuster, which, along with Paramount Pictures and Blockbuster Video, is owned and controlled by Viacom. And in 1998 Bertelsmann stunned the publishing world when it announced plans to buy Random House and merge it with Bantam Doubleday Dell, creating a publishing giant controlling more than thirty-six percent of the U.S. adult trade book market.

There is an argument that the profusion of cable and specialty services provide better programming, but these new services are mostly owned by the same entertainment conglomerates that already control 95 percent of the world's news gathering, current affairs, entertainment, and publishing interests. An entirely different system is taking shape via the Internet, where the big players in the media are planning to feed on big pieces of a bigger pie.

CHAPTER 2

On the Upside, the Positive "Power of the Press"

ON JANUARY 7, 1996, four hundred reporters waited in the cold rain at the Newport, Oregon, airport, for the arrival of a film celebrity, "Keiko," the whale whose plight in captivity was illuminated by the film *Free Willy*. Keiko was first captured near Iceland in 1979, but had lived most of his life at the El Reino amusement park in Mexico City. Now a Hercules C-130 cargo plane, donated for the trip by United Parcel Service, brought the world-famous whale north. Thousands lined the streets, and businesses displayed large "Welcome Keiko" signs. But David C. Phillips, executive director of Earth Island Institute and the Free Willy Foundation, said: "Keiko has become a symbol for the plight of whales and dolphins around the world. We hope [his rehabilitation] will lead to the day when all marine mammals are free from all human exploitation."

Keiko became a world symbol for whales and dolphins because of the 1993 film. That is understandable, since performers make movies into hits and movies make performers into stars. Television, radio, newspapers, magazines, books, the big screen of theater, and the small computer screen hooked into the Internet make that much difference. They, the collective media, provide the public an image of the world, shape public attitudes and actions, and play a large role in how people perceive others as well as themselves. The media can do terrible things and often do, exalting crime, violence, supersexuality, and consumerism, but they can also be incredibly beneficial, making people whale conscious, for instance.

Or bat conscious, free of fright and fear. Consider this from the journal *BATS*, published by Bat Conservation International (BCI): "Perhaps more than any other means, the news media has played a key role in the success of bat conservation and BCI. Today, many people learn for the first time about the importance of bats and the critical need for their conservation through positive articles in magazines and newspapers and from television or radio programs."[1]

It was not always this way. Before BCI was founded, the climate was hostile to bats. Frightening stories about homes "infested" with bats in respectable magazines like *Good Housekeeping* ("Three Years of Terror—A Real Life Ordeal") and *Family Circle* ("The Nightmare House") fanned fear and hate. Austin, Texas, newspaper headlines on the spring return of the city's numerous bats read "Bat Colonies Sink Teeth into City" and "Mass Fear in the Air as Bats Invade Austin."

In BCI's early years the idea of such an organization intrigued editors, and they wanted articles about it. Then serious articles followed. Instead of snarling bats with bared teeth, photos showed the ill-understood creatures in their natural habitat, looking curious, anything but ferocious. Negative stories still appear, but appreciation has grown. When Ann Landers in 1990 ran negative comments about bats, she was flooded with complaints and vowed never to mention bats again.[2]

The media, a plural word for a pluralistic network of words, pictures, and sounds, cover the gamut of communications, right wing to left wing, mass, mainstream, corporate-conglomerate, global, local, traditional, alternative, interactive, and "niche," which means directed toward specialized audiences. The media furnish loads and overloads of information. Anybody can find something wrong with some part or other of the media, but still, as Thomas Jefferson reflected early in the history of the Republic, if he had to choose between government without newspapers or newspapers without government, his clear choice would be to keep the newspapers. Jefferson's principle still applies, for the media have the capacity to make officials and institutions sit up and take notice. The media at their best force the political, social, and economic system to continually examine and renew itself.

I recall the beginning of my career as a journalist, wondering in the early years whatever became of all the words. Did anybody ever read them twice or remember them? Could they possibly make any difference? I discovered in due course that I had chosen the most wonderful way of life. While a columnist for *American Forests,* I received a letter from a woman engaged in efforts to prevent mining in the mountains bordering her hometown, Colorado Springs. "The most beautiful word in the English language is hope," she wrote, "and you have given meaning to it for us here." A column I wrote in 1968 became the rallying point for the heroic and ultimately successful crusade to save Overton Park, the beautiful forest in the heart of Memphis. *American Forests* could hardly be considered a major periodical, but others ignored the pleas of the hardy little band called Friends of Overton Park, so those words, in the best media available, *did* make a difference.[3]

So did the words of Eileen Welsome, whose series for the *Albuquerque Tribune* on human radiation experiments conducted by the U.S. government uncovered a fifty-year-old scandal. Welsome's articles sparked similar stories and investigations in the *New York Times,* the *Boston Globe,* and major networks and a national probe. Follow-up stories showed 235 newborns in five states had been injected with radioactive iodine or iodine. Despite the government's claim that plutonium did no harm to the eighteen patients, records showed that the patient who received the smallest dose suffered radiation damage to the bone from the injection. Defense Secretary Les Aspin ordered the armed forces and the Defense Nuclear Agency to search records back to the 1940s for Americans who may have been used in such experiments. A "human-experimentation hot line" set up by the Department of Energy received ten thousand calls.

To give credit where credit is due, the media have done many good works of this kind. Newspapers and television may be part of the booster system that promotes construction of baseball and football stadiums in cities unable or unwilling to provide decent schools for their children, but they do more than that. For example, in the 1970s, editorials in almost every major newspaper in New York State urged enactment of a zoning plan and a wild, scenic, and recreational rivers system in the Adirondack Park that now help protect twelve hundred miles of rivers and streams. It was not the first time the "power of the press" was brought to bear successfully in the cause of preservation in the Adirondacks.

Nor was it the last. In 1988 the *New York Times* featured an essay by John Oakes on its op-ed page warning of the damage to Adirondack Park from mounting development: "If Governor Cuomo wants to redeem his environmental record, now is the time to halt the park's steady slide into piecemeal suburbanization." That op-ed piece hit the mark. The governor responded with a letter to the editor pledging his commitment to the cause. He wrote that negotiations were under way to acquire a substantial portion of a ninety-six-thousand-acre tract and that he would intervene personally if progress was not soon made.[4]

On the day of Chico Mendes's murder, Marlise Simons, the *New York Times* correspondent in Brazil, called the National Council of Rubber Tappers that Mendes headed "the only group that physically prevented deforestation." In her dispatch she placed responsibility for the violence that claimed Mendes's life on the shoulders of the wealthy ranchers who profited from destroying Brazil's rain forests. She also brought international development banks into the drama: "Both the World Bank and Inter-American Development Bank have lent large sums to Brazil to build a road to Rondonia and Acre that opened up the virgin forests of the western Amazon. But Brazil has not lived up to all the requirements of the loan agreements to safeguard the rights of Indians and other forest peoples. Land speculators have often violently expelled the inhabitants."[5]

The *Times* placed Simons's article on the front page. Within the week other influential newspapers called attention to the plight and struggles of people living in the rain forest. The mainstream media provided activists with new leverage in their efforts to shape policy of the U.S. and the development banks in South America.

In April 1993, Milwaukee experienced the largest outbreak of waterborne illness in U.S. history. More than seventy people died and four hundred thousand were taken ill. In three months, nine *Milwaukee Journal* reporters, led by Don Behm, James Rown, and Marilyn Marchionne reviewed medical journals, EPA technical reports and internal memos, congressional reports, and analyses by citizen-action groups. They interviewed doctors; patients with cancer, heart trouble, and AIDS (considered vulnerable and likely to be affected); government officials; and researchers. They used databases to analyze mail surveys of 440 national health professionals, 858 water-treatment experts, and telephone polls of Milwaukee County residents.

The series they wrote detailed neglect of the nation's water supply by federal and state regulators, misplaced research priorities that ignored microorganisms in water, pork-barrel funding that put public health at risk, and more than one thousand research reports over eight years that pointed out the danger.[6] Consequently the EPA apologized to Milwaukee. Reprints were used as a resource while Congress rewrote drinking-water regulations for 1994, and the state of Wisconsin increased water testing and monitoring and funding for parasite and algae testing.

In South Carolina, the property-tax system in 1993 was a hot topic in the state, a major concern before the session of the legislature. Fritz McAden, editor of the *State*, in Columbia, recognized that his paper had carried only a few surface stories about abuse of the farm tax break by developers and assigned two reporters, Twila Decker and Sammy Fretwell, to work on it full-time. They spent about four months visiting properties, examining county records, and searching the computer database, and they interviewed state and county assessors, lawmakers, county-council members, developers, university experts on farm-use tax breaks, and the governor.

The reporters used their database to determine how much developers in two counties, Richland and Lexington, were saving each year in property taxes and how much the school districts were losing. They came up with startling examples of acreage worth $3 million surrounding a congressman's home and commercial property next to a commercial shopping mall. They used a spreadsheet to rank and calculate the percentage of land in each county getting the tax break—in some counties up to 80 percent. The series detailed how South Carolina, a state near the bottom in education and having trouble in providing basic services, overlooked an estimated $400 million a year as a result of a loose system that a handful of influential legislators refused to tighten. Seventy-five percent of property in South Carolina received the tax break, meaning the remaining 25 percent paid the bulk of the property tax. As a result of their work the governor and key legislators promised to close the loophole, and legislation was introduced in 1994 with strong support.[7]

Many working reporters and editors want to dig deep. That is why they are in the business, trying to follow the best tradition of their profession, not simply to "expose the bastards," but to make a difference in the world by exposing the truth to public view. Critical editorials about the Newt Gingrich 1994–1996 Contract with America alerted people, countering attacks by Gingrich allies on the Clean Air Act, the Endangered Species Act, national parks, and national wildlife refuges.

In mid-1996 media in the Northwest directed attention to Wes Cooley, a freshman Republican congressman representing eastern Oregon, who made his mark by consistently voting for more logging and grazing on public lands until he became a laughingstock for fudging details about his marriage and military service. Reporters pursued Cooley relentlessly until he became an embarrassment to the Republican leadership and was forced to withdraw from the race. In California, Tom Knudson's 1991 series of *Sacramento Bee* articles, "The Sierra in Peril," stirred Congress to initiate the $6.5 million Sierra Nevada Ecosystem Project, which reported in mid-1996 that logging, grazing, water development, air pollution, and urbanization have badly damaged the "Range of Light." Gene Rose at the *Fresno Bee* was, until his retirement, the "conscience of Yosemite," accused by the park concessioner of "smear journalism," and of serving as "pimp for the environmental community."

Sometimes writers are encouraged by their bosses and given the resources for their research, and then supported by them when the going gets rough. Alas, there are those other times . . .

CHAPTER 3

It's More than Reporting and Writing, but a Way of Living

JOHN MUIR in the late nineteenth century loved his life in the Sierra Nevada wilderness in California. It was a refuge from civilization, where he found "divine harmony." Once Muir began serious writing, however, he turned outward, contributing regularly to newspapers and magazines and authoring books, but always in the cause of saving wild places. In a way, he tried to bridge the gap between the outer world of civilization and the natural world as God made it. Fortunately, he was equipped with a vocabulary of science as well as powerful poetry and spirituality in his soul.

Muir is still a model to follow. He may be long dead, but he left an enduring legacy: in national parks of the West that he was responsible for establishing; the Sierra Club, which he founded to champion the outdoors; and the literary imagery of wilderness preserved. As he wrote in *Atlantic Monthly:* "Thousands of tired, nerve-shaken, over-civilized people are beginning to find out that going to the mountains is going home; that wildness is a necessity; and that mountain parks and reservations are useful not only as fountains of timber and irrigating rivers, but as fountains of life."[1]

Another model to follow, Rachel Carson, in our own time wrote: "The beauty of the living world I was trying to save has always been uppermost in my mind—that, and anger at the senseless brutish things that were being done. I have felt bound by a solemn obligation to do what I could— if I didn't at least try I could never again be happy in nature."[2]

Possibly Paul Brooks, who, as editor-in-chief at Houghton Mifflin, worked with Carson on *Silent Spring* and her other books, had her in mind when he wrote in *The Pursuit of Wilderness:* "Conservationists need words because what they are trying to do is to enlighten and inform: to change fundamental attitudes, not because they say so, but because they have the facts that will command such change on the part of any reasonable man [or woman]."[3]

That is what environmental journalism is meant to do. Environmental journalism differs from traditional journalism. It plays by a set of rules based on a consciousness different from the dominant in modern American society. It is more than a way of reporting and writing, but a way of living, of looking at the world, and at oneself. It starts with a concept of social service, gives voice to struggle and demand, and comes across with honesty, credibility, and purpose. It almost always involves somehow, somewhere, risk and sacrifice.

The word *sacrifice* seems to imply suffering and want, but if everybody in the world sacrificed by unplugging television sets for an hour or day or on Superbowl Sunday, or if everybody did not drive for a day or a week or quit driving altogether, burdens would lighten and benefits would grow. Taking less from the warehouse of natural resource and fabricated merchandise enables others to have more. "Sacrifice," surrendering dependence on all the things that actually alienate and destroy, gives time, room, and money for study, exercise, or whatever you prefer.

Many people cannot do those things because they are caught in a system of superconsumerism and resource exploitation that dictates production of useless as well as useful merchandise, marketing, advertising, buying on credit, making wealth without sharing it. "Greed is good," said Gordon Gecko in the film *Wall Street*. Maybe in real life it is not greed, but the inherent goodness of making money. That bias is taken for granted by most media. They would not exist otherwise. Newspapers and magazines and radio and television that try to get by without advertising have a tough time, and those that criticize do not get the advertising, certainly not of their investigative targets.

Thus, in environmental journalism knowing how to order facts in the traditional newspaper "pyramid" style is not enough. The pyramid tells it all in a nutshell in the first paragraph, so the editor can trim from the bottom as needed and the last paragraph or paragraphs become dispensable. In my local newspaper, the *Bellingham (Wash.) Herald*, for example, a Gannett News Service dispatch from Washington, D.C., began: "The House voted to tighten controls on illegal immigration Wednesday, passing a bill to speed up deportations, increase border patrols and deny certain benefits. All but five House Republicans supported the measure, which passed 305–123; 117 Democrats and one independent opposed it."[4]

In some papers that might have been all that ran. The editors at the *Herald* could have cut on the inside page these last paragraphs if they had gotten in the way of advertising: "Democrats criticized the measure, saying it weakens immigration controls on employers who knowingly hire undocumented workers while it strengthens penalties against immigrants searching for jobs. 'This is a bill that says: "Gee, maybe it would be nice if there weren't so many illegal aliens. But now that they're here, maybe we can get some cheap work out of them,"' said Rep. Barney Frank, D-Mass. The bill now heads to the Senate, where its passage is uncertain. Democratic leaders oppose it and hinted Wednesday they might block expedited consideration."[5]

Environmental writing reaches deeper, with beginning, middle, and end integrally joined. It thinks not simply of Who, What, When, Where, Why, and How, but of a species instead of an animal, a forest instead of a tree, and an ecosystem along with species and forest. It examines interlocking systems that touch every aspect of life: science, botany, biology, economics, history, politics, ethics, and religion. It is not necessary to know them all, but the ability to ask questions and digest answers is a skill in itself, the basis of writing with breadth and perspective.

It helps to understand and utilize the power of emotion and imagery, so that every word, phrase, and paragraph contributes to writing that is purposeful, that challenges, motivates, enlightens, and throws light on life. Couple the basic lesson taught by William Strunk Jr. and E. B. White in *The Elements of Style,* "Vigorous writing is concise," with John Muir's admonition, "Dry words will not fire hearts," and you are on the way to turning people on, not turning them off.

"Avoid tame, colorless, hesitating, noncommittal language," advised Strunk and White, but write with discipline: "A sentence should contain no unnecessary words, a paragraph no unnecessary sentences, for the same reason that a drawing should have no unnecessary lines and a machine no unnecessary parts. This requires not that the writer make all his sentences short, or that he avoid all detail and treat his subjects only in outlines, but that every word tell."[6]

Environmental writing, in other words, must be clear and understandable, based on sound data and thorough research, yet reflecting the author's imagination, deep inner feeling, and desire to advance the cause of a better world.

Now and then I ask students in my classes to define environmental journalism, not in so many words, but in words that make sense to them at the outset of their careers. "As we continue to compromise our little planet," wrote Gary Gray, "environmental journalists will remain the eyes through which the public sees the truth." Gray was deeply interested in photography, so he added, "The environmental photographer's task is to reawaken the environmental consciousness we, as humans, all inherit."[7]

Colleen Majors said it this way: "Let the people know. The job of the journalist is to inform the public. The job of the environmentalist is to research the information. Combining these two aspects of writing produces a clear understanding of issues that affect our planet—and ourselves."

Blessed with talent and desire, Gray was at the start of a promising career when he was killed in a climbing accident in the north Cascades. It was a grievous loss for me, as a teacher and a friend. I was pretty tough on him in class, but then the harder a student worked the more I demanded of him or her. I was tough on Majors too, but she kept coming back for more; I would have shortchanged her by going easy. She designed her own major, Environmental Education/Mass Communication, concentrating on producing a weekly radio show, *Ecological Perspectives,* on the campus station. After graduation she started her own audiovisual group working strictly on environmental and social issues and still does so. For her and for others who are making it into green journalism, it is more than a career, more than writing and reporting, but a way of living.

CHAPTER 4

There Is No Dispassionate Objectivity

SAUL ALINSKY in *Rules for Radicals* wrote that "All of life is partisan. There is no dispassionate objectivity." Of course not: what you choose to write about, whom you choose to interview, how stories are presented, and when they are published all reflect prejudices of writers, editors, publishers.

Strunk and White in *The Elements of Style* said it a little differently: "Every writer, by the way he uses the language, reveals something of his spirit, his habits, his capacities, his bias. This is inevitable as well as enjoyable. All writing is communication; creative writing is communication through revelation—it is the Self escaping into the open."[1]

That is how it should be, for the writer, whether journalist, essayist, or novelist, who wants to make something of himself or herself and his or her work. In this respect, I like to cite Bernard DeVoto, who spoke for an entire breed of writers and editors: "My job is to write about anything in American life that may interest me, but it is also to arrive at judgments under my own steam. With some judgments that is the end of the line; express them and you have nothing more to do. But there are also judgments that require you to commit yourself, to stick your neck out. Expressing them in print obliges you to go on to advocacy. They get home to people's beliefs and feelings about important things, and that makes them inflammable."[2]

That was DeVoto's approach and it worked. He was a marvelous writer and historian, a champion of conservation causes until his death in 1955. I met and observed DeVoto in action in 1953 at the Mid-Century Conference on Resources for the Future, conducted in Washington, D.C., under the auspices of the research institution Resources for the Future. Dwight D. Eisenhower was president in a politically conservative period. A major controversy of the time revolved around public lands of the West and whether they ought to be transferred to the states, or at least whether timber and grazing resources should be more intensively exploited. I was in a small section meeting of about thirty people where DeVoto crossed swords with J. Elmer Brock, a Wyoming industry leader, and heard him later in a larger group where he challenged Congressman Wesley D'Ewart, a prominent Montana Republican.

> In effect, the Congressman says, "Cannot we westerners be trusted to take better care of these lands than the government bureaus?" The answer is, "No, they cannot be trusted."
>
> Among the areas Congressman D'Ewart specifically excepts as being protected forever are the national parks. That is not borne out by the history of the Ellsworth Bill [then pending in Congress]. This bill provides compensation to a timber operator on a sustained-yield basis, if his land should be required by the government, in the form either of money or selection from the national timberlands of an equivalent amount of timber—harking back to the operations of the Timberlake Act, under which some of the most grotesque and indecent of all land frauds were perpetrated. . . .
>
> Incidentally, the Congressman was talking almost exclusively about the Forest Service when he mentioned the great distance dividing the lands from the heads of government bureaus. In his own state, the effective control is exercised from the city of Missoula, which he can reach from his own home in two hours by automobile at an expense of sixty cents, and where he can get a ruling which will not involve Washington at all.[3]

That was the way DeVoto spoke and the way he wrote. He had command of his data, but his bold style made editors nervous. In *The Uneasy Chair,* the unvarnished biography of DeVoto, his friend Wallace Stegner wrote that "Ben Hibbs, the *[Saturday Evening] Post*'s editor, got so much pressure from western lobbies and from the bureaus [federal agencies] themselves that he closed the door to DeVoto's pamphleteering and never reopened it." *Harper's* editors said they wished he would not harp on the same old issues all the time. "But that, DeVoto told them, was exactly the point. You didn't mount the barricades until noon and then go out for a three-hour lunch."[4]

Advocacy writing is to the mainstream media and to many journalism schools sheer anathema. They want writing to be free of "value judgments," without evidence of imagination or sense of person. All quotes must come from outside sources, thus somehow eliminating bias. The president of a corporation, or the public-relations person, may lie, but that is not the primary concern. The redeeming element is that he said it— that he said these words in this place at that time. That fulfills the mandate of who-what-when-where-how. Anything else, beginning with interpretation, is suspect. The reporter must never insert herself into the story. To be an activist, personally involved, in an issue is considered gross and improper. It is not "professional." It induces loss of "credibility."

Still, there is a case for objectivity to consider. I could advise that you stick your neck out, as DeVoto did, and go on to advocacy, but you ought to weigh the viewpoint that a reporter and writer should set down the facts as best he or she can, without any injection of self, and allow the reader to reach an independent conclusion.

Ida Tarbell, one of the foremost of the early-twentieth-century investigative reporters known as muckrakers, provides a notable example on the plus side of objectivity. She joined *McClure's* in 1894 and became one of its stars, along with Ray Stannard Baker and Lincoln Steffens. In November 1902 she began her historic nineteen-installment exposé of Standard Oil, supporting all of her statements with painstaking research and hard evidence. "My point of attack has always been that of a journalist after the fact, rarely that of a reformer, the advocate of a cause or a system," she wrote many years later. "If I was tempted from the straight and narrow path of the one who seeks for that which is so and why it is so, I sooner or later returned."[5]

The late Edward J. Meeman, a pioneer in conservation journalism, offered a complementary view when he said, "Democracy requires leadership and this must come from newspapers among others." But he carefully distinguished between editorial and news: "This newspaper leadership should appear in the editorial columns, but it should also appear in purposive, although fair and objective, studies and exposures in major articles or series of articles exploring situations in depth and detail by writers who are not only reporters, but digging investigators and scientific interpreters."[6]

Various people whom I respect share this same view. John B. Oakes wrote outstanding environmental essays while serving as editor of the editorial page of the *New York Times* from 1961 until he retired fifteen years later. He had come up through the ranks as a reporter for the *Washington Post* and as Sunday staff editor for the *Times*. In 1992 I interviewed him about his career and his views on his profession.

> I was brought up in the tradition of objective reporting and still believe that news stories ought to be as objective and non-editorial as humanly possible. Pieces that express the opinion of the writer should be reserved for specially marked magazine pieces and, of course, editorials. I have found myself saying, more than once about a given story, I'm delighted to see this, but it should have been a news analysis, or editorial, or op-ed piece or something else. I would lean over backwards in favor of objectivity, when presenting something as a straight news story.
>
> Let the facts speak for themselves, that's the way it ought to be. The press should be adversarial, but not in its news columns. The public ought to be free to make up its own mind.
>
> It's very difficult. I favor in-depth reporting, giving the background, bringing out the facts—it's when the opinion of the reporter gets into that kind of story, when the reporter tries to push an opinion that I find difficult to accept. If the reporter researches thoroughly, understands the context and history of the issue, and communicates effectively—that is more difficult, yet more effective, in effecting change.[7]

Oakes recognized that opinion-free reporting is not easy. For him the best approach is through in-depth investigative reporting—honest, informed, objective but still adversarial. "Investigative journalism is in the class with news analysis. It's a difficult distinction I'm trying to make, but one cannot write an environmental story in the news columns without expressing a basic point of view of sympathy with the environmental viewpoint. It is impossible to report what's really going on and exposing what's going on without pointing out the antienvironmental actions being taken."[8]

Dan Evans has dealt with the media over a long period of years as governor and as a U.S. senator from Washington State. In delivering the keynote address at the conference on Northwest Media and the Environment at Bellingham, Washington, he said:

> Objectivity, we sometimes hear, is simply impossible to achieve and reporters are really editorialists on the wrong page. But I turn to Webster's unabridged dictionary, which defines reportage as "writing intended to give a factual and detailed account of directly observed or carefully documented events" and objective as "expressing or involving the use of facts without distortion by personal feelings or prejudices."

> This doesn't say you can't have personal feeling or prejudice, but being objective requires trying to disseminate facts without distortion by those personal feelings. We all come loaded with personal feeling, but there are plenty of examples of people trying to be objective, regardless of personal belief. Referees and umpires do it all the time. Good judges recognize their responsibility to judge cases on the basis of law, not their own feelings.

> Environmental advocacy on the news pages is no more valid than business advocacy, education advocation or sports advocacy. We've seen them all and deplore the results when we can identify them. Perhaps we should revert to the common practice of other times and other countries, when and where newspapers were owned by political parties or organizations. When you bought a newspaper you *knew* you were buying an opinion.[9]

Maybe so, but business is almost always interpreted from the business viewpoint. So are sports, which have become more business than sport anyway. And both business and sports are accorded whole sections of the daily newspapers and segments of the nightly news, while the environment rates only occasional coverage, principally when something terrible happens. The strict separation of facts and editorial opinion leads to misunderstanding. Readers and viewers need interpretive voices to guide them through a jungle of facts. The Western European press successfully integrates news and editorials. Its journalists present fact-based reports on international news, balanced by the reporters' well-informed views based on firsthand experience and thorough understanding of events.

John Oakes said he would lean over backward to favor objectivity in the news pages. Still, Timothy Egan's 1995 front-page article in the *New York Times* about a hot issue in the Northwest might have caused Oakes to think further about where reporting ends and interpretation begins:

> Ketchum, Idaho—The high alpine country near the grave of Ernest Hemingway is some of the prettiest public land in America, with its flower meadows, wild horses and views of the tallest mountains in Idaho. Signs inform visitors that it is a land of "many uses," overseen for the public by the Federal Bureau of Land Management. But Congress is now poised to grant ranchers virtual control over this and almost every other part of the 270 million acres of Federal land where grazing permits have already been issued. People who hunt, fish or hike say the concept of sharing the use of public lands is being shoved aside for a small special interest.[10]

The article shows the author's self, or bias, if that is what you want to call it. Clearly, he focused attention on the aesthetics of place, with its flowers, wildness, and vistas, above the values in livestock and grazing. I wish the *Times* and other newspapers published more like it, but this article is the exception, certainly not the rule.

Some able journalists have learned painfully the consequences of independent investigation deeper than the shallow. Philip Fradkin, for one, had initiated the environmental beat on the *Los Angeles Times* in 1970, when he returned from covering the Vietnam War and saw that no one on the paper was writing about the emerging subject. He asked Bill Thomas, then Metro editor, if he could specialize in environmental reporting. Thomas at first turned him down, but Fradkin persisted and produced enough stories of merit to be eventually given the title of environmental writer.

He had a wonderful time, traveling the West and making it his beat. Inevitably he rocked the boat along the way. And then, "In the early spring of 1975, Mark Murphy, the metropolitan editor of the *Los Angeles Times,* called me into his office and told me he was taking me off the environmental beat. He said that I was not objective, that the managing editor could no longer trust my stories, and that I had done a poor job on a recent story. There was no appeal and Murphy would not elaborate further. I felt shocked when Murphy gave me the word. I felt betrayed. . . ."

Steve Stuebner in 1991 had won a string of awards at the *Boise (Idaho)*

Statesman and praise from officials of the Gannett chain for his coverage of the 1988 Yellowstone fires. Suddenly he was labeled as biased and was demoted from the environmental beat to city-county news. And he left.

> The top editors accused me of being too pro-environment. I asked them for proof and they looked back at me with blank stares, blushed and said, "Well, come on Stuebner, you just are. Everyone knows that." And I said, "How come this has never come up at the editing desk? How did you decide I'm too pro-environment?" They had no evidence.
>
> Later I heard the real reason they shifted me off the beat. The marketing director had complained to the publisher and editor that there was too much environmental news in the paper and it was all too negative. Considering the editor hated to get complaints and did his best to kill or emasculate hard-hitting stories, leaving the paper was a very easy ethical decision for me. The *Statesman* had fallen to pieces.
>
> In the very specialized field of environmental writing, only the people who have spent years in the field, examining environmental damage in detail, and who know how to dig beyond the rhetoric, can truly provide a balanced picture and protect the public trust. But it's like leaping into a war zone. . . .[11]

Richard Manning, as an investigative reporter for the *Missoulian,* the daily newspaper in Missoula, Montana, spent many weeks researching and writing a hard-hitting series on the exploitation of Montana forests. The timber industry complained. Then, Manning recalls, "My editors said I was being reassigned because I had lost my objectivity. They alleged I was too inclined to write what the environmentalists had to say and not inclined to write what the loggers had to say. They were wrong, but they and the system that has molded them are managed within the corporate system, groomed, pruned and thinned just like corporate trees."[12]

Kathie Durbin in 1989, after covering drugs, gangs, and minority affairs for the *Portland Oregonian,* welcomed the chance to cover the environment. Teaming with Paul Koberstein, she studied forests along the West Coast and interviewed many people for a six-part series in 1990. The timber industry dispatched an angry eighty-page letter—eighty, not eight—to the editors and made Durbin a special target: "I was attacked by the

Oregon Lands Coalition, a wise use group, which urged its members to call the *Oregonian* and tell the editors they were sick of Kathie Durbin's lies. My editors were nervous, but our report was accurate and overdue. . . . In the process of this trial by fire I learned to be discreet about my own passionate feelings for the forest. Of course I belong to no environmental groups. I don't go to environmentalists' parties. My job is too important to me to take any chances. And I take seriously my responsibility to chronicle the struggle from all sides. I'm a professional journalist. I cannot be a causist."[13] Ultimately Durbin was removed from the beat and resigned.

Philip Shabecoff for thirty-two years worked as a reporter for the *New York Times,* including stints as a foreign correspondent in Southeast Asia. For fourteen years he covered the environmental beat in Washington, turning up major stories. But his editors told him he was "ahead of the curve," stale, biased, too close to environmentalists. When he was transferred to covering the Internal Revenue Service he quit.[14]

Gene Rose joined the *Fresno Bee,* published by the liberal McClatchy chain, in 1960. Twelve years later, after covering major stories, he was assigned to a beat embracing Yosemite and Sequoia/Kings Canyon National Parks and surrounding national forests, his boyhood stamping ground. For years thereafter he was known as a walking encyclopedia of valuable information about the mountains as well as a formidable reporter. At Yosemite he was the "conscience of the park." He spurred concessions reform, shed light on land-planning fiascoes on the national forests, and influenced public opinion for the environment in California.

But he made a few enemies, too, particularly after revealing in 1987 that the Yosemite Park and Curry Company, a subsidiary of MCA, the Hollywood conglomerate, grossed $87 million for its exclusive contract but paid a concession fee of only $585,000. MCA officials accused him of "smear journalism" and fronting for the environmental community. Early in the 1990s, McClatchy toned down its liberal corporate philosophy and replaced George Gruner, the longtime *Bee* editor. When Rose became a target on the inside as well as the outside, he opted for retirement.[15]

♺

The choice of subjects, sources, and words reflects bias. And advocacy goes with it. Ben Long, reporter and columnist for the *Kalispell (Mont.) Daily Interlake* sees nothing wrong there: "First and foremost, reporters must give a damn. I doubt I could ever be a good reporter on stock car racing because I don't give a rip about it. I think I'm a good environmental reporter because that's where my passion is. It doesn't matter what's the beat: an education reporter should want good schools; a cops-and-court reporter should strive for justice, and an environmental reporter should want readers to appreciate their environment and what's going on around them."[16]

Environmental journalism, after all, is not simply about being a competent reporter. "Do not attempt to enter this field," warns T. H. Watkins, professor at Montana State University with many years of experience in environmental writing and editing, "unless and until you feel it in your bones. This is not like accounting, or sales, or computer programming (though I suppose a good accountant, salesperson or programmer has to have a measure of personal commitment, too). It is more like a crusade, a commitment. If you do not care deeply for the fate of the non-human world (a faith that does not exclude the human world, but merely makes equal citizens of all life, as Leopold said), no craft or gimmickry can make up for what you will lack."[17]

Newspapers demonstrate bias daily, with zeal in covering affairs of business and development and through weekly real-estate sections thick with advertising, while ignoring or downplaying the environment and other critical social issues.

Good journalism requires the journalist to be thorough, detail oriented, honest, and ready to defend his or her work. Criticism of objectivity should not be used to rationalize writing "whatever I think or feel" without substance or evidence. Objectivity at its best, as I wrote at the outset, is a means of gathering information, a foundation of reality that justifies feeling.

The journalists I cited above suffered pain, but when one door closes, another opens. There will always be outlets for those guided by Thoreau, who wrote: "There are thousands hacking at the branches of evil to one who is striking at the root." And by I. F. Stone, the nagging conscience of twentieth-century American journalism. Stone quit college, taught himself Greek, and worked as a Washington correspondent and editorial writer. In 1941 he was expelled from the National Press Club for bringing a black judge to the club as his lunch guest. In 1953 he launched *I. F. Stone's Weekly* (later, *I. F. Stone's Bi-Weekly*) and for nineteen years delivered analyses of Washington and global politics found nowhere else. He was hounded by the FBI, excoriated on the floor of Congress, and scorned by colleagues of the media. Stone called himself "a flickering candle in a naughty world." He did not think much of "professional" training or journalism schools that produce people "who know how to run a type-writer" and little more. When he closed shop in December 1971, Stone wrote: "To give a little comfort to the oppressed, to write the truth exactly as I saw it, to make no compromise other than those of quality imposed by my own inadequacies, to be free to follow no master other than my own compulsions, to live up to my idealized image of what a true newspaper-man should be, and still be able to make a living for my family—what more could a man ask?"[18]

CHAPTER 5

Beyond Objectivity, Passion Counts

THE ENVIRONMENTAL JOURNALIST reaches beyond objectivity to examine the world and the universe from the heart as well as the head. Get the facts, but then write them with feeling, your own feeling.

This thought came to me anew as I listened to Kathie Durbin in April 1994 in Reno, Nevada, at a conference of the Association for Education in Journalism and Mass Communication, shortly before she lost her job covering the environment for the *Portland Oregonian*. Kathie said that she had repressed her emotion about unrestrained logging, but, "When the pressure got intense, I would seek out an old growth forest to remind me of what this argument was all about. I wrote poetry about what I was feeling, like the poem 'Objectivity,' and sent it off, wondering if anyone actually published it some timber lobbyist would see it and attack me in print for having and expressing passionate feelings."

But passion counts: it makes the difference and should not be repressed or inhibited. Maybe Kathie did not belong in the newsroom anyway. Thomas Merton, the Trappist monk, in his critical observation of society felt that news as provided to us is merely a new noise of the mind, briefly replacing the news that went before it and yielding to the noise that comes after it, so that eventually everything blends into the same monotonous rumor. "News? There is so much news that there is no room left for the true tidings, the 'Good News,' *the Great Joy*."[1]

The environmental journalist wants to find and feel the Good News and to spread it like the gospel. It is the way to exercise the power in your life, power to join in determining public policy and the course of history.

With power comes a new awareness of human rights, of political and personal freedom.

Rachel Carson rose above the limits of her professional education to pursue the power of service. She was roundly denounced and ridiculed by virtually the entire mainstream media. Nevertheless, through *Silent Spring* and her resolute personality, she showed that a single individual can make a difference in society, rising above herself, above institutions and professions, to challenge an entrenched system.

Kathie Durbin, speaking in Reno, said that deep down she did not want to see anymore forest cut and that she could not bear to drive around the Olympic Peninsula because of all the logging scars. Nevertheless, she would remind herself that she could not be "a causist."

But why not? The best journalism reflects the pursuit of a cause. I. F. Stone followed a lonely road in Washington while publishing his investigative and political newsletter. But he is remembered for both his body of work and the life he lived. As he summed it up: "The place to be is where the odds are against you; power breeds injustice, and to defend the underdog against the triumphant is more exhilarating than to curry favor and move safely with the mob. Philosophically I believe a man's life reduces itself ultimately to a faith—the fundamental is beyond proof—and that faith is a matter of aesthetics, a sense of beauty and harmony. I think every man is his own Pygmalion, and spends his life fashioning himself. And in fashioning himself, for good or evil, he fashions the human race and its future."[2]

The same idea has been expressed by others, in different ways. Ralph Waldo Emerson taught that the one thing of value in the world, above all else, is the active soul, and that each person contains within him or her the active soul, although almost always "obstructed, and as yet unborn." William Faulkner when he accepted the 1950 Nobel Prize for Literature said that only the problems of the human heart in conflict with itself can make good writing, for only that is worth writing about, worth the agony and the sweat. He challenged the writer and writer-aspirant to be unafraid and learn them again, to help humankind endure through reminders of courage and honor, hope and pride, compassion, pity, and sacrifice. On a wall plaque at the Fine Arts Museum in Santa Fe, I found the words of Alice Cunning Fletcher, chairman of the managing board of the School of American Research from 1907 to 1912: "Living with my Indian friends, I was a stranger in my native land. As time went on, the outward aspect of nature remained the same, but a change was wrought in me. I learned to hear the echoes of a time when every living thing, even the sky, had a voice. That voice, devoutly heard by the ancient people of America, I desired to make audible to others."

All these people show how to look beyond objectivity and the limits of professionalism. I do not deny that professionalism is valid, but perhaps it needs to be reassessed and clarified to provide for more open expression. It is one thing to train as a professional by defined rules and rote and then be devoured by a worn-out system, but another to learn from life in a way that enables one to serve society, even when it means challenging the system.

Professions should be standard-bearers of ideas bigger and better than money can buy. So I think they were, must have been, in their early days, all of them: law, medicine, religion, journalism, forestry, education. But time has mellowed them. A professional degree is more of a license to employment than a charge to serve community and humanity without fear or favor. I could equate this statement with any of the professions mentioned, but I have seen the evidence most clearly in those I know best, journalism, higher education, and environmentalism.

My studies of forestry in America show that it began as a social crusade led by Gifford Pinchot, the first trained forester born in this country. Pinchot had thought of social work in the settlement houses as a career, but his love of the outdoors dictated otherwise. He went abroad for his training, then returned to lead a movement aimed at protecting the nation's forests from being devoured and destroyed by big business. Responsible stewardship was his gospel. With support from his friend Theodore Roosevelt in the White House, Pinchot successfully established a national forest system to protect watersheds and a perpetual wood supply. But Pinchot's principles have long gone by the boards.

Stewardship has given way to "management." Students enter forestry schools motivated by love of the outdoors but graduate as managers, technical people, focused, like agronomists, on the production of a crop, principally timber. Over the years I have been in the woods with scores of public and private foresters, and found them generally knowledgeable about commercial species, the timber types of trees, but often ill-versed or ignorant about other vegetative cover, the "weed species" that make an ecosystem whole.

Aldo Leopold, who began in forestry under Pinchot, turned his attention to wildlife stewardship as a profession. Early in his teaching career at the University of Wisconsin he emphasized the management concept, but in time rose above it, evoking the "land ethic" of his classic *Sand County Almanac*. For the most part, however, his profession, like forestry, concentrates on "production" of a crop, in this case favored species, labeled as game and "harvest" by hunters.

An article by Susan Hagood, wildlife issues specialist of the Humane Society of the United States, includes the following:

> Although they know nongame species are virtually ignored and frequently proclaim that the nonhunting public must support wildlife through its dollars, many state wildlife commissions and agencies would prefer that a way is never found to secure the nonhunters' contribution. If it were found, the commissions and agencies would have to change their policies and focus. They would have to address nonhunters' concerns in a meaningful way, which would lead to a reduction in the emphasis on production of game animals, prohibitions against the most objectionable hunting practices, restrictions on hunting on public lands, and other changes in the status quo.[3]

That is absolutely correct, and a large part of the problem derives from the influence of "natural-resource management" that has little to do with stewardship, but sees itself as the means of manipulating nature and converting nature into "resources" for human use and consumption. Most college and university courses in resource management teach objectivity, with little room for sensitivity.

But compassion must be at the root of the revolution of values. I mentioned above that Emerson taught the value of the active soul, and that each person contains within him or her the active soul. Education ought to be an enriching and elevating pathway that frees the active soul, that engenders love of inner self, that explores the wholeness of creation. Compassion and emotion, however, are repressed in the training of professionals. Scientists and educators require evidence, documentation, statistics, quantification, objectivity. While these are essential, there must be more.

I loved my time in teaching but found again and again that education emphasizes the cognitive: a focus on facts, with abilities to analyze, calculate, and memorize, providing a practical means of acquiring information, while largely omitting or denying the intuitive, ethical, and spiritual. The subtitle of Allan Bloom's best-selling book *The Closing of the American*

Mind is *How Higher Education Has Failed Democracy and Impoverished the Souls of Today's Students.* Page Smith said the same in the title of his book on higher education, *Killing the Spirit.*[4]

In 1978, when I received an invitation to come to the University of Vermont for half a year as a visiting professor of environmental studies, I knew little about teaching. I came with hopes of enriching souls, including my own. I had lectured here and there and had spoken on campuses at the first Earth Day in 1970, but being part of academia was quite different. I was assigned to teach two classes, Environmental Journalism and Environmental Politics, but presently found that I had little idea of how to teach, meaning I did not know how to understand students and who they are and what they need and yearn for, or how to connect with them on a learning track we could travel together in mutual respect. I recognized my deficiency in the first session of the journalism class when I talked for twenty minutes and ran out of material; I stared at twenty-five students with eyes wide-open and ballpoint pens at the ready, waiting for wisdom from the expert, and all I could think was, "What do I do now? What else have I got?"

I was ignorant of why students really came to college and what they wanted to get out of it besides a degree. Or about the motivation of their professors, or about tenure, the tenure track, campus politics, a thousand aspects of the academic world that set it apart from other worlds. I found that professors did not see much of students except in classrooms, generally kept their office doors closed and received students strictly by appointment, and scarcely if ever socialized with them, and not much with each other. At Vermont and later, I saw that professors are specialists in their given fields, speaking and writing in their own jargon, without much cross-fertilization of ideas. I met and associated with some wonderful colleagues, who became close friends, but I learned also that higher education can be soulless, cruel, and corporate.

Carl Rogers, the humanistic psychologist, in his book *On Becoming a Person* recalled being offered, early in his career, a full professorship at Ohio State University. "I heartily recommend starting in the academic world at this level," he wrote. "I have often been grateful that I have never had to live through the frequently degrading competitive process of step-by-step promotion in university faculties, where individuals so frequently learn only one lesson—not to stick their necks out."[5]

I saw evidence of that, too, that education trains people to compete rather than cooperate, that it is largely about careers, jobs, serving the needs of employers and institutions, rather than about sharing and serving in simplicity. So it is no wonder that institutions and professions, directed by highly educated individuals, repress emotion and deny imagination, though these qualities open the heart to feeling and open the mind to articulate expression. Nursing educators have shared with me how they tell students they must be detached, objective, and efficient, even with patients who suffer or are dying. There may be well-founded professional reasons for being detached, but if I could not hold hands or embrace a sufferer in need I would work elsewhere.

I have heard the command to "be professional," used in some instances to block expressions of pity, grief, or outrage at wrongdoing, and in other instances to silence dissent. Citizens concerned with destructive forestry practices are discounted. "You don't understand, you don't have the professional background," citizens have been told by trained foresters serving as apologists for the worst kind of abuse in the woods. In fact, in the controversy following my dismissal in 1971 as columnist for *American Forests* magazine, the president of the Society of American Foresters, Kenneth P. Davis of Yale University, said I should never have been given that column in the first place because I lacked the professional credentials.

No, a journalist—or any concerned citizen—has the right to question and comment critically on any issue that affects society and the environment. Wars are too important to leave to generals, the old saying goes, and forests and the environment are too important to leave to foresters, or to any narrowly focused technicians. I appreciate that we continually need new data, valid scientific and technical data, but it takes more—a feeling, a philosophy, love of earth, love of life.

Transformation, whether of an individual or an entire society, depends upon intangible values of human heart and spirit. To say it another way, individual empowerment derives from learning through feeling, independent thinking, and social involvement. The "subjective" embodies power, no longer allowing old-line institutions and their professional experts to define terms and methods for dealing with critical issues. My advice is to use the power of emotion and imagery in what you choose to write and how you write about it. Muckrakers such as Ray Stannard Baker, Upton Sinclair, Ida Tarbell, Lincoln Steffens, and others did, and they made their mark, though mostly in books, magazines, and alternative newspapers rather than the mainstream.[6] Kathie Durbin, after leaving the *Oregonian*, shifted to alternative periodicals, and perhaps for her the best is still to come. Later, in May 1996, she wrote to me about the book she was writing, *Tree Huggers: Victory, Defeat, and Renewal in the Northwest Ancient Forest Campaign.* She had remembered and pondered our dialogue about advocacy journalism, and now *Tree Huggers* represented, among other things, her "evolution from the neutral tone of daily newspaper journalism to a stronger and more directed voice."

At Reno, Kathie said that she had always had a passion for her native Oregon forests; now she can open her heart and say so. She read her poem "Objectivity" and gave it to me as a gift when we lunched together after the meeting. I was thinking of retitling it "After Objectivity," but that really is another poem.

> *Learning to love a clearcut*
> *is possible; the rhododendrons*
> *grow up thickly here*
> *on open hillsides,*
> *smothering charred stumps.*
> *Hemlock stars*
> *the size of fingertips*
> *sprout from tractor scars.*
>
> *A clearcut is more colorful*
> *than a forest: purple fireweed*
> *and red paintbrush shout*
> *among vigorous green seedlings*
> *and you can see the sky.*
>
> *What gives pause is the wide vista:*
> *Naked mountain shoulders*
> *wearing a fringe of spindly trees,*
> *a brown and green quilt spread*
> *ridge to ridge, striped here and there*
> *with the dark green of the true*
> *and natural forest.*
>
> *When you drive by one of these*
> *relict stands, if you slow*
> *and peer inside, you will see*
> *how ferns glow in filtered light*
> *how streams tumble glassy-clear*

over logs and boulders furred with moss
how green suffuses everything

and you'll ache with knowing
the cost of our headlong
conquering rush.

CHAPTER 6

Be Literate, and a Risk Taker, Too

A STUDENT ONCE SAID IN CLASS that she felt like screaming at the television news, when tragedies—fire here, brutal murder there—are covered like a shopping list. Her point was well taken that the word *news* has a cold, uncaring quality. She wanted to write creatively, something of value about the environment, but not news, and definitely did not want to be labeled as a journalist. "If you're a journalist, you have to be confined by facts," she said. "You can't use your imagination all that much. One way or another, you have to be involved, and that restricts your independence, your creative expression. I believe I can be more productive and more satisfied by sharing through my writing the joys I experience when I walk alone in the wilds."

I could understand her viewpoint, and yours as well, if that is how you feel. There certainly is a difference between nature writing, per se, and taking on the issues for the protection of nature. I think of gifted writers, like Annie Dillard and Barry Lopez, who observe, interpret, and philosophize but remain detached from harsh specifics of public policy. That is one way to go, but I do not agree that you have to be confined by the facts to be a good journalist. The facts are a starting point, a foundation on which to build imagination into the work at hand.

That student's comments call to mind the comparison between the celebrated "two Johns" of literary history, Burroughs born in 1837 and Muir one year later. They were contemporaries and friends in sharing appreciation of the outdoors, but opposites in dealing with it. Burroughs wrote to entertain. "I do not take readers to nature to give them a lesson, but to have a good time."[1] Muir, on the other hand, was the evangelist who applied his sermons to political action.

In *The Summit of the Years,* Burroughs acknowledged his constitutional timidity, which led to "shrinking from all kinds of strife."

> I have kept apart from the strife and fever of the world, and the maelstrom of business and political life, and have sought the still waters, and in the quiet fields, and life has been sweet and wholesome to me. In my tranquil seclusion I am often on the point of upbraiding myself because I keep so aloof from the struggles and contentions and acrimonious debates of the political, the social, and the industrial world about me. . . .

> I was never a fighter; I fear that at times I may have been a shirker, but I have shirked one thing or one duty that I might the more heartily give myself to another. He also serves who sometimes runs away.[2]

As for Muir, from his earliest writing he sought to enlighten his readers with his own mountain experience. His series of articles published in the *San Francisco Daily Evening Bulletin* in the years 1874–1875 (reissued in book form more than a century later as *John Muir Summering in the Sierra*) were like letters addressed to civilization, in which he asked his readers to see, hear, and believe in a radically new way. In his foreword to *Summering in the Sierra,* Robert Engberg wrote: "Muir invented a new ethics-centered type of reporting, 'wilderness journalism,' to spread his message. Composed in the field and sent to the publisher without later revisions and redrafting, it retains the freshness and spontaneity that characterizes Muir's best writing. . . . Behind every report about people and places lies Muir's own story of why he quit his solitary wanderings to become the leader of the American conservation movement."[3]

In due course, Robert Underwood Johnson, editor of the *Century,* urged Muir to write about Yosemite, and largely through their collaborative efforts Yosemite National Park was established in 1890. Muir's writing flowed into print continually throughout the rest of his life, but was interrupted by political battles, often successful but ultimately leading to his heartbreaking losing effort to save Hetch Hetchy valley from the dam across the Tuolumne River that ultimately flooded that special part of Yosemite.

Muir and Burroughs traveled together on the Harriman Expedition to Alaska in 1899 (carrying eminent intellectual personalities of the day to explore the wonderland of the North as guests of a multimillionaire), and joined again ten years later at the Grand Canyon and at Yosemite. Muir died in 1914, while Burroughs outlived him by more than six years. Burroughs became a national celebrity, his name a household word. He was a traveling companion of Henry Ford and Thomas A. Edison, two of the most famous Americans of the new industrial age, and his essays were prominent in schoolbooks. Today, however, Burroughs is largely overlooked. I still enjoy reading Burroughs, as I did in grade school, and quote him now and then, but he comes off as pretty tame compared with Muir, whose writing is as vibrant and challenging as ever.

I doubt that John Muir considered himself as either a creative writer or a journalist. He left that for his biographers and interpreters. But surely all writing ought to be literate, manifesting the creativity and imagination of the writer. I mean that journalism can be literature too; everything from obituaries and police news, wherever it appears on a printed page, should be well written, of quality to make the writer proud and the reader responsive.

That is not a new idea. When Lincoln Steffens in 1897 became city editor of the *New York Commercial Advertiser,* he cleaned house of the old staff committed to reporting "strictly the facts" and picked men and women for their unusual literary prose who wanted, openly or secretly, to be poets, essayists, or novelists. He acknowledged a subconscious dread of becoming a professional newspaper man: "I wanted none on my staff. I wanted fresh, young, enthusiastic writers who would see and make others see the life of the city. This meant individual styles, and old newspaper men wrote in the style of their paper. . . ."

You and I may not find this outlook prevalent in the mainstream media, but it is still around, with room for "fresh, young, enthusiastic writers." Publications like *Seattle Weekly* treat their readers like adults, and editors such as Knute Berger still favor writers for their literary prose.

> At *Seattle Weekly* we don't try to be like television because we know we're not. The *Weekly* is for those people who still read, who are willing and able to read stories 5,000 words or more. Thoughtful, literate writing always helps, particularly with our goal of challenging readers, making the world seem more complicated rather than less complicated. That's the difference between us and a lot of other media. We want people to come away thinking there are more sides to a particular subject than they thought. But, then, we find readers are more intelligent and have a longer attention span than some newspapers assume.

Issues that interest me most and that we cover at *Seattle Weekly* involve people. We deal with the environment in human terms. Consider that when people look out their windows at the Olympics or Mount Rainier, they view them as amenities and not as resources. They live in suburbs in hope of finding a nurturing environment, a balance with nature. Now suburbs have become the front line of environmental issues. Covering the conflicts and dilemmas is fascinating work, part of the larger picture of how we cover the environment.[4]

Maybe the most important thing is to have a subject matter that you believe in, that you feel passionate about, a sense of having been singularly chosen by Sigurd Olson, when he said: "Make the wilderness so important, so understandable, so clearly seen as vital to human happiness that it cannot be relegated to an insubstantial minority. If it affects everyone—and I believe that it does—then we must find out how to tell the world why it affects everybody. Only when we put wilderness on that broad base will we have a good chance of saving it."[5]

I urge students to read and draw from the writing of Sigurd Olson, Edward Abbey, Paul Brooks, Rachel Carson, Bernard DeVoto, Aldo Leopold, John Muir, and others who wrote literature even while absorbed with the hard issues. The work of each is invaluable in the study of environmental journalism and advocacy.

Paul Brooks, for example, worked for many years for Houghton Mifflin and eventually became editor-in-chief and was Rachel Carson's editor. During World War II he was chief of the book section of the Office of War Information. Like George Orwell, he got a bellyful of doublespeak: "Of course experts throughout the ages have been aware that they jeopardize their power by giving their secrets to the masses—or even worse by confessing that there *are* no secrets. This axiom is recognized today by the military, by many federal agencies, and by all successful witch doctors. . . . The myth of the expert—fostered by secrecy, sustained by modern techniques of persuasion—is a priceless asset to any public or private operator who would manipulate the environment and at the same time manipulate people to accept the results of his meddling."[6]

As a student of mine in 1991, Sara Olason studied the works of Paul Brooks, which she found "a skillful blending of two kinds of writing: the interpretive, personal and descriptive, with the hard-hitting call to action." In a report for the course, she wrote that Brooks recognizes that political change sprouts from emotional roots, that citizens need a personal connection with wilderness as a basis for action. Thus, according to Olason, "The reader who knows the river as more than a beast of burden is less likely to accept 'harmless' hydroelectric projects; one who has traveled arctic tundra with the caribou may see the land as more than a prospective oil field. There is power in the personal knowledge of nature."

In *The House of Life*, Brooks cited two key aspects of Rachel Carson's work: "the vital role that literature can play in interpreting the natural world, and the enduring ability of one dedicated individual to make an impact on society." In the foreword to an edition of *Silent Spring* issued after it became a best-seller and after Carson's death, Brooks noted: "Rachel Carson was a realistic, well-trained scientist who possessed the insight and sensitivity of a poet. She had an emotional response to nature for which she did not apologize. The more she learned, the greater grew what she termed 'the sense of wonder.' So she succeeded in making a book about death a celebration of life."[7]

Carson had an extensive background in biology, with a master's degree from Johns Hopkins University, and for fifteen years worked for the Fish and Wildlife Service in Washington, writing radio scripts, conservation bulletins, and managing the agency's publications program. By the time of *Silent Spring* in 1962, she was already well known for *The Sea around Us* (which won the National Book Award in 1951), *Under the Sea Wind,* and *The Edge of the Sea.* She was not at heart a crusader, but more like the student who wanted to be productive by sharing the joys experienced while walking in the wilds.

However, when she saw the wholesale destruction of wildlife and its habitat consequent to the use of DDT and other toxic poisons, she committed herself to write the manuscript that became *Silent Spring.* In that landmark book she pieced together evidence from medicine, science, agriculture, and industry for a unified picture, showing problems and goals and the best possible route to attain them. She developed data about the large implications of pesticides that proved convincing in courts of law and before Congress and brought ecology to the forefront.

Carson and her book were criticized and denounced. For one thing, she was not part of the established scientific community. The *New York Times* called the book "wholly inaccurate" and said it "would unnecessarily frighten the readers." *Time* asserted that accidental poisonings from pesticides were "very rare," though Carson and history have shown otherwise.

But she was calm in answering critics and let her attention to scientific detail speak for itself. This is readily evident in listening to the tape of her address to the Women's National Press Club, on December 4, 1962, less than four months after *Silent Spring* was published, a great piece of testimony for the history of environmental journalism. She said the text for her talk derived from an article in the *Bethlehem (Pa.) Globe-Times.* The article began by describing the reaction of farm bureaus in two counties, then continued, "No one in either county farm office had read the book, but all disapproved of it heartily." She cited also an editorial from a Vermont paper, the *Bennington Banner:* "The anguished reaction has been to refute statements that were never made." That, said she, sums up noisier comment heard in the "unquiet autumn," following publication of *Silent Spring.*

In the course of her address she traced public reaction, beginning with the appearance of the first installment in the *New Yorker.* Even before the book was published, editorials and columns by the hundreds had discussed it all over the country. "By late summer the printing presses of the pesticide industry and their trade associations had begun to pour forth a growing stream of pamphlets and booklets to the press and opinion leaders designed to lull the public to sleep from which it had been rudely awakened."

It was a definite pattern of well-known devices to weaken a cause by discrediting the person who champions it, undermining the message by attacking the messenger, a standard procedure experienced by virtually every crusader. In her case, Carson was derided as a bird lover, fish lover, cat lover, "a devotee of some mystical cult that has to do with laws of the universe to which critics are immune."

The industry misrepresented her position. She did not oppose the use of chemicals, but many of the modern pesticides that control insects badly and inefficiently and create serious side effects. "They are," she said, "based on a low level of scientific thinking. . . . Inaccurate statements in reviews of *Silent Spring* are a dime a dozen." One example was a review in a chemical journal that called listing sources "name dropping." The complete and specific references listed in fifty-five pages of notes were "padding to impress the inexperienced with its length."

She showed the influence of the chemical industry behind the critical reviews and media attacks and the comments of scientists. Research supported by manufacturers, she said, is not likely to be directed at discovering facts unfavorable to the continuance of current practices. Not then, and not now. She cited a 1962 report by a committee of the National Academy of Science on the effects of pesticides on wildlife, a study frequently cited by industry to refute *Silent Spring.* The committee study mentioned only some damage to some species of wildlife, without documentation, but that study was underwritten by trade organizations like the National Agricultural Chemical Association, leading Carson to ask: "Do we hear the voice of science or industry? Is industry becoming a screen through which facts must be filtered so that the hard uncomfortable truths are kept back while only the harmless morsels are permitted to filter through?"

Rachel Carson died in 1964 at the age of fifty-six. Whole books have been written since then interpreting her life and work. I doubt she ever thought of herself as an environmental journalist, but I cannot think of a better exemplar.

Marjory Stoneman Douglas was another inspirational personality who used words to command changed attitudes. With her pen and passion, she created the Everglades as we know them now, reshaping the public image of the place from an obstacle-to-progress to a world treasure of untamed nature. Douglas began her career writing society news and editorials for the *Miami Herald* (which her father founded), then as a columnist taking on moral issues, condemning prison conditions and urging women's suffrage. She knew her way around Miami, but little about the wilderness at Miami's back door: "When Hervey Allen [editor at Rinehart of the Rivers of America series] asked me to do this book, I was overwhelmed with the realization that although I had lived in South Florida for many years and had known some part of the Everglades, I had no idea at all what they were or where I could begin to write about them."[8]

With poetry in her prose and spiritual power, she showed the Everglades as more than a swamp to be dredged, filled, and turned into real estate, but as the exciting "river of grass." Since the publication of *The Everglades: River of Grass* in 1947, that book has projected an image of hope and heart—time and again cited to help save Everglades National Park. In 1985 the National Parks and Conservation Association initiated the annual Marjory Stoneman Douglas Award to honor the citizen of the year for his or her work in behalf of national parks. She was named the first winner.

In April 1991, Douglas celebrated her 101st birthday. Wearing a big straw hat and dark glasses, she started her second century by planting trees at a nature center in Miami named for her and pledging to keep up the fight for her beloved, beautiful Florida. She was almost blind and mostly deaf, but that did not stop her. "It's the greatest opportunity anyone could have," she told a cheering crowd of friends and fans, then adding, simply and confidently, "The future is ours!" And so she believed and preached until her death in 1998 at age 108.

Sigurd Olson also was more than a writer but a participant, an activist, a champion of the Boundary Waters Canoe Area, and a leader in the movement to establish Voyageurs National Park. Through his books, including *The Singing Wilderness, Listening Point,* and *The Lonely Land,* he gave voice to the north country in the same sense that Douglas gave voice to the Everglades. Life was not always easy when many of his neighbors were more interested in mining, logging, motorboating, and snowmobiling than in saving wilderness. In the 1930s and 1940s he was threatened with dismissal from his position as professor and then dean at the community college in Ely, Minnesota. At public meetings and hearings he was treated to hoots of scorn and derision.

But he would not be denied. In *Troubled Waters: The Fight for the Boundary Waters Canoe Area Wilderness,* the authors note that when Olson rose to testify at a congressional field hearing in Ely in 1977, "wave after wave of boos and jeers rolled over the auditorium." After a few final hisses, Olson began. He was seventy-eight, but his strong, clear voice echoed through the hall, drawing attention away from the persistent palsy in his right hand:

> I support the Fraser Bill [sponsored by Congressman Don Fraser of Minnesota] whose purpose is to eliminate all adverse uses from the BWCA and give it complete wilderness status. The time for action and immediate passage is now.
>
> I have crisscrossed the BWCA and its adjoining Quetico Provincial Park by canoe countless times since my early guiding days. This is the most beautiful lake country on the continent. We can afford to cherish and protect it.
>
> Some places should be preserved from development or exploitation for they satisfy a human need for solace, belonging, and perspective. In the end we turn to nature in a frenzied chaotic world, there to find silence—oneness—wholeness—spiritual release.[9]

Olson was prominent in national councils of the Wilderness Society and the National Parks and Conservation Association; he came to Washington as an adviser to Secretary of the Interior Stewart L. Udall. He died at the age of eighty-two in 1982 the way he might have wished, while snowshoeing near his home in Ely. I knew Sigurd Olson as a man of poise and presence, who had faith in himself and in the ability of people to respond to a message of consequence. He did not become a serious writer until he was fifty. He had been a guide, a teacher, and dean of a community college. He persevered, insisting that his writing must be purposeful and elevating, which explains why his nine books are still read and quoted.

Edward Abbey, starting with *Desert Solitaire* in 1968, gave artfully detailed descriptions of the Slickrock country of southern Utah, but then with *Monkeywrench Gang* and other works he gave even more. He was funny, irreverent, cynical, and sensitive, turning on many readers, particularly young readers, to join the radical edge of the environmental movement. A writer without passion, he felt, is like a body without a soul. In *One Life at a Time, Please,* he wrote: "Am I saying that the writer should be ... political? Yes sir, I am. . . . By 'political' I mean involvement, responsibility, commitment: the writer's duty to speak the truth—especially unpopular truth. Especially truth that offends the powerful, the rich, the well-established, the traditional, the mythic, the sentimental. To attack, when the time makes it necessary, the sacred cows of his society. And I mean all sacred cows: whether those of the public-lands beef industry or the sacred cows of militarism, nationalism, religion, capitalism, socialism, conservatism, liberalism. . . ."[10]

The common thread through the careers of these people is not simply their competency in using the English language, but rather in their willingness to take a strong position and to declare themselves without equivocation. All of them were "balanced": they balanced their indoor time for reading and writing with time outdoors to appreciate the finite of God's earth and the infinite of God's heaven. The lesson I see is to avoid getting hung up on "creative writing," as you studied it in college.

Creative writing in colleges and universities generally deals with literature, notably fiction and poetry, sometimes drama, and nonfiction to a lesser degree. Courses in these areas can be helpful, but some scholarly professors of English tend to shelter themselves and their students from the cruel, cold vocational world.

Take, for example, the case of Jeff Rennicke, who wrote to me in 1989. He was already the author of five books, magazine articles, and contributing editor of *Backpacker, Canoe,* and *River Runner.* We had met several years before when he worked for the American Wilderness Alliance in Denver and as a wilderness guide. He had read about my environmental-journalism program at Western Washington University, which reminded him of his days at the University of Wisconsin:

Back in 1976, when I enrolled in the creative writing program at the University of Wisconsin–Madison, I began a crusade for just such a program at that school. It has always been my contention that quality nature non-fiction writing is a legitimate literary genre and, perhaps more importantly, that writers who were trained to bridge the gap between the biologists, geologists and ecologists of the world and the general public could play a valuable role in environmental education. It was, perhaps, an idea that had not yet reached its time. No program was created and I muddled along as a creative writing major taking as many ecology and wildlife courses as I could get away with.

Studs Terkel, social critic and oral historian, and his pal and admirer Mike Royko of the *Chicago Sun-Times* probably would see it a little differently. In 1984 Terkel won a Pulitzer Prize for *The Good War,* but the book was panned in some scholarly quarters. This inspired Royko to do a syndicated column taking on "The Professors."

When the professors were asked to comment on Studs' award, oh, how they whined. As one whiner from Northwestern put it: "I don't find him an interesting writer at all." Of course he doesn't. That's because the whiner is a college English professor. And Studs doesn't write like an English professor. If he did he wouldn't have written an oral history of World War II, as told by people who were involved in it.

Instead he would have written a novel about a college English professor who is struggling to complete the great novel that everyone has always expected of so gifted a writer. But he's suffering from writer's block, and his marriage has become boring, and he's having an affair with a gorgeous graduate student, and he's struggling with the fear of impotency, and he wonders if his teen-age daughter respects him. So he goes off to Paris to pull himself together, and while there he meets the beautiful and fascinating . . .

Thank you, Mike Royko, but I still recommend that hopeful environmental journalists read fiction, poetry, and the best nonfiction—including Studs Terkel—to enlarge and enrich their capacities of expression. Be literate, I say, and a risk taker, too.

CHAPTER 7

When Journalists Speak Truth to Power

ON A HOT DAY in the summer of 1844 the editor of the *New York Evening Post,* William Cullen Bryant, took a long walk through the city searching for a future park on ground still unbroken. Then he returned to the office to write an editorial, which he titled "A New Park." It appeared in the edition of July 3, warning that booming Manhattan was in danger of losing its last chance to acquire territory for recreation and pleasure grounds. Bryant's proposal stirred public interest, earning the particular support of Andrew Jackson Downing, the noted landscape architect of that period. Consequently, legislation authorizing acquisition of some of the necessary land was enacted in 1851, though Central Park, the most valuable undeveloped parcel of real estate in America, was not completed until a few years later under Frederick Law Olmsted, the landscape architect and apostle of parks and open space.

This likely was Bryant's most important single contribution to the cause of conservation, but certainly not the only one. In his long career as editor of the *Post* he wrote descriptions of significant natural areas within reach of New York, including the Palisades, the Delaware Water Gap, and the Catskills. Bryant, lover of the country, influenced readers to look at America as a place to cherish and protect. He was one of the first to recognize the pioneering ecological work of George Perkins Marsh. Possibly there was someone before him, but William Cullen Bryant impresses me as the first environmental journalist of note.

Bryant began his career as a Massachusetts whiz kid who wrote *Thanatopsis* (in 1817, when he was seventeen), opening an epoch in American verse. He was bard of the early Republic, "father of American song." As a poet he was immersed in forest solitudes and the flowing of time; wilderness groves, with lodges of Indians, for him were "God's first temples." On reading Wordsworth for the first time, "a thousand springs seemed to gush up at once in his heart, and the face of Nature, of a sudden, appeared to change into a strange freshness and life." Van Wyck Brooks in *The World of Washington Irving* wrote that many poems had been written in America before him, but with few exceptions were in the classical, mechanical modes of Queen Anne's day in England:

> He was the first American poet who was wholly sympathetic with the atmosphere and feeling of the country and who expressed its inner moods and reflected the landscape, the woods and fields as if America itself were speaking through him. . . . The grave, austere and sensitive Bryant sincerely expressed a whole-souled joy alike in the American spirit and the American scene. . . . There were few American writers indeed who did not lose all their American moorings when they set foot in Europe, and especially England, whereas Bryant was free as an American and as a poet, and he only felt abroad, in the course of many journeys, the absence of the wild scenes he loved at home.[1]

Bryant was many-sided, knew botany and Greek, and translated Homer. As a lawyer he came to New York at age thirty-one, but presently joined the *Evening Post*, reviewing books. In 1829 he became editor-in-chief and remained for nearly fifty years, promoting reforms and free discussion of ideals. Bryant was a friend of artists of nature, notably Thomas Cole, principal figure of the Hudson River School, and of John J. Audubon, who lived in upper Manhattan, in the area later known as Audubon Park. Sometimes Bryant joined the young editor of the *Brooklyn Eagle*, Walt Whitman, on explorations of natural New York. Whitman admired Bryant, calling him, in *Specimen Days in America*, "bard of the river and wood . . . touching the highest universal truths, enthusiasms, duties. . . ."

Whitman also exalted nature. He liked to read the great poets in the open air, within the sound of the sea. The poetic form that he gradually evolved he called "oceanic," with verses that recalled the waves, rising and falling, now and then wild with storm. In *Specimen Days*, Whitman recorded a rail journey across America in 1879. The views made him wonder if "the people of the West know how much of first class *art* they have in these prairies—how original and all your own—how much of the influence of a character for your future humanity, broad, patriotic, heroic and new." He wanted "new words in writing about these plains, and all the inland American West, [for] the terms far, large, vast, etc. are insufficient."[2]

Those early editors, Bryant and Whitman, clearly were more than the newsmen we have come to know in our time. But they were journalists, in the best sense, whom I recommend for reading and study. Study the lives and work of creative men and women who have made a difference. Times and techniques may change, but fundamentals remain of philosophy and expression. Good writing lasts forever, and much of it grows better with time. The same for good research and reporting: they are never out of style, and I cannot think of any substitute for them.

Find your own role models in skill, courage, commitment to the public interest and a healthy environment. As a start, I offer Bryant and other favorites of mine. Note that some were trained as journalists and worked in the news business, while others came from altogether different roots, but they shared the singular quality of motivation to rise above the average and to be heard, in a public interest extending far beyond their own.

In 1876, two years before the death of William Cullen Bryant, another New Yorker with considerable in common with him, George Bird Grinnell, joined the staff of *Forest and Stream* as "natural-history editor." He was twenty-seven, studying for his doctorate, and already quite accomplished. Grinnell had received his first formal education and introduction to natural history at the private school conducted at the Audubon place by the widow of Bryant's old friend, John J. Audubon. He had traveled in the West, observing and writing about Indians, including a two-volume study of the Cheyenne. In due course he became editor-in-chief and principal owner of *Forest and Stream,* for its day a formidable environmental journal. Through its pages he directed a steady sequence of dramatic campaigns. One was to protect Yellowstone from poaching, leading to the Lacey Act of 1894, which eliminated hunting in national parks. Another was aimed to end market hunting (killing game for profit). It was a revolutionary idea, but led to the Lacey Act of 1900, making a federal offense the interstate shipment of game killed in violation of state law. Grinnell was closely allied with Theodore Roosevelt in his conservation crusade and was prominent in virtually every major conservation organization.

Grinnell made a reputation as a big game hunter but lost his interest in the sport and turned to preservation. He organized a bird-protection society, which he called the Audubon Club, the first organization anywhere to carry this name; through the pages of *Forest and Stream* he enrolled fifty thousand members, mostly schoolchildren. Later he led the effort to establish Glacier National Park, where Grinnell Glacier, Grinnell Lake, and Grinnell Mountain memorialize his active commitment. When Calvin Coolidge presented him the Roosevelt Memorial Medal at the White House in 1925, the president told Grinnell: "Few have done as much as you, and none has done more, to preserve vast areas of picturesque wilderness for the eyes of posterity in the simple majesty in which you and your fellow pioneers first beheld them." Grinnell died in 1938, in his eighty-ninth year.[3]

The years from about 1880 to 1915, Grinnell's heyday, saw the establishment of national parks and national forests, the advent of forestry, and the birth and growth of the environmental movement. It was the period of populism and progressivism, marked by women's suffrage, civil service, municipal home rule, prison reform, and child-protection laws. It was the time when muckrakers of the media flourished, and influenced the course of history. Yet the periodicals for which they worked were mostly weeklies, monthlies, and alternative media, rather than "mainstream" daily newspapers.

With credit to his confreres, Lincoln Steffens was master of the muckrakers. He was a reporter's reporter, who did his share of uncovering timber and land frauds, and a lot more besides, exposing the "shame of the cities" (the title of one of his books), interpreting national politics and ultimately global geopolitics. He did not start out as a reporter at all, but as the son of wealth, who, after graduating from Berkeley, continued studies in Europe largely for the sake of study. But when he returned from abroad he found a letter waiting from his father: "By now you must know about all there is to know of the theory of life, but there's a practical side as well. It's worth knowing." His father enclosed one hundred dollars, which he hoped would last the young Steffens in New York until he could find a job. He applied to the newspapers of the city. They all turned him down, except, at last, the *Evening Post*, William Cullen Bryant's old paper, where he started as a freelancer and ultimately became a star reporter.

Steffens was energetic and imaginative, perceiving more than news in the news. In 1897 he joined a group that took over the *New York Commercial Advertiser*, the oldest newspaper in New York, down to twenty-five hundred in circulation and no influence. As city editor, he built a staff of fresh, young, enthusiastic writers who attracted a new readership. Then Steffens went on to magazine work with *McClure's* and later *American Magazine,* both distinguished by strong staffs of investigative journalists, the celebrated muckrakers who exposed corruption in diverse settings across America. Steffens himself was not an environmental writer, but he tracked political corruption wherever it might lead. Thus, in his autobiography he relates his adventures in covering timber frauds in Oregon, as perpetrated by railroads and budding timber baronies in harmonious collusion with public officials:

> The famous timber fraud prosecutions were by President Roosevelt's attorney general's department of corrupt acts and policies by the Federal Department of the Interior. Individuals and companies involved were some of them residents of Oregon, Washington, California, and other western States, and the State officials and local political parties played a part. Senators, representatives, and appointees to Federal office from these States had built up, protected and used the Federal departments to further the frauds, so that this whole story was a clear sight of the interlocking of the local, State, and Federal machine as all of one system. Just as we had observed that a railroad commission, whether State or national, established to regulate railroads, came finally to represent the railroads; as a public utility commission came to act for the companies against the consumers; and as the police appointed to arrest crime were corrupted to license criminals—so a Federal department created to execute land, timber, and mineral laws in the public interest was organized (by political appointments) and bought by systematic bribery to take the part of the land grafters, timber thieves, and big mine-jumpers.[4]

'Twas ever thus, then as in our time, but mainstream journalists of Steffens's day did not deal with bribery and corruption built into the system, and they do not much now either. Luckily, Steffens was bold and independent and dared to show the weakness in reform politics, the same problem late in the twentieth century, when the environmental and other social movements hesitated to criticize friends in public office. Steffens saw and showed them as they were: "TR was a politician much more than he was a reformer; in the phraseology of the radicals, he was a careerist, an opportunist with no deep insight into the issues." And as for

Woodrow Wilson: "He had ideals; they were high and they were sincere, but they were so high that he did not expect to realize them. He worked for them, but as a practical man he could yield to facts, and so long as he could feel that he had done his best, he was satisfied. I cited other Americans of this type, reformers who fought for the right, and drove out the rascals, and came into power—and themselves fell. And never knew it."[5] These brief excerpts are from *The Autobiography of Lincoln Steffens,* the one book in journalism that I commend above all others, for it is full of adventures in journalism and in living; it teaches the journalist to be resourceful, unafraid, and "to tell it like it is."

Irving Newton Brant was another who made telling it like it is his life's work; he challenged readers and the system, and I would not be surprised if inspiration came from direct contact with Steffens. In the *Saturday Evening Post,* for example, Brant wrote: "The Petrified Forest of Arizona is being looted and smashed to pieces by the motoring public of America. . . . the Government of the United States is virtually on the side of the looters."[6] Brant, who was born in 1885, began his newspaper career as a schoolboy, working for a small-town Iowa newspaper his father published. Subsequently, he spent thirty years as a reporter, foreign correspondent, editorial writer, and editorial-page editor for major newspapers, including the *Des Moines Register,* the *Saint Louis Star Times,* and the *Chicago Sun.*

Brant was a formidable figure in conservation during the 1930s and 1940s, collaborating with gutsy Rosalie Edge and Willard Van Name in the Emergency Conservation Committee (ECC) and as an adviser to President Franklin D. Roosevelt and Secetary of the Interior Harold L. Ickes. Van Name was a biologist continually in trouble with his superiors at the American Museum of Natural History, but loved and respected by his cohorts at the ECC. Mrs. Edge described him as one who "lives literally with the poverty of St. Francis and gives all he has." Brant wrote: "Brilliantly endowed with insight and foresight, Van Name had been the first to call public attention to virtually every assault on natural resources in the 1920s. He was correspondingly unpopular among the exploiters and short-visioned."[7]

Mrs. Edge was a wealthy New York matron turned social activist. Her favorite project was the protection of hawks in migration across eastern Pennsylvania from hunters, which led her to purchase the prime shooting zone and transform it into the present Hawk Mountain Sanctuary. The three principals kept the ECC small and intimate. "It could strike hard on any issue without being toned down by the conflicting interests of a large board of directors or a diverse membership. This was particularly valuable at a time when almost every nationally organized conservation body was in the paralyzing grip of wealthy sportsmen, gun companies, or lumbermen who were devastating whole states. . . ."[8]

Mrs. Edge used Brant as the ECC's principal pamphleteer—for mailings to lists of activists who would respond to calls for letters and telegrams. Thus, he was projected into almost every nationwide conservation fight for more than thirty years. Then, with Roosevelt's election in 1932, Brant found new and bigger opportunities. FDR took a personal interest in conservation policy, and so did Ickes, the self-styled "curmudgeon"; soon Brant was writing speeches and strategy papers for both. The following excerpt from Brant's book *Adventures in Conservation with Franklin D. Roosevelt* shows the extent of the access and influence he enjoyed: "During a two weeks' stay in Washington in January and February of 1936, I spoke to Secretary Wallace [Henry A. Wallace, secretary of Agriculture] about the unwillingness of the FS [Forest Service] to sanction the transfer of national-forest lands to national parks. He suggested a three-way discussion, to be held at lunch with him and Silcox [Chief Forester Ferdinand Silcox]. We had the talk, and after its close I secured an appointment with President Roosevelt to tell him about it."[9]

The subject at hand was the proposal to establish a national park on the Olympic Peninsula in Washington State. Brant's subsequent monograph, "The Olympic Forests for a National Park," published by the ECC in 1938, and his influence with the president proved instrumental in the establishment of Olympic National Park. In the monograph he wrote:

> If the Mount Olympus National Park is made adequate to preserve the finest trees of the peninsula, it will preserve the Roosevelt Elk. If it is made adequate to preserve the elk, it will preserve the finest of the Douglas firs, the Sitka spruces, the giant cedars and hemlocks, beneath which the elk gather their browse of vine maple, salmonberries, deer fern, moss and fungus.

> The people of the Olympic Peninsula, of the state of Washington and of the United States have a varying yet a common interest in the preservation of this last wilderness, this colossal jungle of the northwestern cool tropics, this final habitat of one of the continent's noblest mammals.

Let this land, which belongs to the American people, be placed beyond the despoiling ax and saw, beyond the hunter's rifle, and we shall have for our own enjoyment, and shall hand down to posterity, something better than an indestructible mountain surrounded by a wilderness of stumps.

Brant was involved in a range of social issues. The American Civil Liberties Union lauded him as a lifelong friend and advocate of civil liberties. As an editor he developed an interest in early American history that led to his definitive six-volume biography of Madison; his best-known book may be *The Bill of Rights: Its Origin and Meaning,* published in 1965. He remained active and involved until he died at Eugene, Oregon, in 1976 at the age of ninety-one.[10]

Where Brant's important work came before World War II, Bernard DeVoto's followed after the war. From the late 1940s until his death in 1955 at the age of fifty-eight, he was by all odds the most productive, influential environmental journalist. How influential? In 1957 Sen. Richard Neuberger of Oregon called DeVoto the most effective conservationist of the twentieth century, and, if you ask me, that could well be true. Wallace Stegner said it best: "His conservation writings record a continuing controversy unmarred by any scramble for personal advantage or any impulse toward self-justification, a controversy in every way dignified by concern for the public good and for the future of the West from which he had exiled himself in anger as a young man."[11]

DeVoto's most widely read material probably were his Easy Chair columns in *Harper's,* but he was distinguished as a historian who won a Pulitzer Prize in 1948 for *Across the Wide Missouri.* Though he left his native Utah to live in the East, mostly at Cambridge, Massachusetts, he wrote columns such as "The Anxious West," "The West: A Plundered Province," and "The West against Itself." He taught conservationists the value of the media, with strong, critical, widely cited columns and articles about proposed dams in Dinosaur National Monument, the pitiful postwar state of the national parks, and the political campaign of western stockmen to take control of national-forest grazing lands. He did not hesitate to anger people, as when he wrote an Easy Chair column called "Outdoor Metropolis," ridiculing coastal Maine as "a jerry-built, neon-lighted overpopulated slum," inciting the Maine Tourist Bureau to withdraw its advertising from *Harper's.*

I suspect that editors in the East never fully fathomed DeVoto's western crusades. They could better comprehend the celebrated elegant piece he wrote in *True* on how to make a martini. Nevertheless, at a ceremony in 1955, Louis Lyons, director of the Niemann Fellowship at Harvard, presented DeVoto a bound volume of the November issue of *Harper's* containing his twentieth-anniversary essay, his 241st, with this inscription from the editors: "To Bernard DeVoto, seasoned practitioner of the journalistic craft, widely ranging in competence and punctual in deadlines, as resolute in his approvals as in his dislikes, partisan of sound sense and adversary of cant, friend of the public lands and enemy of the lukewarm martini, who in the twenty years he has occupied the Easy Chair has never learned to write a dull sentence."[12] He could not write a dull sentence because there was not anything dull about him, either in print or in person. I met DeVoto several times and remember him exactly as Lyons described him. He was always willing to declare himself, with vigor.

Richard L. Neuberger was also an environmental journalist of note. Born in Portland in 1912, Neuberger became a student journalist at the University of Oregon; as editor of the student paper he campaigned for abolition of mandatory military training and compulsory student fees. His grades were low, and he left without graduating, but that did not stop him from writing for the *Portland Oregonian*, the *New York Times*, and for major national magazines (including *Esquire, Harper's, Holiday, Reader's Digest*, and the *Nation*). In the pre–World War II era he was the foremost media interpreter of environmental issues in the Northwest. He grew from an observer of politics into a participant, first as a member of the Oregon House of Representatives in 1941, then, after returning from military duty, the state senate in 1949, and in 1954 as a member of the United States Senate, breaking a Republican monopoly on Oregon politics, based largely on his conservation platform against the Eisenhower administration.

While in Washington until his death in 1960 Neuberger was associated with every positive piece of environmental legislation and was known as "Mr. Conservation." Yet he still thought of himself as a writer, enjoyed corresponding with writers, and introduced meaningful articles into the *Congressional Record*.

"Say nothing, and say it well," Neuberger was advised by an older U.S. senator interested in his budding career. He wondered whether he belonged in politics, whether it was proper to mix his craft as a writer with political candidacy. But, "When I see Oregon's teachers paid the lowest salaries on the Coast, when I see a private utility company selling the power from the dam at Bonneville which the people built and paid for, when I see a Japanese-American soldier with forty-one blood transfusions denied a hotel room on a rainy night, when I see a million-dollar race track rising while veterans cannot construct homes—then my blood pressure rises too, and I wonder if any case is strong enough to impel abdication in favor of those who tolerate these things."[13]

Edward J. Meeman was another vintage journalist of both the prewar and the postwar eras. He was the rare example of a daily newspaper editor who recognized the big story in conservation and spread it unashamedly across the front page. Meeman was born in 1889 and began his newspaper career in Indiana, influenced by Eugene Debs, the socialist leader. In 1921 he went south to Tennessee as the founding editor of the *Knoxville News-Sentinel*. During the next decade he played a prominent role in the movement to establish the Great Smoky Mountains National Park. So did his newspaper, with propark front-page editorials. He wrote one telling readers that, unlike logging payrolls that last only a few years, the national park would endure forever and grow in value. In his autobiography, *The Editorial We,* he wrote: "Yes, our newspaper did a lot. Yet it was no more than a newspaper ought to do. When citizens work for the public, they are volunteers. They do it over and above their regular occupations. But public service is the family business of a newspaper."[14]

Meeman in 1931 shifted to Memphis as editor of the *Press Scimitar,* where he waged two memorable crusades. On one hand, he challenged the entrenched political machine of E. H. "Boss" Crump that controlled the city of Memphis. More than Crump himself, according to Edwin Howard, in the foreword to Meeman's posthumous autobiography, Meeman attacked the public indifference that made Crump's power possible: "His strategy was to convince the people of Memphis that they were free—free to govern themselves, free to choose democracy over a paternalistic but oppressive dictatorship, free to create a better government than the machine, for all its pretensions of efficiency, could provide—and to make them want to exercise that freedom."[15]

It took Meeman seventeen years to bring the machine down. The victory came with the 1948 election of Estes Kefauver, who dared to run for the United States Senate without Crump's support. During the campaign Crump ridiculed Kefauver as a "pet coon," but the latter made points by donning a coonskin cap and declaring, "I'm not Boss Crump's pet coon."

Meeman also led the movement that gave Memphis the 12,500-acre state park that now bears his name. In his address to the National Council on

State Parks in 1958, Meeman said: "I will not recount all the difficulties which you can imagine we had to overcome in the creation of a park close to a great city. But they were overcome by the magic formula: (1) Keep the goal steadily before you, (2) take one step at a time, (3) ask the cooperation of everyone whose cooperation you need and have faith you will get it."[16]

Meeman until his death in 1966 influenced the entire Scripps-Howard chain to treat the environment as an important issue and to give annual awards for the best environmental articles published in any newspaper. His guiding principle was: "Citizens working alone can do much; a newspaper working alone can do much; citizens and their newspapers can do anything."[17]

In the period of the 1960s and 1970s, I do not believe that any journalist in America exercised greater influence on environmental policy than John B. Oakes, editorial-page editor of the *New York Times*. I first became acquainted with his work in the 1950s (before his appointment as editor), when he wrote a monthly Sunday column titled Conservation, on the back pages of the *Times* travel section. Oakes had joined the *Times* in 1946 after serving in the military during World War II and four years as a political reporter at the *Washington Post*. His job initially was editor of the review-of-the-week section; the conservation column was a sideline, but this did not keep him from scoring strong blows. With the announcement of the dismissal of Newton B. Drury as director of the National Park Service, Oakes took up the issue of proposed dams in Dinosaur National Monument in Utah, a major issue of that time: "If Congress should approve construction of the Dinosaur dams, it will release the floodgates for renewed attacks on many national parks—Grand Canyon and Glacier, to name but two that have already been threatened in the same manner. Mr. Drury's departure may forebode a new stress on the promotion of organized recreation in our parks and monuments, and a slackening of interest in the preservation of untouched areas of wild and natural beauty for themselves alone."[18]

In 1956 his column commended new legislation introduced by Sen. Hubert Humphrey to establish a national wilderness-preservation system. It was the beginning of the long political fight leading to passage of the Wilderness Act in 1964.

During the fifteen years he ran the editorial page (starting in 1961), Oakes editorialized about civil rights, the presidency, foreign affairs, politics, and the Wilderness Bill, defining an agenda of public policy. A single editorial, "Along the Wide Missouri," reprinted and widely circulated, proved a key factor in stopping the Corps of Engineers from building Fort Benton and Cow Creek dams. When he retired his colleagues paid editorial homage: "He could not and would not prettify the scene. But he dignified it, with a conscientiousness and with standards that were unyielding and with a boundless confidence that if only sound values and solid information could be located in the confusion of events, the citizen reader would distinguish the right from the wrong and uphold the public good."[19]

Even after retirement Oakes contributed powerful opinion pieces to the Op-Ed page (which he had started in 1970), including "Watt's Very Wrong," when James G. Watt's nomination was pending in the Senate; "Pork—U.S. Prime," about the ill-conceived Tennessee-Tombigbee barge canal and waterway; "Japan, Swallow Hard and Stop Whaling"; "The Attack on Alaska's Parks"; and "Adirondack SOS," which, as mentioned earlier, in short order elicited a letter to the editor of the *Times* from Gov. Mario Cuomo pledging renewed commitment to preserving the Adirondacks.[20]

Reporters can do outstanding work too, though they rarely get the chance to, or exercise enough initiative on their own. Nevertheless, Dick Smith joined the staff of the *Santa Barbara News Press* in 1948 and proceeded to make the backcountry of the Los Padres National Forest his special beat, roaming the trails and canyons with camera and notebook. He was the untiring guardian of wilderness, "the conscience of the county." He studied the California condor and helped gain recognition for it as a species in need of special protection. He sparked the effort to designate the San Rafael Wilderness, the first one reviewed by Congress and set aside under the 1964 Wilderness Act, and wanted a large adjacent area added to it. When he died suddenly in 1977, the mayor proclaimed Dick Smith Week, and the city mourned. All kinds of groups and the elected officials of Santa Barbara County supported the wilderness extension, which became the Dick Smith Wilderness.

Another exemplar, Michael Brown, made the country aware of Love Canal and the consequences of dumping toxic wastes. As a reporter for the *Niagara Gazette,* he wrote more than one hundred stories piecing together the grisly saga of enormous amounts of chemicals dumped in a residential area by Hooker Chemical Company. His investigation and reporting of miscarriages, birth defects, cancers, and other grave medical problems led the State of New York in 1978 to declare an emergency and permanent evacuation of two hundred homes. He subsequently traveled into every section of the country, showing Love Canal as only one of many "toxic time-bombs waiting to go off," then wrapped it up in his book *Laying Waste: The Poisoning of America by Toxic Chemicals.*

Robert H. Boyle, editor and writer for *Sports Illustrated,* devoted his talent to protection of the Hudson River and the Hudson River valley. His book *The Hudson River: A Natural and Unnatural History,* first published in 1969, details the uniqueness of one of America's celebrated rivers, but it does much more. It recounts successful public efforts to prevent a powerful utility from defacing Storm King Mountain and to gain enforcement of state and federal antipollution laws. Boyle and his writings have been central to all these efforts, and to the future of the Hudson.

But not all environmental journalists came up through journalism. Harry Caudill, author of many fine articles and of five books, trained as a lawyer. He actually practiced within a mile of his birthplace (he was born in 1922) in Letcher County, Kentucky, but was also a legislator, a professor of Appalachian studies at the University of Kentucky, and an active writer with a mission. In assessing his most important work, *Night Comes to the Cumberlands,* Henry David wrote: "Mr. Caudill's richly informed and sobering account of the Cumberlands' painful plight is the product not only of thorough research, but also of an intimate firsthand knowledge of the region and its people."[21] Caudill repeatedly made the connection between plight of the land and plight of people; he showed that a million Americans in southern Appalachia were living in squalor, ignorance, and ill health, the consequence of a failed education system and the destructive practice of strip-mining coal.

The book led to federal programs to help Appalachia, but I believe Caudill was disillusioned by the failure of these programs to make any difference. But then, as Lincoln Steffens noted, the interlocking local, state, and federal machine is all one system used to further the fraud. Caudill died in 1990, of a self-inflicted gunshot wound to the head after suffering from Parkinson's disease. One year later the Letcher County Library undertook to fund a new headquarters to be named the Harry M. Caudill Memorial Library, which seemed appropriate considering his conviction that education and an access to books are basic to solving the dilemma of Appalachia, a region of intrinsic natural beauty subject to endless cycles of exploitation by corporations headquartered elsewhere.

Dorothy Day was yet a different kind of journalist, but one whose life and work I find relevant and inspirational in dealing with the environment. As a young writer in the 1920s, exploring social activism and religion in Greenwich Village, she worked for a time for the socialist *Call,* then for the radical literary magazine the *Masses,* and contributed occasional articles for Catholic magazines. In 1932 she reported the Hunger March to Washington, which the popular press brushed off as a ragtag parade of dangerous radicals, ignoring its proposals for jobs, housing, and health care. So the next year, when she was thirty-five, she launched the *Catholic Worker.* It cost fifty-seven dollars to print twenty-five hundred copies of the first issue, and it sold for a penny. The purpose was not to report news, but to create news.

Her essays, which ran for thirty years under the heading "On Pilgrimage," bring a timeless basic message to every social cause and to every activist. As her daughter, Kate Hennessy, wrote on the occasion of Dorothy's hundredth birthday: "She turned the life of poverty into something dynamic, full of richly simple moments for those who have nothing."[22] For Day, it was only a matter of knowing where and how to look. She wrote of how, on her way to mass in downtown Manhattan, she was greeted by the globe of sun, one street wide, framed in early morning mists. She saw the Franciscan spirit in one man who washed and dried her black cat, then anointed it with warming unguent for a bad cough, and also in another man, Big Dan, who took the blanket off a bed to cover an old horse.

> There is poverty and hunger and war in the world. And we prepare for more war. There is desperate suffering with no prospect of relief. But we would be contributing to the misery and desperation of the world if we failed to rejoice in the sun, the moon, and the stars, in the rivers which surround this island on which we live, in the cool breezes of the bay, in what food we have and in the benefactors God sends.

> Love and ever more love is the only solution to every problem that comes up. If we love each other enough, we will bear with each other's faults and burdens. If we love enough, we are going to light that fire in the hearts of others. And it is love that will burn out the sins and hatred that sadden us. It is love that will make us want to do great things for each other. No sacrifice and no suffering will then seem too much.[23]

Near the end of her life Day received considerable recognition, but she brushed it off. "Too much praise makes you feel you must be doing something terribly wrong."[24] When she died in 1980 at eighty-three the *New York Times* eulogized her as "a nonviolent social radical of luminous personality." The *Catholic Worker,* which still appears regularly in continuation of her work, seems insignificant and inconsequential alongside the mainstream media, but only when measured in material terms. Dorothy Day learned from the Gospels that the most important events take place on the margins of history, in obscure, unexpected places. Her writing, with spiritual response to social problems, grows more meaningful as a guide to self-fulfillment.

Finally, in this little survey of my hall of heroes and heroines, I arrive at Samuel H. Day Jr., no relation to Dorothy, whom I first encountered in the late 1960s when he was editor of the *Intermountain Observer,* a lively fortnightly published at Boise, featuring articles on welfare by welfare mothers, on prisons by prisoners, and on the environment by an actual environmental activist, Pete Hennault. I really came to know Day, however, by reading his 1991 autobiography, *Crossing the Line: From Editor to Activist to Inmate, a Writer's Journey.* I learned in its pages that Day was born in 1926 into privileged comfort as the son of a diplomat. Though he planned to follow his father into the State Department, instead he joined the Associated Press in San Francisco, then went to Idaho as a reporter and editor, and founded the *Observer.*

As a subscriber at the time, I remember it as literate and innovative; it reached a circulation peak of four thousand in 1973, but it failed to attract advertising and Day closed shop. He left Idaho to become editor of the *Bulletin of the Atomic Scientists,* where he learned about science, technology, academia, and nuclear-weapons laboratories. Atomic energy was viewed as the global savior, safe, easy, and "too cheap to meter." Time, however, has shown nuclear development dependent on huge government subsidy, while incidents and accidents like Three Mile Island and Chernobyl have led to cancer and ill health, and now nobody knows where or how to dispose of the waste.

Samuel Day raised questions about nuclear safety (the Atomic Energy Commission claimed that a reactor accident more devastating than a flood or earthquake was unlikely to happen in a million years) and endorsed total nuclear disarmament over the "arms control" approach of the liberal scientific community that ran the *Bulletin.* He was reminded sternly that it was not a "political" magazine and went on his way. In 1977 he joined the *Progressive,* at Madison, Wisconsin. As managing editor, he continued the antinuke crusade, nurturing an article by Howard Morland that on the face of it seemed to reveal important secrets. The government tried to block publication, calling the article a blueprint for construction of a thermonuclear weapon. But the *Progressive* would not be intimidated. Day and colleagues demonstrated that the basic scientific concepts already were in the public domain; they insisted that the government should not be allowed to stifle public awareness of the H-bomb program by claiming "national security." After the government finally dropped its case, the article was published in April 1979, dispelling the secrecy mystique protecting the nuclear-weapons program.

Day became a full-time antinuclear activist, since 1981 a prime mover in Nukewatch, a nuclear-disarmament group, protesting CIA recruiting and military research at universities and getting arrested for civil disobedience. His autobiography, in fact, began as a prison journal after he was sentenced to serve six months for cutting his way into a nuclear-missile launch site. Certainly he traveled a long way from his upbringing and from conventional journalism: first, as he wrote, through passages of inner struggle, then into deep fear, followed by calm of the action itself, exhilaration whatever the outcome, and sometimes painful satisfaction of having, as Quakers say, "spoken truth to power."

Journalists should speak truth to power. It is not easy; it takes a special person to grow into it. Samuel Day, Dorothy Day, Harry Caudill, and all the rest have each been that kind of person. It requires something more than professional skill. Samuel Day wrote: "By fits and starts I crossed the line from observer to doer, from dispassion to passion, from agnostic to believer. You cannot do this work for long, I am convinced, without religion of some kind. I tapped into a secondary source. I came to believe not in God but in those who believed in God—people of deep religious faith who had been moved to action by the call of the Holy Spirit."[25]

Personally, I agree with Samuel Day, but I will not here prescribe religion, or faith, of any kind. Let me call it a calling of spirit, and to anyone who hears it, I say, give it room to deepen and to grow, and draw from it.

Part II

LESSONS FROM A

CAREER OF

COMMITMENT

You Can't Make an Omelet Without Breaking Eggs

BECOMING AN ENVIRONMENTAL WRITER was never something I planned or studied for. Now, in retrospect, I appreciate the value of designed and disciplined course work, but in my case it was, for want of a better word, an accident. Writing my first column, my first book, and attaining my position in higher education may all have been dreams, or beyond my dreams, but never the consequence of deliberate decision or design. Luckily, searching for new ideas led me to discover scenes and places and opportunities I never knew existed.

Experience has taught me there is no magic formula and no magic either. Almost everything I have done, or accomplished, came the hard way. The difference for me came when I chose as a writer not to be an observer only, but an advocate and participant, involved with people, groups, and live issues. The more involved, the more meaningful I felt my writing became. Now I cannot separate writing from issues that I write about; it is the cause that counts.

I began my professional career in journalism in the year before World War II as a copyboy at the *Washington Post,* for fifteen dollars a week. I stayed until I got a better job for the old Hearst International News Service, for eighteen dollars a week. Both those assignments were wonderful training—there is a lot to be said for starting at the bottom.[1] Then I became managing editor of a weekly newspaper in Pennsylvania. I was twenty-one and was hired for twenty-five dollars a week, later raised to thirty-five dollars, an aspiring young journalist working for cheap, but that was good training, too. However, I soon joined the Army Air Corps (later the Air Force) a step or two ahead of the draft, and trained as a navigator. I spent the war years in ferrying and transport missions across oceans and continents, high adventure, although the only shooting I did was of celestial fixes through the bubble of an octant.

Following the war I returned to the *Post* as a reporter. At first I covered local news and wrote obituaries. I was one of two reporters who stayed on duty until three in the morning, mostly to be there in case of late-breaking news. Then opportunity came my way. One afternoon, while walking through the lobby of the Willard Hotel, I ran into two pilots I had known in the military. They now were civilians too, preparing to fly to Prague the next week on a civilian mission for UNRRA, the United Nations relief agency. Their charter plane would be loaded with hatching eggs to help regenerate Czech agriculture. They said they needed an experienced navigator and wondered if I could join them.

It was not easy, but I walked across the street to ask permission of my employer. The *Post*, as it happened, editorially supported UNRRA; the owner and publisher, Eugene Meyer, was personally committed and had been involved in the beginning of the relief agency. So I was given leave of the obituary page for a while. I filed my first story by wireless from Prague in time to make the Sunday edition. The timing could not have been better: it was Easter Sunday, 1946. The Czechs loved the hatching eggs, and the editors in Washington evidently loved my dispatch, which they featured at the top of the front page with my photograph. I wrote other stories with impressions of Prague and a few weeks later rejoined the charter crew on a mission to Warsaw, where I interviewed leaders of the government and the opposition as the basis of a five-part series.[2]

It was heady stuff. I drew better assignments on some days, but on other days it was back to the obits and the local civic associations. That was my job. Perhaps I was too impatient, too eager to get ahead: I accepted a position elsewhere. Before I left, the city editor of the *Post*, Ben Gilbert, took me to lunch. "The boss wants you to stay," he said. "If you stay, we'll give you a raise and better assignments."

I did not stay, as probably I should have. The new position (as managing editor of the daily newspaper in Spartanburg, South Carolina) did not turn out well, probably because I was not ready for it, and within a year I was back in Washington. This time I got a job working in public relations for the American Automobile Association (AAA). I stayed with AAA for ten years, much too long, but there is no rewriting one's life, and somehow every experience has something positive to it.

I recall one evening, during intermission of a concert at Constitution Hall, meeting Katherine Graham, the daughter of the *Post* publisher and later her father's successor. She asked what I was doing; when I explained, she snickered about what a letdown it must be from working at the *Post*.

There was much in what she said, but every bit of experience, whether plus or minus at the time, adds to the writer's experience and perspective. While at AAA as a writer and publicist my assigned specialty was the field of travel; I was spared promoting freeways or apologizing for them. I was asked to develop an antibillboard legislative and publicity campaign to protect roadsides from blight, so I became aware of conservation groups interested in this phase of landscape protection and began communicating with them.

I traveled around the country and learned a lot about it. I discovered national parks and their problems. The parks clearly were significant touring destinations, but their postwar popularity was soaring beyond adequate staffing and protection. Bernard DeVoto wrote a classic piece on the subject, "Let's Close the National Parks," in *Harper's*.[3] I met DeVoto and other individuals in and out of government who played particular roles in park policy, including the publisher Alfred Knopf, who was chairman of the National Parks Advisory Board, and Wallace Stegner and Sigurd Olson, authors who concerned themselves with preservation of nature. I became acquainted with the conservation column by John Oakes in the *New York Times*. I came to it because it was in the Sunday travel section, which I read regularly as part of my work; the column was buried in the back pages, but it was alive with news of goings-on in America that I found in no other paper.

During my ten years with AAA, I developed an expertise in travel and tourism. Editors and writers would call about trends and article ideas. *Holiday,* an elegant upscale magazine of the postwar period, sent an editor to consult me about how to structure a proposed series of offbeat motor tours and to ask me to write the first three articles (which AAA permitted, providing that it was mentioned and the articles were written on my own time). Then *Woman's Day* asked me to do a piece on travel planning. As these avenues opened, I recognized that I could do something more in my life than publicize and promote automobile clubs. In the late 1950s I went on my own and never looked back. From the beginning I was lucky enough to get assignments for travel articles from *Holiday, Woman's Day, Parade,* and *Changing Times,* all respectable magazines, and to have articles accepted by travel sections of the *New York Times,* the *Christian*

Science Monitor, and the *Chicago Tribune.* Out of the blue a friend steered me to an editor at Doubleday, for which firm I wrote my first books, two travel guides.[4]

I thought of myself as a travel writer, but saw many stories in national parks, national forests, and conservation generally that were not being covered but needed to be written. I wrote cover articles for *Parade,* one called "The Battle for Gettysburg" about the invasion of the battlefield by subdivisions and tourist traps, another called "What's Happening to Our Shoreline?" which Sen. Richard Neuberger of Oregon introduced into the *Congressional Record.* There was nothing unusual about that—congressmen load the appendix of the *Record* with all kinds of relevancies and irrelevancies, but I admired Richard Neuberger as a writer with a cause who made his mark in public life. I listened to an intensely impressive speech by Gaylord Nelson, then a new senator from Wisconsin, in which he warned a Washington, D.C., audience that conservation of woods, lakes, streams, and other natural resources constituted the most urgent and crucial domestic issue facing the nation. But to find a report of his remarks in the *Washington Post,* I had to look to the bottom of the obituary page, where it lay buried below the deceased, like a dead issue. It struck me that as long as the media treat the environment as an incidental "story" to be covered now and then, the public will remain in the dark, unable to participate intelligently in the process of decision making. I saw a void and the challenge to fill it.

One step led to another. Following a pack trip in the Bridger Wilderness and surrounding national forests in western Wyoming, I proposed a book to Doubleday, which became *Whose Woods These Are: The Story of the National Forests,* published in 1962.[5] Coward McCann asked me to write two juveniles, for children eight to twelve or so: one about Virginia (where I lived), the other called *The Varmints: Our Unwanted Wildlife.* Then the editors at Doubleday asked if I would write a book about the Great Smoky Mountains of western North Carolina and Tennessee. My initial thought was to make it something of a history and travel guide, but when the National Park Service proposed to construct a disruptive road across the mountains, I wanted my book to speak for preserving and protecting wilderness. When *Strangers in High Places* was published in 1966, park officials responded in mean spirit by banning the book from sale in the park. But the road was not built, which counts more. Moreover, that book has remained in print, now for more than thirty years, through new editions and printings. It proves to me that I was right to choose not to be an observer only, but an advocate and participant, involved with people and live issues.

That year, 1966, was a big one for me. I became a columnist for *American Forests,* the monthly magazine of the American Forestry Association, with the chance to offer my own opinion on conservation and natural-resource politics. The editors of *Holiday* noted the natural-beauty movement and asked me to analyze it, in Washington and across the country. I observed President Lyndon B. Johnson in a bill signing at the White House, interviewed cabinet members, senators, congressmen, industry and conservation leaders, and visited the Grand Canyon and redwoods. It was a great writing exercise: twice the editors returned what I considered the finished manuscript, raising pointed questions, forcing me to learn more about my subject. The feature that emerged, "The Politics of Conservation," dealt with public desire to meet the onrushing environmental crisis and the inadequate, sugar-coated response of politicians and public officials. I have been writing the same theme, with variations, ever since.

Soon after that article appeared, I received a letter from Clare Conley, the editor of *Field & Stream,* whom I had met at a dinner in Washington. "When are you going to write something like that for us?" he asked. I was not a hunter, nor much of a fisherman, and was barely acquainted with *Field & Stream,* but it struck me as a welcome opportunity to reach an important audience of outdoors people.

I researched and wrote two articles, and then, when the conservation editor died, Conley appointed me to succeed him. As a contributing editor, I worked at home but also had a base at the magazine's office in New York, plus assured income and an expense account, and latitude to pursue other activities. Between 1967 and 1974 I wrote seventy-five conservation columns and more than a dozen features. Though a stranger to the outdoor sports, I found hunters and fishermen receptive and responsive to the conservation message. They wrote to me of their concern over degradation of particular places they cared about—and they needed something more than cues on how to kill a deer or skin a bear. They needed to be told who was responsible for the loss of hunting grounds and fishing streams and actions they could take to save what was left.

I wrote about the effects of logging on wildlife, drainage of waterfowl breeding areas of the northern prairies, the threat of dams at Hells Canyon on the Idaho-Oregon border, the ill-conceived Cross-Florida Barge Canal, and environmental issues in Alaska. I investigated illegal eagle killings in

Wyoming and defended professional game biologists in Oklahoma from petty political interference. I investigated and wrote about politics, bureaucracy, and corporate power, naming the wrongdoers, trying to involve and activate readers so they would not feel helpless against the odds. Conley encouraged me, every step of the way.

In autumn preelection issues of 1968, 1970, and 1972, *Field & Stream* published a special feature, "Rate Your Candidate," showing readers how to evaluate congressmen and congressional candidates on crucial environmental concerns. The 1972 article rated the performance of every member of the House and Senate, stirring loud complaints from those with low grades, including Congressman Gerald Ford, of Michigan, who later became president, and Sen. Bob Dole, of Kansas, who would run for president.

But anyone who dishes it out must prepare to take it as well. Freedom of expression is more of a goal than a given. Thomas Jefferson recognized the constant effort required, when he wrote: "No experiment can be more interesting than that we are now trying, and which we trust will end in establishing that man may be governed by reason and truth. Our first objective should therefore be to leave open all avenues of truth. The most effective hitherto found is the freedom of the press. It is, therefore, the first shut up by those who fear the investigation of their action."

In 1971, although still going strong at *Field & Stream*, I was having trouble with my other connection, at *American Forests*. I believe the column of independent ideas was popular with readers—that was never the issue. The editor, James B. Craig, was continually supportive; so was the executive director of the association, William E. Towell. The time came, however, when I stepped on the wrong toes, by criticizing the clearcutting and overemphasis on timber production that I found all across the national forests.

Craig talked to me about it several times; he did not want to interfere with my writing but explained that he was getting pressure and finally asked me to turn to other issues for a while, and I agreed. The president of the association, Charles Connaughton, after all, was a high official of the Forest Service (regional forester in the Pacific Northwest), and the board of directors was composed largely of foresters, forestry professors, and timbermen. I had no idea of the travail I was causing, however, until I received a phone call from one of the few nontimber members of the board, Professor Ernest H. Linford, head of the journalism department at the University of Wyoming, a former chief editorial writer of the *Salt Lake Tribune*. He read (and then sent) to me a memorandum from Towell to members of the board reporting Towell's directive that I was "not to write critically about the U.S. Forest Service, the forest industry, the profession or about controversial forestry issues" and my agreement to it. To Linford, a journalist, this was censorship, and he wanted to confirm my acquiescence to it. It was all news to me, and I was angry at Towell's presumptive misrepresentation. I wrote memoranda of protest to both him and Craig. I could not accept the censorship and was fired. The Towell memo, dated March 4, 1971, follows:

TO: James B. Craig

FROM: William E. Towell, Executive Vice President

SUBJECT: Mike Frome's Column in AMERICAN FORESTS

The formality of this memorandum is to clarify for the record the decisions made regarding Mike Frome's column in AMERICAN FORESTS Magazine. It will be your responsibility to see that these decisions are carried out.

It is hardly necessary to review the background and reasons for this action, except to say that Mike's column frequently has been personal and inflammatory, particularly with respect to the Forest Service; and, in the opinion of many, sometimes contains outright inaccuracies or harmful innuendoes. For the protection of the Association itself, it is necessary to require certain editorial restrictions on Mike in the future. It is my understanding that Mr. Frome has agreed to these restrictions as a requisite to his continued service as a columnist with AMERICAN FORESTS:

1. Frome's column is to be censored by you as Editor to insure that it is not in conflict with established AFA policy position.

2. Frome, in the future, is not to write critically about the U.S. Forest Service, the forest industry, the profession or about controversial forestry issues.

3. A disclaimer is to appear permanently on Frome's column that he is a paid columnist and does not speak for the Association.

I am very pleased, as was the Board, that Mike has agreed to this censorship and wants to continue writing for us. He is a very effective and popular writer who has been and can continue to be a great asset to our magazine.

CC: Officers and Directors W.E.T.

The episode presently reached the media. Stewart Udall and Jeff Stansbury in their column for the Los Angeles Times Syndicate wrote as follows: "HOW TO KILL A CONSERVATION ORGANIZATION. With no great pleasure we write this obituary for the American Forestry Association (AFA). It is not dead in a literal sense, but its leadership has sold out its birthright and therefore its future claims to our attention. . . ."[6]

Living Wilderness published an extensive review of "The Strange Case of Michael Frome, Lover of Trees and *bete noire* of the Lumber Industry." An introductory editorial note included the following:

> We always thought it was to the credit of the American Forestry Association that it published Mike's column, which began in 1966 and was preceded by occasional articles going back to 1959. Here was convincing proof that the association could look objectively at itself and its many close friends in government and industry and fight for change where change was needed. With at least seven industry representatives and several former officials of the U.S. Forest Service among its officers and directors, the association needs to show this kind of independence.

> To us, it is indeed sad that this relationship has ended. It is especially sad for what it seems to tell us about the internal problems of the American Forestry Association, once thought to be a strong voice for conservation and now, perhaps, something less than that.[7]

The association actually was hurt more than I was. Members wrote letters of inquiry and protest, but received no rational reply. For example, when Gary Soucie, conservation director of Friends of the Earth, wrote Towell that he was shocked by the Udall-Stansbury revelation of censorship, Towell replied: "Thank you for your opinion. I am well aware that censorship is a serious affair, public issues or otherwise. But, there are aspects of this situation which did not appear in the newspapers, and I am sure your reactions would be different if you had the whole story.

However, I choose not to make a public issue or prolong this one by disclosing internal affairs of the American Forestry Association." And to Beulah Edmiston, a reader in Los Angeles, Towell wrote:

> Thank you for your comments about Mike Frome's column in *American Forests.* No, Mike Frome will not be censored (we don't believe in censorship either), but his column has been discontinued.
>
> Please keep in mind, Miss Edmiston, that *American Forests* is not a news publication. It is a membership service of the Association governed by a policy making Board of Directors. Mike, or anyone else working for the Association, must conform to the basic policy and philosophy as laid down by the Directors. Mike chose not to do so and his column was terminated.
>
> Sorry to lose you as a member, but no individual can be independent of the organization for which he works.[8]

The dismissal taught me a great deal: I could stand up and take it, I could survive, and I must continue to call the shots as I see them—to demonstrate that it can be done. And, after all, I still had *Field & Stream* (where one of my colleagues, Dick Starnes, wrote a lovely tribute, "How the Clearcutters Tried to Gag Mike Frome").

Field & Stream was much larger and more influential, but changes were taking place there, too. CBS, then the owner, shuffled management at the top. Conley was fired, and the new editor, Jack Samson, reversed course, directing that I write in generalities, instead of holding institutions and individuals responsible for deeds and misdeeds. For him and the owners of the magazine, that made sense. Those outdoor magazines, *Field & Stream, Outdoor Life,* and *Sports Afield,* are cogs in corporate conglomerates without roots in the outdoors. They help sell firearms and fishing tackle for advertisers by stroking readers, not stirring them up, in the same way that women's magazines merchandise cosmetics and fashions through happy imagery.

Early in 1974 Samson ruled out plans for another preelection "Rate Your Candidate" feature because, he wrote: "This is definitely not the year of the environment. The energy crisis has caused a backlash. . . ." His reference was to the Arab oil embargo initiated in 1973 by the oil-rich nations of the Middle East in retaliation for U.S. support of Israel. The oil companies made the most of it, beating the drums for exploration and exploitation of new energy sources, including those in Alaska. I might have seen that it was not the year for me either. In October, Samson wrote me that management wanted "a modification in the editorial approach" and that I had written my last piece. From then on environmentalism at *Field & Stream* would be expressed in affirmative answers to such questions as "Oil and Water: Can They Mix?" An editorial by Samson in January 1975 sounded to me like an Exxon annual report: "Our nation has its energy problems, and the welfare of 100 million depends on us working with our vital industries to see that the environment is protected, not upon those forcing those industries to come to a complete halt. . . . We are in a serious recession now. But stop all development of resources in the name of preservation only and we answer to several million unemployed."

There were various speculations as to why I lost my job. *Time* did a feature, "A Voice in the Wilderness," quoting Clare Conley: "We got vibes from CBS that they didn't want trouble with Pastore [Sen. John Pastore of Rhode Island, chairman of the subcommittee with jurisdiction over broadcasting regulations.] The word was 'Do what you have to do, but take it easy,' " to which the magazine added: "That Frome refused to do, with the result that he lost his biggest platform."9

Many friends and organizations protested my dismissal. "We tout our system as being one of freedom for the individual, and we particularly tout our freedom of speech and expression," wrote Tom Bell in *High Country News*. "His [Frome's] experiences give the lie to just how much freedom we really do have." That was a thoughtful, considerate critique but not wholly correct: I did not lose my right of free expression, I was just fired from one publication that I had lucked into. I learned and benefited from the experience.

Peter Harnik, director of Environmental Action, in a letter to CBS chairman William S. Paley, wrote: "Michael Frome's dismissal lends credence to the growing popular conception that the media today exists more to mollify the public than to educate. And it bolsters the feeling that the last place people should turn to for 'real' news and analysis is the major networks and magazines."

That is about right, no less now than then. Henry David Thoreau followed a simple creed: "The only obligation I have a right to assume is to do at any time what I think right." Thoreau spoke for all of us who want our words to rise above the mediocre. Yet it grieves me that able editors are not free to grant freedom to their authors. In 1977 I wrote about national parks for *Mainliner,* the United Airlines in-flight magazine. After it appeared, I received a nice note from Fred R. Smith, editorial director of East/West Network (which then published the magazine for the airline): "A few short things were cut for space and we elided the discussion of redwoods as United didn't want to be involved in the controversy. Otherwise, I think you will agree it is a great picture issue."

In 1982, to cite another example, the editorial director at Du Pont called to ask if I would write an article on the Delaware River for the company's external house organ. I was then spending a year as author-in-residence at the Pinchot Institute for Conservation Studies at Milford, Pennsylvania, in the Delaware River valley and was interested in the region. The article was intended to describe the improvement in water quality in the river over the course of recent years. I would gladly do it, I advised, if I could make my own investigation and determination. But no, that was not the point of the story: Du Pont's own experts had already made the judgment on water quality, and the writer was expected to interview and record statements of company-chosen authorities. Clearly it was best that I bow out at the beginning, for, while flacks and hacks can make "a great picture issue," there ought to be more to a writing career.

"People have to know what other avenues, if any, are open to outspoken environmental writers such as you," wrote Donald McDonald, editor of the *Center Magazine,* published by the Center for the Study of Democratic Institutions, in a letter to me early in 1975, "what other recriminatory actions have been taken against other writers who 'name names'; the degree to which writers self-censor their own work, anticipate trouble and sanitize their writing to the point of banality; the connections between congressmen and special business interests (mining, lumbering, etc.), and the mass media with its cross-ownership of interests."

His letter led to an assignment to write an article, which appeared under the title, "Freedom of the Press—For Those Who Own One," and then to another assignment for the same magazine, for an article about whistle-blowers in the federal government, which I prepared with the aid of a grant from the Fund for Investigative Journalism.

The *Center Magazine* ceased publication, alas, but there will always be other outlets. When one door closes, another opens. The next outlet may not be as significant as the last, but one never knows where it may lead. After *Field & Stream,* I became a columnist for *Defenders of Wildlife,* with a message in every issue for eighteen years. I also wrote columns for the *Los Angeles Times* and *Western Outdoors,* each of them for five years. I loved the work and had fun speaking out. Jack Brown, the editor of *West-*

ern Outdoors, wrote in the November 1985 issue: "Probably the most consistent generator of both gripes and praise is The Environment Column by Michael Frome. As our resident gadfly, Michael manages to sting bureaucrats where it hurts and to puncture the stuffing out of the stuffiest organization leaders."

Through it all I traveled to marvelous wild places all across America, and elsewhere in the world as well, more than a full share for a lifetime. I associated with and interviewed people at many different stations in life. I feel that I have been blessed, with miracles in my life. I treasure those special moments, as when I came to New York in 1981 to receive an award from the American Society of Journalists and Authors for the best magazine article of the year. I stood up to receive my award and speak my piece in a ballroom filled with maybe four hundred people, fellow authors, editors, and agents. Then in 1994 I was awarded the Jade of Chiefs and inducted into the Circle of Chiefs by the Outdoor Writers Association of America at its annual convention. There was vindication in it, for when I was dismissed from *Field & Stream* the editor there, Jack Samson, put a stigma on me among the outdoor fraternity. But when Joel M. Vance presented the award he spoke of me as follows: "He's what all good conservation communicators should be, a gadfly to some, an inspiration to others. You can't, as the old saying goes, make an omelet without breaking some eggs, and our new Chief has cracked more than a few vulnerable shells in his career. . . . Let's just say he has been a consummate head-knocker."

I suppose that I might advise students to be careful to avoid mistakes, but I would rather say, "Do what feels right, in your heart, without ever regretting it." In September 1994 I was surprised to receive a note, out of the blue, from Ben W. Gilbert, under whom I had worked almost fifty years earlier, when he was city editor of the *Washington Post* and I was a cub reporter. He was living in Tacoma, in western Washington: "It has been a long time since you did a stint as a reporter on the *Post.* I have noted your existence from quotes here and there, but did not know you had made the trek west as I did ten years ago." He hoped that we might meet, then concluded: "The news business lost a very promising person when you left, but I think you are doing more good monitoring the environment." So it turned out right for me. Life has a habit of working that way.

CHAPTER 9

Finding Hope in the Classroom

IN 1980 I RECEIVED A LETTER from Lucy P., telling about herself and asking advice on whether, and how, to make a career in environmental writing. She was recently graduated from the University of Tennessee and already had worked six months as a reporter for a daily newspaper, with occasional chances to cover environmental events and issues.

Lucy wrote that she would like to work on the staff of a publication dealing with the environment, or perhaps do graduate studies in science writing. Her questions included: "From your experience, do you think there is a demand right now for people who can write well about environmental concerns? Are there trade journals or other sources where job opportunities in science or environmental writing might be included? What general advice would you have for someone in my position?"

Over the years I have responded to those and similar questions many, many times. Most, but not all, have come from young people somewhere near the beginning of their professional careers. In the process of working through them all, the raw materials for this book germinated and grew. When Lucy wrote to me I was busy doing the kind of work in environmental journalism to which she aspired. In addition, by the time of Lucy's letter I already had tasted teaching, two years earlier, as a visiting professor in the environmental studies program at the University of Vermont, and had lectured at various other schools.

Then in 1982 I came to teaching on a committed basis and worked at it for fourteen years at the University of Idaho, Northland College, and Western Washington University. I came to teaching late, but thoroughly enjoyed practicing both professional disciplines. Journalism in one sense is a form of teaching, and education a form of communication. "Learned institutions," wrote Jefferson, "ought to be favorite objects with every free people. They throw that light on the public mind which is the best security against crafty and dangerous encroachments on the public liberty." The same goes for the media, too, for all their weaknesses still safeguarding public liberty by throwing light before the public mind.

I wrote Lucy that practical experience is imperative, as a complement to the scholarship derived from her academic studies. That was my feeling, and to a large degree so it remains. For a long time I felt a difference between education and real learning: that the former tends to be theoretical, a process of memorization of established formulas leading to the certificate required for professional employment, while learning, on the other hand, is a self-assigned responsibility, a personal adventure. I could cite the case histories of John Bartram, the pioneer botanist of colonial times, who began as a farmer, observing life forms as he turned the earth, without anyone to teach him; Mark Twain, who had only a third or fourth grade education; John Muir, who walked away from the University of Wisconsin to pursue studies in what he called the "University of the Wilderness"; and Roger Tory Peterson, who built his fame as a self-taught naturalist and illustrator with an inspired system by which people could identify birds alive in the wild instead of dead on a specimen tray.

I learned that I was wrong. Mark Twain may have been gifted, but he matched his gift with sheer diligence. For almost all students the combination of solid course work and practical experience is best. Some begin weak in their writing skills and need to work harder than others. Guidance and disciplined thought help them improve and avoid the impoverishment of sloppy writing. Sara Olason Noland, a former student of mine at Western Washington University, made a strong point in a letter to me early in 1998: "I am so grateful to have had an education both in science and journalism. Getting a degree (two in my case) pushed me onto the path of loving to learn, to think critically on my own, come to my own conclusions, and know how to act from there to help make things better. Being able to think critically and do my own research enriches my job and my personal life. I feel I can contribute instead of just going along for the ride."[1]

I could have told Lucy that some of the finest American writers got poor grades or flunked out. In due course, however, I discovered that it is not that simple, that I myself still had lessons to learn—and that some of the best would come from students. I remember that one student in his or her evaluation of a seminar on current issues I conducted in 1983 referred to my approach to teaching as "untutored." That was probably true. One day in the journalism course I taught that year I made reference to the inevitable tribulations awaiting students in "the real world." But Cindy Teipner piped up, "But, Michael, this is the real world," and then, during the rest of the semester, she showed me the realities of students living beyond the classroom.

Over the years I developed a level of understanding and communication with students. We had potluck socials, went on field trips, and celebrated Earth Day with hammer dulcimers, fiddles, guitars, songs, and speeches. At Idaho, Jim Tangen-Foster took courses with me, but he was also my racquetball instructor in the extracurricular fitness program; it was hard to think of him as a student, since I learned so much from him. Lynn Kinter also took several of my courses. One day, in the first of them, I assigned the class to write a letter to the editor. She came to me with a question. "Michael, how do I write a letter to the editor? The only writing I've done has been for term papers." Two years later, however, she became editor of the *Idaho Forester,* and when she graduated and returned to Wyoming started a newsletter, "New Sage," for the Friends of Wyoming's Wild Desert. Her primary interest was botany, not journalism, but still while on the way to studying for a doctorate she became a regular contributor of science articles to the *Casper Tribune,* the major daily in her state.

It is not easy for them, yet down through the years I have watched students accept responsibility for themselves and change their lives in positive, fulfilling ways. I can illustrate by recalling the first environmental journalism course I taught, while at the University of Vermont in 1978. I came to the classroom with plenty to learn about teaching and advice from all kinds of people. "Throw the textbooks out," a biology professor, Hubert Vogelmann, had strongly suggested. "Tell about specific issues in which you've been involved. Tell the human stories of the real-life world." That was one approach. I myself wanted to see every student publish at least one article in a worthy publication, but a magazine editor to whom I outlined that goal had laughed and predicted I would be lucky if one student succeeded even once.

He came close to being right, but I never felt that I was wrong. During the semester students took on tough projects and did well with them. Then in August, I received a welcome letter from Cynthia Jaffe:

> While sitting at the desks in the [Burlington] *Free Press* Capitol Bureau the other day, it occurred to me that you might like to know

where your efforts landed one of your journalism students this year. You once mentioned in class that a colleague of yours had challenged you to get even one of us published. Well, you did, and more than once.

In those last days of May after finals, I had a talk with Jim Welch, Desk Editor of the *Burlington Free Press*. He offered me tremendous opportunities, all on the basis of that one Richelieu column [about a water-control project that would have seriously degraded Lake Champlain]. I was almost too honest about my limited journalistic capabilities, yet he seemed to have high expectations of my capabilities. I've been writing freelance for the *Free Press* and [the alternative] *Vanguard* on topics—mostly environmental—centered in Central Vermont, particularly Washington County around the capitol. Jim has been fantastic about referring assignments to me, so that digging for stories has not been entirely my burden. The reporting, interviewing, attending hearings/meetings and deadline writing have been the most intensive and exciting learning experiences I've ever had—just as you always told us they could be.

I really believe I was not competent when I began, in terms of journalistic style. But concentrating on the lesson I had when you helped me reorganize the Richelieu article, and "studying the market" prolifically, it began to come easily after only one week.

There's a lot more to tell, but it's all part of my novice's enthusiasm. I've still a ways to go, but I wanted you to know where your encouragement and energy went for one grateful protegee.

Sorry to say, I lost touch with Cynthia, yet I feel that her testimony is valid and valuable. It is not expertise in journalism, per se, that counts, maybe not even environmental journalism. The skills will come, with good class work and once you realize the power of your own life, have faith in yourself and in people, and believe that through your writing you can influence positive change in society.

Critics say that college students cannot spell, do not know history or geography, and are driven by the desire for self-gratification. Maybe so, but I have seen enough of them using their research and communication skills to speak and act responsibly with thoughtful, positive ideas. In my files I find that one wrote in an essay, "The desire to gain knowledge is the first step toward making a difference," and another, "The courageous first step begins with both the development of an individual's true sense of human dignity and the identification of humanity's place in nature." A third cited Whitman: "Faith is the antiseptic of the soul." They wrote further that awareness alone will not yield action, that they find traditional teaching methods wanting, that they want channels through which to act upon their awareness.

"A Writer Finds Hope in the Classroom" is the title of an article of mine about my graduate seminar on current issues.[2] I expressed the theory that students learn best by doing, that it takes the pursuit of real issues to comprehend the process of decision making and how to influence it. The students were doing that, through term papers carrying such titles as "Soils as a Resource System," referring to the Palouse dry-farming environment in which the University of Idaho is located; "Acid Rain: A Threat to the United States"; "Small Scale Hydro Power: An Update, Focusing on Idaho Rivers"; "Buffer Zones: Can They Help Our National Parks?"; "Freedom of the Hills: Is Management Necessary?"; "Sustaining Professionalism"; and "The New Interior."

"The New Interior" was a view of Yellowstone grizzly management, well researched, but written as a fictional thriller. The story in brief: The park superintendent favors Alternative D, the proposal "to eliminate grizzly bears from the Yellowstone ecosystem." So does the secretary of the interior, but he wants to wait until after the election and opts for Alternative A, a continuance of the present policy. However, a new secretary is appointed and decides to make Alternative D operational without public notice. This is accomplished by the interior's newest division, the clandestine OCO, the Office of Covert Operations, staffed by ex-CIA agents posing as park rangers. After clearing out the bears, they find they must now turn to human protestors. "The maneuvers in Yellowstone were not winding down," wrote the author in his chilling conclusion. "The war had only just begun."

This student had devoted a lot of himself and his mental energies to the project. Nor was he alone. "Class discussions allowed me to become more aware of the issues," wrote one student. "By increasing knowledge and understanding, my interest has grown. I have become more aware of the importance of keeping up with current events."

The most precious lesson that I have learned is to have faith and to keep the faith—in myself and in my students. Thus, my goal in teaching has been to help open hearts so that students may look inside themselves and write with feeling, evoking and articulating their own particular talent or genius, qualities waiting and wanting to make each of us complete.

I have believed that since I first read *The Autobiography of Lincoln Steffens* in high school and was inspired by the crusading life of that pioneer muckraker. I loved the early section of the book about Steffens's arrival in New York to look for a job as a reporter. Nobody wanted to hire him, but one city editor weakened, "I'll give you a chance strictly on space—paying you only for what you bring in." He was off and running; without asking or waiting for assignments, he knocked on doors of important people and delivered exclusives and scoops. Soon the editor called him in to say: "Steffens, you're making more money than anybody in this office. You're going on salary." From then on he made a career of probing power without fear of the powerful. Steffens could hardly be called objective, but he pursued his work to influence the course of events, rather than merely report them.

Lincoln Steffens came to his career with a solid education in this country and abroad, and went on from there. Though I never heard from Lucy P. again, I hope she knocked on doors too, and that the right one opened for her.

The Story That Evolved into a Career

"PANTHERS WANTED—ALIVE, Back East, Where They Belong" was the headline of an article I wrote for *Smithsonian.* It was just one story, but it proved to be a chapter of something larger, a body of work that kept growing and evolving as part of my career. I can trace it back to the research for my book *Whose Woods These Are: The Story of the National Forests,* in which I wrote:

> Gracing the foreground of the historic gateway to Pisgah National Forest [in western North Carolina] is a roadside souvenir and refreshment stand. Here you can buy a Coke, hand it to a bear through the bars of his cage and watch him drink it. The purpose of his presence is to attract your interest and trade. Western North Carolina has a variety of such crude attractions. One is the reptile "garden," which everyone who loves the wild creatures should see, not because it is good, but to observe how the animals, assorted scraggly deer, a bear and snakes, are cared for. There are the "Twin Yona" (*yona* is Cherokee for bear) caged on the roadside in the Indian Reservation between the national forest and Great Smoky Mountains National Park. And like displays of wildlife before gift shops and gasoline stations in Maggie Valley.[1]

I was still thinking like a travel writer looking at tourist traps. Subsequently, I wrote an article for *Changing Times,* the Kiplinger magazine, titled "America the Beautiful—Heritage or Honkytonk?" about the spread of tourist blight.[2] I used the same material about the caged bears (plus other examples, including Gettysburg, Pennsylvania; Mount Rushmore, South Dakota; and Yellowstone National Park). I reported interviewing the North Carolina Wildlife Resources Commission, which conceded the bears were kept in "deplorable, unsanitary and inhumane conditions" but was unwilling or unable to intervene in the bears' behalf. I found the roadside zoos dismal and disturbing and went around to various conservation organizations, hoping they would take up the issue and help make something of it. The only organization expressing interest was an outfit that I barely knew called Defenders of Wildlife. The executive director, Mary Hazell Harris, shared concern over the caged bears and reptiles, and then proceeded to enlighten me about her organization's major cause, the defense of predatory wildlife, particularly from federal "animal damage control" agents who used steel traps, poisoned baits, and aerial gunning, and were known in places as "gopher chokers."

So I started learning and writing about predators—certainly nobody else was. My first piece for *Field & Stream* began:

> The tragic fiasco of Federal predator control as we know it today began half a century ago, during World War I. At first it was a means of eradicating wolves in order to save beef for our troops and allies. Then the sheepmen enlisted the government in a program to kill coyotes in their behalf. Wars have come and gone, but we have been struck with predator control programs ever since.

> Now the government has admitted that the principles in predator control are wrong, a needless annihilation of millions of animals, a waste of money, a political boondoggle. The Secretary of the Interior has acknowledged a fifty-year blunder by an agency of his Department. This he did by accepting with praise a report of his Advisory Board on Wildlife Management, a document which constitutes a penetrating criticism of past performance, and by directing major reforms, overhaul, and a new approach for the future.

> It is now three years since Secretary Stewart L. Udall received the historic Leopold Report, so named for Dr. A. Starker Leopold, the distinguished wildlife biologist who served as chairman of the Advisory Board. It is two years since Secretary Udall ordered the old Branch of Predator and Rodent Control (PARC) to be renamed the Division of Wildlife Services and to have its functions recast. But is

it that simple? Can deep-set prejudices be reversed, and political opposition overcome by an executive order? If we have been damaging the natural resource for half a century and longer, can we stop overnight—or will it take another half century?[3]

I tapped into the same idea in 1969 when I wrote *The Varmints: Our Unwanted Wildlife*. It was a book for children, covering twelve North American species (including badger, bear, coyote, fox, mountain lion, wolf, and wolverine), but adults read it, too. Then in January 1977 I wrote the piece for *Smithsonian*, which began:

> On a July evening in 1975, five Great Smoky Mountains National Park maintenance workers were lounging on their bunkhouse porch watching a doe and two yearlings. Suddenly the deer fled into the forest and a large, grayish cat with a long tail emerged from the woods and bounded after them. The five men followed quickly, but found nothing more than tracks along a creek. They were convinced, however, that they had seen a panther hunting its traditional prey.
>
> The report they filed in late September 1975 triggered a new sense of awareness of the largest, rarest and most secretive of the wild American cats. The Eastern panther was thought long ago to have followed the trail into oblivion of the great auk, Labrador duck, heath hen, passenger pigeon and sea mink. Recent sightings by some professional biologists, wildlife personnel, and forest and park rangers show this not to be the case. The Eastern panther may be coming back from the brink of extinction for a second chance.
>
> The 1975 observation in the park and concurrent reports of panthers along the Blue Ridge Parkway in North Carolina stimulated me to investigate the whereabouts of the big cat, one of the least known of North American mammals today, not only in the Southern mountains but throughout its range. I found these lonely wanderers of our mountains and forests more widespread than I could possibly have dreamed. The numbers of animals must be dangerously low, but they apparently are breeding and the long thread of life, though tenuous, remains unbroken.

I rewrote the lead for an epilogue to a new edition of *Strangers in High Places*, reprinted in *National Parks* in June 1980. In books and magazine articles I wrote about grizzly bears, eagles, and wolves, and sometimes critically of public policy and of wolf management by federal and state agencies. I met and interviewed scientists and read their published works. I particularly respected and admired John Craighead and Frank Craighead, twin brothers who studied Yellowstone grizzlies for more than a decade, tagging and tracking them with radio transmitters, attempting to quantify the age and sex ratios of the grizzly population and compiling data on social organization, feeding habits, and other aspects of grizzly life history. Their Yellowstone field work was terminated in controversy by the National Park Service in 1971. Maurice Hornocker, who had served as member of the Craighead research team before achieving a reputation on his own as the leading scientific authority on mountain lions and other large wild cats, became another source, and later a colleague at the University of Idaho whom I could always consult. I wrote about the Craigheads in *Defenders,* later republished in *Chronicling the West,* citing an article by Hornocker in the *Wildlifer,* the professional journal of the Wildlife Society:

> The Craigheads stuck to what they believed and paid a very dear price. Their research was stopped. A large segment of the profession ostracized them. They were criticized by many. Yet, on principle, they endured and never faltered in their position.

> Many of the lasting contributions in biology and wildlife management have been made by individuals willing to endure criticism and hardship for what they believed. They have been capable of rising above professional jealousies, conflicting personalities, opposing agency positions, and non-support from their own organization or agency.

> These individuals have placed the resource itself uppermost in their work and in their recommendations, regardless of any "agency" position. They have been men of principle, and because of this the rewards of their profession have been denied them. Yet most of us are employed by public agencies in which "going along" is rewarded far more frequently than any stand on principle. This is a sorry state of affairs.[4]

In 1986 I received a memorandum from Hornocker congratulating me on the Marjory Stoneman Douglas Award that had just come to me from the National Parks and Conservation Association for my work in behalf of national parks. "Congratulations," he wrote. "The system works!"

That was a reminder that just as he and the Craigheads, despite the odds, worked through the system as scientists, so must I as journalist.

I wrote many articles and essays about national parks, starting in the late 1950s, in likely newspapers and magazines and in unlikely ones like *Sohioan* and *Travel Agent*.[5] In the *Washington Post,* I began an article: "Our national park system is now engulfed by the gravest threats in its entire history of more than a century. Pollution of air and water, commercial encroachment, overuse, improper assignment and lack of field personnel to protect the resources are some of the critical problems that must be faced and solved in the 1980s—that is, if our parks are to remain unspoiled, peaceful havens for travelers in search of inspiration and wholesome recreation." And in the *Chicago Tribune,* I wrote:

> I propose to close Yellowstone National Park for five years to automobile traffic. Let visitors enter on foot or shuttle bus—maybe not even shuttle bus. Use that period to develop a whole new system of circulation, and to decide how the park should be used, based on veneration of Yellowstone as a sacred place. But that's only the first step in regreening the national parks.
>
> I propose to eliminate half the overnight facilities in Yosemite National Park, and all the cars.
>
> That's for John Muir, who lamented allowing those "blunt-nosed mechanical beetles" to puff their way into the valley and mingle their gas breath with the breath of pines and waterfalls.
>
> I propose to close the transmountain road across the Great Smoky Mountains and by so doing make the wonderful wilderness of southern Appalachia whole again.
>
> In the regreening process the administration of every park will focus on the mountains, canyons, forests, prairies, songful rivers and the natural life systems they support. Their welfare will come before commerce and crowds. The same principle will apply to the national historic and prehistoric sites; Americans will learn at last to walk lightly over the dead and to treat the ancient battlefields and structures of mud, stick and stone as documents in trust.[6]

At *Field & Stream* the Army Corps of Engineers was a favorite target. Whenever I criticized the corps for its environmentally damaging construction projects, readers would send cheering messages with data for even more criticism. There was so much interest and solid material that the editor, Clare Conley, approved my writing a series of three articles, titled "Dam the Rivers, Full Speed Ahead." The October 1970 article appeared with this subhead: "The Corps of Engineers has been called the most powerful, pervasive lobby in Washington. Even presidents have been unable to subdue its force. What chance have conservationists against its relentless development of our waterways?" The next article, one month later, appeared with this subhead: "Where the Corps of Engineers is concerned, the public can never be too much on guard, for damming rivers is its way of life and it is not likely to give up on a fight. Here are the Fifteen Most Unwanted Projects today. Watch them!" And the last article in the series, in December 1970, included this subhead: "To date, the Corps of Engineers' most prominent projects have involved changing the natural, often drastically. Must it remain on this course, or is there hope that someday it will work to clean up the mess man has made?"

Soon after my dismissal from the magazine four years later I was thoroughly surprised to receive a letter from Maj. Gen. J. W. Morris, director of civil works (and later commander of the entire corps), in which he wrote:

> The honest, constructive and sincere criticism of public programs and of those who are given the responsibility to administer those programs is essential to the healthy democratic process. The public interest is often difficult at best to establish and without discussion of all aspects and viewpoints it becomes almost impossible to define. Your published articles and personal communication with the Corps of Engineers have been appreciated. Your integrity, candor, the reliability of the information you have printed, and your willingness to listen to and consider other points of view is most commendable. . . . We will look forward to reading your articles in other periodicals and to hearing directly from you where a particular situation can best be brought to our attention through direct communication.[7]

I cherish that letter as fan mail, to be sure, and have it framed. I am proud that someone whose organization I criticized in print would respect my integrity, reliability, and willingness to listen to and consider other viewpoints. That is an award in itself. I think it comes from believing in what I was trying to do and believing the system works. That letter on the wall keeps the lesson fresh.

History and Ethics Help To "Write Whole"

ONE DAY AT THE UNIVERSITY OF IDAHO I was asked to speak to a forestry class on wilderness preservation, a subject especially dear to me. To help me prepare, I was given a copy of the course syllabus, in which I found a statement emphasizing strict adherence to objectivity. "Since the assigned theme is wilderness," I told the class, "let's take a break and be subjective today for a change." Then I asked the students to picture in their minds the most wonderful natural place they had ever known and, once they had that fairly fixed, to write a descriptive paragraph about what they saw. In due course all the students read aloud their little essays, which proved to be imaginative, creative, and realistic, and I believe the students felt good about themselves.

To me that exercise was consistent with sound forestry and a compatible philosophy of love of earth and sky. Wilderness identifies human hope with human fate; it celebrates the human condition and human potential, requiring a subjective, rather than objective, value system. I think that philosophy and ethics provide a foundation for technical and professional studies and careers. Everybody who gets anything done in behalf of any part of the environment has drawn from intangible values of human heart and spirit. And a review of history shows these values to be central to the conception and development of environmentalism, as evidenced in the lives, work, and words of Emerson, Thoreau, and John Muir, and of scientists from George Perkins Marsh (the "father of ecology") and John Wesley Powell to Aldo Leopold, Paul Ehrlich, and Edward O. Wilson.

I have learned that both philosophy and history are relevant to environmental journalism. For one thing, much of the damage to the environment is slow in human eyes, more like erosion than a landslide, and most people are too busy or too mobile to notice. Stories such as the disappearance of open space would be vivid if reporters took the time to get historical perspective and saw more of the big picture. A good exercise is to imagine what an urban neighborhood was like a century ago: that is the contrast and speed of change the environmental writer needs to capture, looking backward and forward, exploring issues that take time to unfold.

Awareness and appreciation of the breadth of history help to "write whole." I found a choice example in an article by Ted Steinberg, professor of history and law at Case Western University. He opened the article with a quotation from *Newsweek,* in the aftermath of Hurricane Andrew: "Andrew was what the insurance companies call 'an act of God,' an act for which no mere human can be held to account." Then Steinberg showed this was not true at all: "The opinions of *Newsweek*'s editors aside, there is no questioning the role that human social and economic forces—poorly enforced building codes, low federal standards for mobile homes, eviscerated zoning laws—played in the calamity. Most students of natural disaster would agree that events like Hurricane Andrew are not entirely natural, but human complicity in such events has been slighted."[1]

Although hurricanes are seen as "chance occurrence of natural extremes," Steinberg asked questions about the unnatural history of natural calamity, by looking closely at south Florida's high-risk environment: How do risky humanscapes come to be? Who benefits from their construction? When disaster does strike, how is the human dimension of calamity obscured and denied in order to foster more economic growth and land development?

Steinberg explained that hurricane-prone south Florida has long been a disaster waiting to happen, mainly because private developers have sought to maximize tourist and agricultural potential by building in areas susceptible to hurricanes and flooding, and have been helped with subsidies from federal and state governments. "Natural disaster has a very shadowy history in south Florida," he wrote, "rooted in years of denial for the sake of profit." After the disastrous 1926 hurricane, the *Miami Herald* concluded that, fearful as a hurricane might be, "there is more risk to life in venturing across a busy street." And the *Miami Daily News,* two months after the Labor Day disaster, declared Miami had withstood the storm's test. The *Daily News* claimed that more people die in traffic accidents in a single day than died in the storm and that "The chief suffering from any hurricane is caused by hysteria."[2]

But Steinberg recorded that when Miami Beach encouraged further development of waterfront property in 1948 by extending the bulkhead line seaward, allowing hotels to expand and enclose their lots, they not only closed off public access but also increased the amount of public property in harm's way. Beach erosion was not new. It had developed as early as the 1910s and intensified after the 1926 hurricane. The city installed groins to help trap sand and save the beach; so many had been built by the 1970s that the beach looked like a military obstacle course. But mainly it was the building of hotels and other structures too close to the water that caused the beach to disappear.

After Hurricane Donna in 1960, President Eisenhower declared the Florida Keys a disaster area, opening the way for millions of dollars to help rebuild bridges, highways, and water lines in this hurricane-prone area. Federal funds continued to flow into south Florida in the aftermath of Hurricanes Cleo in 1964 and Betsy in 1965. After Betsy, a long lull in storm activity, coupled with population growth and development, especially during the 1980s, paralleled the evisceration of building codes. Dade County repeatedly acquiesced to the construction industry looking for cheaper, quicker ways to build. Consequently, Hurricane Andrew destroyed approximately 90 percent of the 10,593 mobile homes in Dade County.

> Ample evidence exists that from early in the twentieth century until well into the 1960s, south Florida's real estate and tourist interests, sometimes with the help of a complicit press, downplayed the danger of hurricanes. In addition, both state and federal governments further disguised the true risks of living in south Florida, especially in the years after World War II, to bolster private development in hurricane-prone areas by shifting the cost to the public sector. Downplaying the threat of hurricanes while simultaneously subsidizing further development in risk-prone locales may well have helped to encourage people to settle and sit tight while in the path of danger.

Environmental journalism needs to explore that history and expose it fully to public light. Environmental journalists ought to know the history of journalism, of how the press began in America as an antagonist of British rule, and as the watchdog over misuse of power, protected in the Constitution and Bill of Rights. They should know of the technological advances in the late nineteenth century that led to inexpensive mass magazines that focused on graft, corruption, and social problems, and of twentieth-century crusading journals such as the *Nation, New Republic, New Masses,* and *InFact.* Recognizing and reviewing the work of the editors and writers of these publications provide fitting context for crusading to come.

Part III

The Green-Ink

Primer

Take One Step at a Time

IT HAS BEEN SAID that becoming a professional writer is at least as difficult as becoming a surgeon. Writing, especially writing about the environment, demands hard work, persistence, patience, and a thick skin—it does not happen overnight. One of the basic lessons is to take it all in stride, one step at a time.

This is something you do out of choice. It gives purpose to life. Each piece of writing is a gift to people who do not recognize corruptions passing under their noses, or who do not have adequate data to evaluate what they see—so keep the faith, with pride in whatever you do. Never, ever, sell yourself short. Do the best you can, then improve on it, one step at a time.

Be yourself, whoever you are, without trying to be anybody else. Sonia Slater, a student of mine, had the right idea when she wrote: "It is difficult to set aside fear and apprehension, but I *am* charting my destiny—one book, one class, one interview, one meeting, one conference, one conversation, one heartbreak and one success at a time. A report card cannot determine how educated one has become; a letter grade cannot interpret intelligence. I have learned to reach out from the safe channels and challenge myself without the need to meet the expectations of an impersonal system."

Define in writing your long-term goal. Set it down in your journal, to revisit over time. Then follow with *short-term objectives,* individual actions leading to the goal. Cover subjects you want to write about, where you want to get published, and what you need to learn to make that happen. Allow flexibility to change later, but include a deadline for each. Limit your objectives to the realistic and attainable; otherwise you are apt to face discouragement and disappointment in yourself.

Start small, maybe a letter to the editor, and take a bigger step next time, on the principle that success breeds success. Celebrate every chance you get. Failure is not so bad either; it creates another chance to succeed.

Sure, you are competing with others, including professionals who have more experience. But consider that so much has been written already that ongoing battles almost come across as old news. Now it is your turn to come up with new data and refreshing new ways of saying things.

Learn to show your work and to take advice. When you get the same critical comments from different readers they must have a point to reckon with. But keep writing, moving ahead.

Keep a journal. That is your place free of editing for the private and unpublishable, for thoughts and feelings, for sorting positives and negatives, insights into hopeless situations, for clarifying attitudes and ideas to express in print outside the journal.

Good reading makes for good writing. T. H. Watkins feels that for every two hours you spend writing every day you must spend twenty-two hours in reading. Read *everything,* he advises, and read all the time. Read fiction, nonfiction, in different fields: "Read poetry, read it aloud, and feel its rhythms, the smell and taste and sound of words. Read the back of cereal boxes, if you have nothing else. The good stuff will seep into your head and sooner or later leak out on paper."[1] Reading quality writing of others enhances your own skill and talent.

Focus on principle, rather than personality. In environmental journalism you are likely to upset somebody, but writing in one sense is outreach to adversaries, recognizing that people who disagree are not evil.

Be affirmative, focus on solutions, not simply on problems, with abiding belief in people to make the solutions come true. It may take years to build a cathedral, but construction begins with a vision and each small step marks an advance in making that vision real.

Focus on discipline. Show patience with yourself, but be persistent, working through trial and error. Discipline is a must; there is no other way. Get a daily work plan. Four hours, two hours, one hour, whatever time you have, whatever works. Write a page a day, as someone said, and at the end of a year you will have a 365-page book. The more writing you do the more proficient you will become.

Think and live environmentally. Be informed by reading newspapers, journals, and books. Actively support change, with your time and money. Focus on elements central to life, living simply, or at least simpler, removing distractions and superfluities.

Cooperate with others. And others will cooperate with you when you need it. There is plenty of room at the top. Those you meet on the way up you are apt to meet again on the way down.

Cultivate a smile and good humor. Life is grim enough, so lighten up. Take the issues seriously, but not yourself. Learn to laugh.

Get outdoors. Balance the introspection of writing by going outdoors. Camp, canoe, kayak, hike, walk, or sit in the park—whatever works. Know and appreciate the world you are trying to rescue and you will do better by it. Thomas Jefferson, in a letter to his granddaughter Cornelia Jefferson Randolph, wrote: "I rejoice that you learnt to write for another reason; for, as that is done with a goose quill, you now know the value of a goose."[2] You do not have to write with a goose quill, but it helps when you know the value of the goose.

Stories Are Where You Find Them

THE STORY BEGAN for Eileen Welsome, a diligent young reporter on the staff of the *Albuquerque Tribune,* in 1987, when she spotted a reference to human beings injected with plutonium in a declassified report on animal experiments at the Weapons Laboratory at Kirtland Air Force Base near Albuquerque in New Mexico. She shared this finding with her editors, who agreed that Welsome had turned up something serious to pursue.

From that start, Welsome proceeded to review declassified government documents and classified documents obtained under the Freedom of Information Act, plus congressional reports, oral histories, medical records, and funeral-home records. She interviewed retired and active scientists, historians, physicians, librarians, genealogists, and surviving family members of five people who unknowingly had been injected with plutonium between 1945 and 1947.

The series uncovered a fifty-year-old scandal.[1] Welsome's research showed that the patients had not been told the truth about the original injections of the 1940s, nor had they given their informed consent. In the early 1970s, when follow-up studies were made, survivors and family members were deceived again about the true purpose of the studies. In fact, surviving relatives had not even known of their loved ones' involvement in the experiment until they were contacted by the *Tribune.* Now for the first time human faces were connected to a still unknown number of Americans used unwittingly in radiation experiments during the Cold War.

The story began for Rachel Carson in January 1958 (though concern for the issue was already deep in her conscience): "Olga Owens Huckins told me of her own bitter experience of a small world made lifeless, and so brought my attention sharply back to a problem with which I had long been concerned. I then realized I must write this book."[2] Those are the powerful opening lines of *Silent Spring,* which Carson undertook to write when she was fifty and already a well-known author. She had tried in vain to interest magazines in an article about the damages caused by DDT and other chemicals. Friends questioned whether she could write a salable book on such a dreary subject, but she felt there could be no peace unless she plowed ahead—for the next four years of committed research and writing.

Stories are where you find them. The best ideas for environmental journalism come from personal experience, on the job or in the community; from reading newspaper articles, government documents, technical and scientific journals; from the Internet; from reading environmental publications and knowing active environmentalists, or from being an active environmentalist oneself. Two of the most valid starting points are "Write about what you know" and "Write about what you care about."

Based on his years in covering the environment for the *New York Times,* Philip Shabecoff believes that:

> Many if not most investigative stories come from tips from people who are involved in some way, don't like what they see and think the media can help change the situation. Because the *New York Times* is such a powerful medium, I was often approached by people who wanted to expose what they believed was some wrongdoing. For example, when the leadership of the EPA during the early years of the Reagan Administration tried to reverse the policy of requiring the phaseout of leaded gasoline, a political appointee in the agency with brain and conscience and who was aware of the effect of lead on children, told me about it. When the same administration and its allies in Congress were trying to open the Arctic National Wildlife Refuge to oil development, an environmental group gave me a report from Fish and Wildlife Service officials in Alaska which detailed the negative impact of such development on wildlife in the Prudhoe Bay vicinity. The report had been suppressed by the right wing leadership of the Interior Department.[3]

"You have to read absolutely everything, talk to anyone who offers himself or herself, and keep alert," counsels Gregory McNamee, who gave up a successful editing career to concentrate on environmental writing in Arizona. "Not everything is breaking news; sometimes a writer must allow coincidence to play while the subconscious does its work."[4]

In McNamee's case, he recalled a film-producer friend, making a documentary on indigenous peoples in southern Sonora, asking if McNamee knew anything about buffelgrass. Like everyone to whom the plant is not familiar, he thought it must be "buffalo grass." But the producer went on to say the Indians of southern Sonora were worried about the grass's rapid growth in the nearby desert—they knew there is a price to pay for trying to improve on nature. Soon after, a pilot on returning from Alamos exclaimed, "You ought to see all the buffelgrass being planted around Hermosillo and south!" Then a Mexican soil chemist said he had been visiting his family in Sonora and helped a neighbor plant, yes, *Zacate buffel,* this new "wonder crop." Three mentions in three weeks, and McNamee set to work reporting and writing a revealing feature, a warning that such efforts to make the earth "more productive" are apt to create a backlash.[5]

For Philip Shabecoff, one particularly memorable story—about a toxic-waste dump located in the middle of an industrial town in Connecticut—began with a phone call:

> I was told about it by a whistleblower in the EPA who had been contacted by a citizen activist in the city. It involved a waste disposal company that was illegally storing hazardous waste on the site and was also secretly discharging wastes into a bordering river without treatment. The site was in the immediate vicinity of several schools, a hospital and several restaurants.
>
> The EPA, the state environmental agency, the city government and the local newspaper all knew at least something about what was going on but did nothing about it. The owners of the waste dump were substantial contributors to political campaigns. The local congressman, who was chairman of an environmental subcommittee, had started an investigation of the site, but was in the middle of a reelection campaign and was saying and doing nothing about it.[6]

It was painstaking work for Shabecoff, researching documents, interviewing on and off the record, cross-checking statements, looking for inconsistencies, double-checking scientific and technical aspects. But it added up to a front-page story in the *New York Times* that jumped to a full-page spread inside.

It took a lot of work for Bruce Selcraig, too, to produce the exceptional story headlined "The Filthy West—Toxics Pour into Our Air, Water, Land" that covered the entire front page, plus five full inside pages in *High Country News*. The lead read: "When the wind blows eastward across Utah's Great Salt Lake, which is to say most of the time, a long yellowish plume of chlorine often drifts from the stacks of a giant magnesium factory on the desolate west side, across the saline waters, fouling the view and sinuses of anyone in its path. Upon first sniff, downwinders wonder who spilled the Clorox. About 30 miles to the south, in the pleasant small town of Grantsville, a bus comes through several times a day to ferry workers to and from that massive plant. It's not an easy bus to miss. You can smell it coming."[7]

Selcraig was writing about the processing plant of the Magnesium Corporation of America, the largest releaser of chlorine, and the largest industrial air polluter in America. But that story began with Selcraig's computer savvy, tapping into the annual Toxic Releases Inventory, or TRI, issued by the Environmental Protection Agency. Established in 1986 in the wake of the 1984 Union Carbide accident in Bhopal, India, which killed more than thirty-five hundred people and injured tens of thousands more, TRI requires twenty-three-thousand-plus facilities in twenty manufacturing industries to report their release of 341 chemicals, in twenty-two chemical categories, to the air, land, and water, and by underground injection. It has become the best barometer of industrial pollution in America and a useful tool for prying information out of corporations reluctant to speak.

From the TRI, or its computerized version, anyone can find a particular polluting pulp mill, smelter, or refinery, or the nation's most polluted ZIP code, or the company emitting the most neurotoxins and ozone depleters in all fifty states. Thus, Selcraig learned and wrote: "Six of the top 20 companies with the largest toxic releases to the land, usually in the form of enormous slag piles, are smelter operations in the West. The Coastal Chem site in Cheyenne, Wyoming, is the fourth largest disposer of toxic waste by underground injection—over 20 million gallons of chemicals beneath the ground."[8]

The largest federal polluter in the West is the Naval Petroleum Reserve at Tupman, California. Another big one is the federal prison at Florence, Colorado, which released ninety thousand pounds of toxins in the process of making furniture.

A sidebar on mining pollution gave mining companies a chance to say: "The slag is out in the open. There's no release to the environment. If properly handled it's only hazardous by legal definition." But Selcraig also quoted Philip Hocker, director of the Mineral Policy Center, an environmental watchdog group promoting mining reform: "This quantifies for the first time the threat these mines present to the people of the West. The idea that slag is somehow benign and that the companies shouldn't have to report it is immoral."[9]

Maybe it takes "a nose for news," or a sense of what editors want at a particular time, or what people will read, or what the writer wants most to say, or a combination of them all that works. When I first began freelance writing in the late 1950s, I contributed a number of articles to *Parade,* the Sunday supplement. During that time I was in Gettysburg, Pennsylvania, for another article when the superintendent of Gettysburg National Battlefield, J. Walter Coleman, took me around and astonished me with the sight of intrusive commercial developments and the warning of still more coming within the park boundaries. That visit led to the cover story in *Parade:* "Neon Signs, Junk Yards and Dollar-Grubbing Are Invading Many Great Shrines. And the Most Hallowed of All Is Being Desecrated in . . . the New Battle of Gettysburg."[10]

I was already absorbed with parks and preservation, and now I learned that I could actually sell articles about my concerns, even to unlikely periodicals. *Changing Times,* for instance, was mostly about personal investments, but Herbert L. Brown Jr., the editor, and his successor, Robert W. Harvey, encouraged me to write "America the Beautiful—Heritage or Honkytonk?"; "America the Beautiful—Let's Not Lose It"; Why Are We Ruining Our National Parks"; and "America the Beautiful Needs More Friends."[11]

In the course of finding stories I also found people, particular individuals to remember and cherish, who made the research more a joy than a chore. In 1970, for example, I read a news report about an airline pilot, W. Lain Guthrie, a veteran of more than thirty years, who was fired for refusing to follow orders to dump excess fuel over Miami. "I should be criticized if I did dump in the air," Captain Guthrie told the press calmly. "I don't know why I didn't stop earlier. Why should we dump muck on people's houses?"

I felt I had to know this fellow. I am not sure if I looked him up in the telephone book or called the airline, but he was easy to reach. Soon he came to my house, fascinating the whole family, and later I went to his house, south of Miami. He was conducting a lone-eagle campaign on his own time and money. He had been moved by the death of a fellow pilot in a crash due to "poor visibility," very possibly traceable to human-caused smoke. He had found his own horizons in the sky disappearing. "The smoke is getting so thick in some areas that pilots not only can't see the horizon, but can't see other planes soon enough. The official accident reports simply quote the weather as haze."

Eastern Airlines reinstated Guthrie after three months and assigned him to work on pollution problems, along with flying the big jets. In 1973, when he reached the mandatory retirement age of sixty, he felt free to spend more time on his campaign, lecturing at colleges and for civic groups. At his own expense he produced and distributed an ingenious little booklet, "Captain Guthrie's Dictionary of Words and Phrases," including zestful definitions such as "Pollution control: elaborate scheme for planned dumping." In retrospect, I wish I had been able to write more about Guthrie, more *for* him and his good cause. In any case, I can look back at him and many others as sources, contacts, and, better yet, companions on the same trail.[12]

⊸

In summary, I offer a few tips on finding story ideas and working them into print.

Build your contacts as a volunteer. If you do not know where to begin, volunteer to work on media projects for the local Audubon or Sierra Club chapter or for a local grassroots group, or for the group's newsletter. It is a way to learn the issues, contribute constructively, see your work in print, and build contacts and confidence.

Get a good subject, a cause you care about, and stick with it. Say it is grizzly bears, eagles, wolves, dioxins, the Hudson River, or the Grand Canyon: you can never know, or write, everything about the subject, but you will never run out of challenge either. In due course, you will become the expert and opportunities will open for you.

Read everything, as Greg McNamee and T. H. Watkins suggested: newspapers, magazines, the Internet, new books, old books, and government reports. Read about the profession of writing so you can match your ideas with the literary market you want to write for.

Finding the story idea is only the beginning. Get ready for the hard work. Next comes research to show you have done your homework. You do not necessarily have to talk tough, but there are times when it helps. Listen to Shabecoff on his investigation in Connecticut:

I did not take no for an answer when people declined to talk. I kept coming back for more answers as I pursued new threads of the investigation. When the congressman refused to talk I threatened to write a story saying he was deliberately turning his back on a dangerous situation in his district in order to win an election and thus was able to gain access to his documents.

I read all documents, interviewed all potential sources, no matter how unpromising they seemed. When I had documentation of abuses, I tried to confront company management, but they refused to be interviewed—which I duly noted in my story. I also made sure I was informed about the scientific and technical aspects of the story—what chemicals were being dumped and what were their dangers? Was there evidence of health effects? (There was.) What did the law prescribe? What were the institutional responsibilities and how were they being followed?[13]

Look to your models, who show how to write with clarity and authority, who shape ideas into timely and timeless writing, provocative, with strong voice and viewpoint.

See the story in print, in your own head. From the very concept of the idea, visualize the audience it is meant for, and how it relates to the lives of readers. Visualize the publication (or the book), complete with cover, headlines and subheads, photos, and graphics. Once you get a framework on paper, share it with friends and family, if you think they can help, but you may be better off showing it to an editor or teacher. Set a target date to complete and submit the story. Get it in print, when you can, and move ahead to the next one.

Conducting Interviews and Investigations

ANYTHING YOU WRITE, for any medium on any subject, ought to be an adventure for both you and your reader. Your challenge is to capture the reader's attention in the opening paragraph and to hold it all the way to the conclusion. You can do this by humanizing your writing, for readers like real people.

As Amy Morrison, a student, discovered: "Putting oneself in an article—using the page as a sort of mirror reflecting the author's experience—makes for first-rate writing. The reflection the reader beholds should bridge her (or him) with the author. Connecting with the reader is an essential of communication. Technical writing doesn't connect, it doesn't communicate; it alienates. I needed to 'de-technify' and personalize my writing. I needed to learn how to connect with my reader—how to write for people rather than for universities."

One of the best ways to enliven your work is through interviewing. The interview is research, investigation that takes you out of books and gives your work an up-to-date, human dimension. The interview develops evidence that supports assumptions, or shows that your assumptions were all wrong.

All writing is investigation of one kind or another, searching for answers, usually of others, but sometimes of oneself as well. In journalism, "investigative reporting" has come to be considered almost a distinct discipline, requiring a special approach and training. While I am all for efforts of Investigative Reporters and Editors (IRE) to promote professional skills, I believe that all reporting is investigative in nature—asking questions, and digging deeper with more questions when need be. IRE provides excellent materials through publications and web pages, but here I want to share particular experiences and pointers of my own and others.

First, with reference to interviewing, if you prepare fully and keep your ears open, many times you will get more than you expected. For example, in 1987 while researching for my book *Regreening the National Parks,* I interviewed Stewart L. Udall at his law office in Tucson. I had known and respected Udall over the years and had interviewed him while he was secretary of the interior under Presidents Kennedy and Johnson. He was always frank and open, sometimes, I thought, to his own disadvantage. In this case, I asked Udall about references by Robert H. Boyle in his book *The Hudson River* to citizen efforts to block construction of a power plant proposed by Consolidated Edison at Storm King Mountain and a Hudson expressway. Governor Nelson Rockefeller of New York and his brother, Laurance, renowned as philanthropists and conservationists, supported both projects. Udall at first sided with the citizens, but (wrote Boyle) the Rockefellers persuaded Udall to switch gears and allow the U.S. Army Corps of Engineers to grant a dredge-and-fill permit. "I allowed Laurance Rockefeller to hornswoggle me," Udall conceded willingly. "Laurance had done a lot. We had worked together for seven years. He was a 'good guy'— although I increasingly had a lower regard for him. This was something he had worked out and about which he, in effect, said, 'I've done a lot of things for the parks and now I want you to give this your blessing.' I shouldn't have done it, but I'm talking about the kind of personal relationships you develop."[1]

During the course of this visit we discussed various aspects of history. A favorite picture hanging on his wall showed Udall with Robert Frost, the celebrated poet and teacher; William O. Douglas, associate justice of the Supreme Court and champion of the environment; Earl Warren, the chief justice who led a progressive court; and Howard Zahniser, executive director of the Wilderness Society and principal author of the Wilderness Act of 1964. Udall made it a point to associate with such people, much to his credit. But there were always the pressures, from industry and from politicians speaking on their behalf. For example, where President Eisenhower had turned off the flow of federal dollars to build dams in the West, Kennedy during the election campaign promised to turn it back on. Then it came time to deliver. As Udall told me, Ted Sorenson, one of Kennedy's chief lieutenants at the White House, insisted, "We have to keep that commitment to the West."

Udall always made an interview easy. Most people do, no matter who they are. Almost everybody welcomes the chance to be interviewed by someone genuinely interested in him or her. Often it is the interviewer who makes things difficult, either by going in unprepared, or with readiness to talk rather than to listen.

David Helvarg, one of the top environmental journalists of the 1990s, tries to read in advance everything possible about his interviewees, particularly their own materials. His 1994 book, *The War against the Greens: The "Wise-Use" Movement, the New Right, and Anti-Environmental Violence,* is filled with effective interviewing of people with whom he would logically disagree. "I try never to debate, but to get them to open up," explains Helvarg. "I look for some subject of common interest that encourages them to talk freely." In his book Helvarg records his visit in 1993 to Bellevue, Washington, to interview Alan Gottlieb, a guru of the wise-use, property-rights movement operating under the aegis of his Center for the Defense of Free Enterprise and Citizens Committee for the Right to Keep and Bear Arms. "I talked to him about guns, since he was author of the *Gun Rights Fact Book* [as well as *The Wise Use Agenda*]," Helvarg later recalled, "but he wanted to talk about direct mail. That told me a lot, too."[2]

Thus, Helvarg was able to write, with confidence, of Gottlieb: "He was one of a handful of direct-mail fundraisers columnist George Will once called 'quasi-political entrepreneurs who have discovered commercial opportunities in merchandising discontent,' " and to describe him as "a diminutive, forty-five-year-old businessman with the attentive-wet-eyed look of an intelligent mole."[3]

Practice cannot quite make interviewing perfect, but it certainly will help. So will the following guidelines.

Study your interviewee in advance. The more you know, the better his or her answers will be. When you can say, "I read your last book and wonder about . . ." or "In your speech last month you said, . . ." that person will feel you have done your homework and deserve a full response.

Go in prepared, with notebook, pen or pencil, and tape recorder.

Make a list of five or six questions. Other questions will come to you. The better the questions, the better the answers.

Get off to a good beginning. Get there five minutes early. Dress appropriately. Make the interviewee comfortable by showing respect, without argument, no matter how you feel about the subject. You are there to get that person's viewpoint; keep your role of asking questions.

Establish eye contact and stick to the subject. Ask for an example, or ask, "When did that actually happen?" Do not be shy: if you do not understand an answer, ask again, and do not be brushed off. It would be far worse to try to write something later that you do not fully fathom.

Ease off before leaving. Close with an open-ended question, like, "Do you think we have covered everything?" Or, "Anything you would like to add?" If you have done a good job to this point, you may get something special that comes to the interviewee's mind. Ask who else to talk to.

Keep the door open for future communication. Call back, or send an e-mail, for clarification, if you need it. Drop a note of appreciation. You may have a valuable contact and source.

About the tape recorder: be sure that it works, you know how to work it, you have more than enough tape for the interview, and set it close to the subject without it being obtrusive. Always ask if it is all right to use it. In 1983 I went to the Maine woods in company with two employees of International Paper, Ron, a forester, and Paula, a public-relations representative. We drove through the forest to overnight at a company cabin. We had positive dialogue until I mentioned that I would like to bring out my tape recorder and spend the evening interviewing Ron. Quickly, Paula interjected, "What questions are you going to ask Ron?" He was flustered, intimidated by the idea of a recorded interview without a script, and I gave it up.

It was the only time that happened to me, but it showed me not to depend only on the tape recorder, which is never always foolproof anyway. Keep notes, too. If the interviewee goes too fast, ask him or her to slow down, or to wait a minute until you catch up.

Build your own shorthand system with abbreviations and shortcuts. I use 2 for "to," 4 for "for", g for "ing," t for "the", "pk" or "pkg" for package, and make up others as I go along.

As soon as the interview ends, transcribe it while you can still decipher your notes and integrate them with what you observed and remember but did not write down. Figure what is important and set aside the rest. Is it okay to clean up the grammar? Yes, as long as you honor the sense of the interviewee's words and respect his or her position. Considering that oral and written communications differ, exact quotes are apt to make the person appear inarticulate. There is nothing wrong with moving the quotes to connect, as long as you recognize the obligation to represent the voice of the interviewee accurately. If in doubt, call back to clarify or rephrase.

Save your notes. Sometimes an editor will ask, "Exactly what did that person say?" Or a magazine researcher will ask, "Do you have a record of it?" Over the years I have saved a lot of notes and correspondence to track where I have been, whom I met, and how conditions have changed. I cannot remember ever being challenged legally to produce notes, but it happens on occasion to writers. If there is a court order to turn over your material, at least the documentation will be there. If you do not have documentation, it looks like you just wrote from memory.

The better the sources, the better your story is likely to be. It takes time and experience to learn the field and to develop a trusting relationship so that contacts are willing to share valuable information that is not in the press releases. I recall once speaking at a seminar of reporters covering the environment. Several of them complained about the inadequacy of response to their queries by public-relations personnel of the Forest Service. That was their grievance. But why should a reporter rely on a spokesperson whose basic mission is to generate a favorable image for his or her employer? The reporter needs to connect with experts at various levels within the institution and in the field around it, to find the people he or she respects and cultivate genuine relationships with them.

In an earlier chapter I quoted Philip Shabecoff recalling experiences at the *New York Times*. Because the *Times* is such a powerful medium, he was often approached by people who wanted to expose what they believed was wrongdoing. True, it is easier for the *New York Times*, but the principle remains the same. As Shabecoff said, "Many if not most investigative stories come from tips from people who are involved in some way, don't like what they see and think the media can help change the situation." And if they believe you can help, they will share their information with you.

Learn the Freedom of Information Act. That, too, can pry records and data loose from public agencies. Sometimes merely writing a letter citing the act to the appropriate public official will suffice. That failing, ask a congressional office to intervene in your behalf. A lot depends on the issue and the politics of the congressperson, but he or she likely has more clout than you do, plus a yen to badger bureaucracy. There are times when agencies resist even a legal challenge to yield information, but keep prying and trying, for there is always a way and somebody, somewhere, who wants to help.[4]

But I agree with Shabecoff that many if not most investigative stories come from tips from people who are involved and think the media can help. Law enforcement officers say much the same about leads in their work. I learned that while interviewing revenue officers and moonshiners in the mountains of western North Carolina for my book *Strangers in High*

Places: The Story of the Great Smoky Mountains. "They answer the phones themselves and speak in hushed tones, for they may be receiving tidings that will never be offered again. One caller, a jealous woman, in a fit of spite may disclose the location of her own husband's illegal whiskey operation. Another may be a defeated ex-sheriff hoping to punish his political foes. Or a religious zealot stirred to passion against a neighbor who has fostered the whiskey sin. Or a moonshiner double-crossing a competitor in order to improve his own selling position."[5]

In the case of public agencies, and I believe of private corporations, tips and leads come from personnel who believe in what they are doing and feel let down by superiors. Once, while a guest of the Weyerhaeuser Company, observing their extensive operations in the Northwest, I was invited to dinner by a vice president and the manager of pollution controls. We had a drink, dinner, and dialogue, when the manager said, "We have the technology to do a good job, but we're not using it. You must force us to."

Years later, in mid-October 1993, another Weyerhaeuser vice president, Charles W. Bingham, told the conference on Northwest Media and the Environment, at Bellingham, Washington, that industry must improve its resource-management practices to meet public expectations and "must work to make the media a part of the solution—a catalyst in rebuilding trust. . . . The journalist has an obligation to be prepared, to listen carefully, to present a balanced point of view. The industry has an obligation to be open, honest and straightforward about everything—the mistakes as well as the well-dones—to earn that respect."[6]

Bingham said that journalists rarely view the industry as a "source" for environmental information, that they much prefer government and activist groups because they are "more accessible." He could well be right. Thus, a good guideline in conducting investigations and interviews is to give what you consider the other side a fair shot. That is good journalism. Follow Bingham's counsel to prepare and listen carefully, for you may come away with more and better information than you expected.

But what if the party, whether industry, government, or whomever, is not open, honest, or straightforward? What if the spokesperson at hand stonewalls, refusing to provide the data requested, or giving what is plainly a runaround? When that happens, you can be sure that party is covering something that needs to come to light. Here is one prize example from my own experience and from Mr. Bingham's own industry.

In *Field & Stream* of July 1969, I reported receiving word from concerned citizens that the Tennessee Game and Fish Commission had granted permission to Bowaters Southern Paper Corporation, part of a global conglomerate, and a subsidiary, the Hiwassee Land Company, to spread poison grain in a ten-county area for the benefit of a pulp-producing monoculture, while in the process of eliminating native hardwoods. I noted that members of three hunting clubs had taken separate tours of a particular area outside Chattanooga, and all had found dead animals, including dogs, birds, and rabbits. Though I wrote only one paragraph about this case, as part of a larger story (on citizen concerns around the country), it evoked an anguished letter of protest from Bowaters's public-relations manager, accusing me of "misleading statements and fabrications."

He wrote extensively, telling me the grain was poisoned with a pesticide called zinc phosphide, scattered judiciously to protect young pine plantations from hungry voles, rodents of field and forest, and moreover that federal and state biologists had inspected the treated area and found nothing wrong. He provided the names of ten experts capable of providing testimony. I did indeed check with several of them; they unanimously gave Bowaters a clean bill of health, and so did the Tennessee Game and Fish Commission and the regional office of the federal Fish and Wildlife Service.

I might have thought I was on the wrong track, but then another witness rose to be heard. Soon after my column appeared, the American Forest Institute, a public-relations front of the wood-products industry, issued a public report of a survey on the widespread damage caused by pernicious voles throughout America. The principal source of the "survey" was none other than Bowaters Southern, and, would you believe, the chairman of Bowaters and of the American Forest Institute were one and the same.

I contacted a newspaper reporter listed by the Bowaters public-relations man. The reporter responded that he was not up on the affair, but sent revealing clippings, including one quoting a company official admitting that mistakes had been made in spreading the poison. I contacted another reporter, Buddy Houts, of the *Chattanooga News–Free Press,* who assured me the grievances of the citizens were valid. Then one of the leaders of the group forwarded a private letter from a federal field biologist who wrote, "All of these people [who made reference to the disappearance of quail, rabbits, and songbirds] cannot be wrong." The regional director of the Fish and Wildlife Service refused to make available a copy of this biologist's official report—clearly in violation of the Freedom of Information Act.

As I wrote above, when officials insist on hiding something, they invariably have something damaging to hide. Once, in the mid-1980s, I was writing a piece about the salaries of executives of national environmental organizations, which I suspected were beginning to resemble salaries of corporate executives. The figures were all readily available except for the National Wildlife Federation, which tried to brush me off by saying, "We don't give out that information." The federation clearly had something to hide, and I got the figure anyway, of the salary plus surprisingly generous benefits, but they never knew how.

In the Bowaters case I turned to people I knew in both the Fish and Wildlife Service and the Forest Service and to scientists for guidance, particularly on the subject of zinc phosphide. They steered me to literature published by the National Communicable Disease Center of the Public Health Service; National Pest Control Association; Northeast Regional Pest Coordinators; California Agriculture Experiment Station at the University of California, Davis; and Hanna's *Handbook of Agricultural Chemicals*. Although Bowaters and friends insisted that zinc phosphide kills only voles, virtually every piece of current literature stressed this to be an intense, extremely dangerous, and long-lasting poison.

In the course of my study, I went to Chattanooga, reviewed the scene, and talked with people. Then I described it all in detail in a subsequent issue of *Field & Stream*, with these conclusions: "On the day that I arrived in Tennessee, Bowaters announced postponement and possible cancellation of its second poison attack on the voles. This was wise: Total annihilation programs for rodents are rarely successful; declines are followed by greater reproductive success. Instead of search for panaceas in the bag of trick poisons, one might suggest careful research and serious self-searching concerning forest management practices that may account for high vole populations."[7]

In reviewing these experiences two further guidelines come to mind: First, build contacts with public employees as sources of public documents and data. Most of them take seriously the Code of Ethics for Government Service, which opens: "Any Person in Government Service Should: Put loyalty to the highest moral principles and to country above loyalty to persons, party, or government department." Second, go to public-information offices for leads and answers, but also find and get to know technical specialists tucked away in offices and cubbyholes. Officials high on the ladder are subject to political influence and pressure, but at all levels most personnel are committed public servants who want to share information in the public interest. Where they feel constrained, they may give clues or cryptic tips on what to look for and where. Occasionally the public employee will excuse himself to the toilet, leaving the writer to peek at the document on the desk. Or the document may arrive in the mail in a blank envelope. Some public employees walk a risky path as whistle-blowers, but Sen. Patrick Leahy of Vermont has defended them, declaring, "Disclosure of waste and abuse by government officials should be seen as a sincere commitment to making government more responsive to people's needs and worthy of their trust. Taken in this light, such disclosures can strengthen and improve government, not weaken or disrupt it."[8]

Listen to private citizens who care. They may not always be right, but almost always are worth hearing and heeding because they know the issues, have assembled information, and have established their own contacts within agencies.

It is best to quote a source, whenever you can, because it makes an article much more credible. However, if dealing with a whistle-blower or someone sharing a confidence, your obligation is to protect the source. If you use what that person has given as the basis of further interviews, research, and corroboration, his or her bosses will never know, and others may well provide you with additional inside information.

Should you let a subject or source review a work in progress? Various publications and writers have their own criteria. Sometimes it can be a bad idea to share something critical. But if you are going to be critical, then be sure you have everything right—or else everything is likely to go wrong, particularly your credibility and reputation. Major magazines have their researchers, or "checkers," working on articles before publication to protect *their* credibility, but the checkers expect you to be reliable. By and large, I have always felt that I benefit from the subject's response to a manuscript. And I still control the final draft.

You should also verify what you have been told: the statement may come from a prominent public official or the president of an important corporation, but that does not necessarily make it the truth. Remember that you are more than a "he-said, she-said" reporter in a hurry; you are an investigator and interpreter.

Now that you are in the process of writing the interview, work back and forth from direct quotes to indirect quotes, maybe two paragraphs one way, and then two the other way. I am not teaching grammar here, but the uncertainties and errors of students remind me to remind you that to introduce a direct quote, use a comma if the quote is a single complete sentence: The child said, "The river overflowed." Commas always go inside quotation marks at the end of the quote, followed by attribution. "Pull over," said the policeman. For quotes of more than one sentence in a paragraph, use a colon.

Take in and record the setting. I mentioned the photograph in Stewart L. Udall's office in reflecting his personality and interests. Another time I interviewed Donald Hodel, one of Udall's successors as secretary of the interior. Hodel wore western boots, had a fire in the fireplace, and a photo of himself climbing in Yosemite, which I found useful in my story.

I mentioned cleaning up the grammar, but there are times when you want to evoke the feeling that goes with the words. In writing *Promised Land: Adventures and Encounters in Wild America,* I went to float the Stanislaus River in California with Mark Dubois and his wife, Sharon Negri. Mark had been a key figure in protesting construction of the New Melones Dam. In the spring of 1979 he climbed to a remote spot above the Stanislaus and chained himself to a boulder, threatening to stay until covered by water rising behind the dam or until he received official assurance the reservoir would not be completed. This excerpt from the book opens with Mark talking:

> "One of the things I recognized after I came out of the canyon on my little camping trip, I was blown away by all the coverage I got. I recognized, ah, for three months the lower canyon had been flooded and we took reporters up. We told them all about it and they said, 'No story, kids, it's just too—a few inches a day are getting flooded and it's just trees. What's the story?' When I was ready to go down, all of a sudden they were ready to cover me. I said, 'Look, I'm going to join my friends in the canyon. They're suffering the same fate.' 'Oh, they're just going to fill it with water, that's all that's going to happen.' I recognized how homocentric our society is. Most folks don't understand that other life has a value. Everything else is for our benefit. . . ."

> Sharon had been listening thoughtfully. Not that she lacked her own ideas or ability to express them, far from it, but when Mark gets talking—listening becomes a treat. Now, however, she felt moved to interject: "Last night when we were paddling on the river

and after going over all that I kept thinking, *Why aren't more people as devastated about this as I am?* When I watch television and I see what happened in Nazi Germany I can't believe that the rest of the world just sat back and watched. As the river was being flooded, I asked, *Why aren't more people screaming and saying, 'No! This is absurd and this can't happen!' "*[9]

Philip Shabecoff sums up his thoughts on interviews quite well:

> Interviews should be conducted politely, with a sympathetic understanding of the interviewee's point of view. But the interviewer should be persistent in requiring the interviewee to answer the questions and not to dodge them. Another basic rule is that there are no dumb questions, only dumb answers. Off-the-record interviews should generally be avoided, though there can be exceptions if they will lead to specific information. Be punctual, dress properly, be aggressive with a polite smile.

> People don't talk in quotes, especially people who would rather not be quoted. A reporter learns which sources can give the kind of quotes he wants. I could always count on specific politicians or environmentalists to provide me with intemperate rhetoric. . . . One builds contacts by working assiduously at one's job, by honoring commitments on secrecy and attribution, by listening with a sympathetic ear to all sources, and by doing an honest, fair and accurate job of reporting and writing.[10]

That, I believe, has always been the hallmark of Philip Shabecoff's work, and I hope that I honor him professionally and personally by recording it here.

CHAPTER 15

The Essential Computer

THE COMPUTER and its little built-in companion, the modem, are essential for writing, research, and communication in our time and likely forever. The journalist and author cannot be without it. Maybe a poet can, but knowing how to use a computer is about as important as knowing how to spell and punctuate.

I try to remember that my laptop, the only computer I own, is not God and the World Wide Web is not heaven. I want to assay the computer ecologically and environmentally, and to use it to my advantage, without being used or abused by it. But, still, I cannot function effectively without it.

I wish that I had started using the computer and Internet earlier so that I could do more with them now. At least I have encouraged students to learn computer skills and to keep learning. In applying for jobs, it helps every time. It helps even more with experience in Pagemaker, or some other software to use in computer layout. In my professional lifetime, from the time of the manual typewriter, carbon paper, mimeograph, Linotype, and "hot lead," I have witnessed fantastic change, and more of it clearly still under way. It pays to keep up.

Editors these days hardly ever want a typescript by itself. In the least, they expect a manuscript on diskette along with hard copy; it is also possible to send it via e-mail, from computer to computer, or via FTP, or File Transfer Protocol, on the Internet, without even the disk. With e-mail, the writer can not only submit a manuscript, but also receive edited copy and review and return it in an hour.

In addition, Internet search engines such as Yahoo and AltaVista and many web sites open access to limitless literary and environmental resources. "The Internet is the hermit's salvation," in the view of writer Richard Manning. "It allows me to do research at libraries and to contact sources all over the world, which means I can do what I do from a quiet spot in the woods. Further, it is largely free, meaning I have access to some of the resources of a fully employed reporter without paying the same costs of my independence."[1]

Personally, I try to scan the *New York Times* and the *Washington Post* several times a week. I tap into a variety of web sites run by for-profit and nonprofit organizations with clues and news the *Times,* the *Post,* and other mainstream media are apt to ignore. EnviroLink, started in 1991, operates its own on-line news wire service to break stories otherwise ignored by the wire services. American Rivers' web page gives daily reports on river issues around the country and weekly congressional reports. People for Puget Sound, in Seattle, provides news and alerts, plus on-line publications *Habitat Report* and *Native Neighborhoods,* and an on-line directory of opportunities for volunteer shoreline stewards.

A growing community of on-line activists, policy advocates, and public-interest organizations has turned to the Internet, communicating without benefit of editing by the mass media, and, in the process, opening new opportunities for computer-literate journalists. Jay Townsend, of Greenpeace, calls it "the ultimate freedom of the press," enabling people to read about an issue or protest that may not otherwise be reported. He cites a case history:

> In the summer of 1995, French military boarded and seized the Rainbow Warrior which was in the South Pacific protesting French nuclear weapons tests. Many television networks just aired a clip of the dramatic video of a French commando breaking in the ship's bridge door and throwing in a canister of tear gas. Wanting more information, supporters flocked to our Web page to read news releases and diary entries by the Rainbow Warrior's crew, view maps and photographs from our protest flotilla and even download that video clip of the tear gas assault. We offer far more comprehensive intelligence about issues, surpassing the typical who, what, when, how and digging into the why.
>
> In a matter of weeks, we gathered tens of thousands of signatures with an on-line petition opposing French nuclear testing, and we're zapping out thousands of electronic Action Alerts on other topics on a regular basis.[2]

More specific to journalism, the National Press Club (NPC) web site serves fresh transcripts of its Washington, D.C., luncheon speakers and the weekly NPC *Record*. Poynter Online, in Saint Petersburg, Florida, a school for journalists and teachers of journalism, provides research files, bibliographies, library information, and links to other on-line publications. One of the best Internet services comes from the Investigative Reporters and Editors and its affiliate, the National Institute for Computer-Assisted Reporting, with tips about advanced reporting, contacts with whistle-blowers, and links to other journalism resources. Discussion groups enable people to ask for advice and tips, pick up job postings, and join discussions about current controversies.

But there is a shadowy side to these computer goodies. Sometimes, while working at home alone, I think that my little computer reflects an unreal world that undermines schools, libraries, and human communication—like progress without people, substituting codes and numbers for human faces. When Bill Gates, the Microsoft mogul, promotes computers in the schools he does not say that looking at a computer for hours causes eyestrain and back strain. Or that book literacy is more important than computer literacy and that, absent the language and educational base that comes from reading, the reduced mental scope of computer users may make their computers largely useless to them.

Jerry Mander, a reformed advertising executive, in *The Case against the Global Economy*, argues that the new electronic technologies primarily serve to accelerate centralized corporate power at the expense of local community-based interests.[3] Time will tell if he is right or wrong. For the present, Mander and others who share his concern can take some comfort in the work of NetAction, founded by a former *Fresno Bee* reporter, Audrie Krause. "NetAction Notes," a free twice-monthly electronic newsletter, shows activists how to use the Internet for community organizing, outreach, and advocacy, while the Consumer Choice Campaign works on issues like Microsoft's potentially anticompetitive practices.

Somehow, even with the blessing of the information revolution, people all across the world are working longer hours, under worsening conditions, with less security, fewer benefits, lower pay, and less power. I hate to say it, but this goes for writers, too, maybe especially for writers, who are subject to publishers' demands for the control of all rights, and thus control of all profit from secondary uses in electronic media. Little wonder that all the writers' organizations have objected and resisted. Representing their members' desire to share in the revenue, the organizations established the Authors Registry to collect fees for electronic and other uses, much like ASCAP has done for years in the music business.

Nevertheless, whether or not we call it a blessing, the computer is a fact of life. It is best not to get hung up on a machine when the weather outside is favorable, but otherwise treat the computer like a messenger in writing, researching, and marketing your own good words. And copy everything on a zip drive or floppy disk as back-up protection, just in case . . .

How to Ask the Science Questions

IS THE EARTH'S CLIMATE WARMING? Are spotted owls in danger of extinction? Are trace concentrations of dioxin dangerous to human health? How do we know and who do we believe? How much does the journalist need to know to be comfortable and credible?

In preparing this chapter I asked friends, professional colleagues who work at it and care, whether they consider training in science important to the environmental journalist and, if so, how important. Here are the views of three of them, experienced journalists and authors, in advance of giving you my own, and of discussing further science, scientists, and communication skills.

Richard Manning states:

> Scientific education is vital, and this is one of my favorite sermons. I never cease to be amazed by the gulf between scientists and the rest of us, and can't help but believe a lot of our political problems could be solved by narrowing that gulf. The scientists, especially the new breed under the banner of conservation biologists, have many of the answers the political debate needs, but I think they've simply grown impatient with our ignoring them. That needs to stop. It seems that the task of environmental writing can be defined as translation, as communicating the wisdom of science to the rest of us. It is our job to narrow the gulf, and a writer cannot do that without attending always and forever to his or her scientific education.[1]

Steve Stuebner declares: "It's worthwhile to get some solid background in science in college. I took a lot of environmental studies classes at the University of Montana, and learned a few things that have helped me in my reporting, such as the chemistry of air pollution and forest ecology. It helps your credibility when you're talking with biologists or engineers and they see that you have some knowledge of technical issues. But you've got to make those technical issues clear and understandable to the public. Don't write for your sources, write for the public."[2]

And Philip Shabecoff: "Scientific training would be particularly helpful for covering the complex environmental beat but it is not necessary. A good reporter covering any beat knows how to be a quick study and learn the essential information to write an accurate and informative story. More important than training is the ability to know what questions to ask and then to be persistent in getting the answers."[3]

All the comments of these professionals are valid, though I concur with Shabecoff that knowing how to ask questions and where to find the answers can prove more valuable than scientific training. Education can teach critical thinking skills. Questioning and persistence, wherever the trail may lead, are at the root of good journalism and good science.

I myself have known many scientists over the years, through interviews, working with them on issues, and even editing *their* work for popular publication. Science ought to be the essence of inquiry, open-ended, though it tends at times to be dogma, ruled by rules, knowledge based, without always recognizing the incompleteness of knowledge, or that scientific knowledge can never be more than approximation, not absolute truth. At last the new type of scientific thinking (to which Manning referred above) stresses consideration of systems as a whole and the linkage of systems at different levels, including human concern and involvement in public process. We do need new data, valid data, but it takes something more to serve society, for science hardly stands alone.

"Imagination is more important than knowledge," is one of Albert Einstein's quotable quotes. Aldo Leopold, in his teaching at the University of Wisconsin and in *A Sand County Almanac,* demonstrated that emotion and aesthetic sensitivity can be wholly compatible with good science. He was neither bland nor impersonal, but an advocate, a crusader.

Like Leopold, his contemporaries, Olaus Murie and Adolph Murie, saw preservation of wild, unmanipulated nature as a "wise use," the essence of wisdom, of human intellectuality and ethics, as well as of science. Olaus overcame the opposition of utilitarians, commercial and political, because he wanted to save the Alaska Arctic slope as a part of the book of life, page after page vibrant with grizzly bears, wolves, caribou, moose, Dall sheep, polar bears, eagles, peregrine falcons, seabirds and songbirds, and with the native people who have dwelled in the north country for countless centuries. Later, in the foreword to *A Naturalist in Alaska,* Adolph's best-known book, Olaus described his brother's way of living out among wild animals, trying to think as they do, establishing an intimate relationship that reveals the motivations of creatures in all they do. Such intimate contact, he noted, leads to an understanding of nature desperately lacking in their time—and still lacking in ours. He continued: "What is much needed today is more mutual respect among the exponents of science, philosophy, esthetics, and sociology. Although we are beginning to think in terms of human ecology, it is now time that we recognize all elements of the good life and give them the emphasis they deserve."[4]

That is what science should do. I do not ask scientists to be anything but scientific, in the same way that I expect a reporter to be a good reporter and avoid peddling propaganda—which should not be necessary if research is thorough and fair. Still, a personal ethic counts as much as professional training.

Society needs the scientific research that foretells significant changes we cannot see. Scientific investigation becomes even more valid when factored into public decision making and public policy. Peter H. Raven, director of the Missouri Botanical Garden, delineated what I consider a model of scientific responsibility in discussing "The Politics of Preserving Biodiversity." Citing destruction of old-growth forests of the Pacific Northwest, he said:

> This significant regional problem has been disguised as a battle between the undoubtedly hardworking people employed by the lumber industry in the Northwest and a romantic obsession on the part of environmentalists with the northern spotted owl. . . .
>
> These ancient forests have been attacked in a frenzy of greedy exploitation, in which they are cut as rapidly as possible and sold as unprocessed logs to Japan to maximize short-term profits. The clearcutting practices ignore the health of the regional economy, which depends on the long-term sustainability of the forests.
>
> Today, strong links need to be rebuilt between biologists and conservation groups, which depend directly on information developed by systematic biologists and stored in museums and similar institutions. . . . Political leaders are hungry for authentic expressions of opinion from informed people, and we need to take part in the political process at all levels to make that process work.

We must begin to give credit to our colleagues who do speak out, often making severe professional sacrifices in the course of doing so. We need to approach the media, the politicians, one another—anyone who will listen—and try to improve the sustainability of the world.[5]

Rachel Carson in the early 1960s opened a new era in communication of environmental science. Farley Mowat, the Canadian, used his training in wildlife science to write *Never Cry Wolf* and other fine books. Others, including Paul Ehrlich, Eugene Odum, Edward O. Wilson, Norman Myers, John Craighead, Frank Craighead, Hugh Iltis, Michael Soulé, and Peter Raven himself, deserve credit for speaking out, often with professional sacrifice.

Some have proved to be excellent and influential writers, while others want to and could be, provided they learn to shed scientific, academic jargon and communicate in the vernacular with personality and personal anecdote. Joseph Palca described his learning experience in the November 3, 1989, issue of the "AAAS Observer," a newsletter of the American Association for the Advancement of Science (AAAS). Palca, as part of an AAAS mass-media fellowship, was interning at a Washington, D.C., television station. His job was to assist the television reporter working on science and health stories. He learned that the reporter conveyed the essence in two minutes of what researchers had taken twenty minutes to communicate. "His report would not be acceptable at a scientific meeting," wrote Palca, "but the story was accurate, to the point, and appropriate for its intended audience. Scientists in journalism must leave behind their need to tell the whole story, and concentrate on providing the essential."[6] Palca himself completed his doctorate, worked as a television producer for a time, then for *Science,* the AAAS journal, and at last listening was reporting science on National Public Radio.

With due credit, there is a considerable difference between covering science and the environment. I realized this anew on reading *A Field Guide for Science Writers.* The essays by thirty-plus writers of prominence include valuable guidance and pointers, but I noted recurrent themes born of institutional mainstream, including warnings to watch out for the environmentalists—for "they have *an agenda.*"

I certainly hope that environmentalism brings an agenda with it and that it may always be open. On the other hand, the *Field Guide* shows science writing heavily impacted, or influenced, as the case may be, by corporations, trade associations, educational institutions, and government agencies flooding writers and editors with press releases, news and feature stories for magazines, speeches, radio and television reports, and video news releases to provide television viewers with stories the stations are unable to cover for themselves, plus research magazines, newsletters, newspapers, and brochures. But, then, consider everything at stake. The federal government alone spends about $40 billion a year on civilian science and technology programs, ranging from the space program to public health and weather forecasting, plus another $30 billion on military research and development. "That's why many of these agencies hire science writers—either as full-time employees or as free-lancers on assignment—to help explain what they do to the taxpaying public," explains Rick E. Borchelt, special assistant for public affairs at the White House.[7]

Academia, trade associations, industry, and government prefer to hire communications specialists who are writers with experience, so they know how to "place" stories and "pitch" stories to the media. Michael Ross, who worked for the Lawrence Livermore National Laboratory (on nuclear-weapons design, magnetic fusion, and Star Wars antimissile defense) before switching to IBM's Almaden Research Center in San Jose, tells *Field Guide* readers what writers do at technology companies: "News releases, fact sheets, marketing documents, trade journal features, and—for internal use—lists of expected questions and suggested answers are the most commonly assigned publicity writing tasks. . . . Be realistic and aim for the right audience. Before you even start writing a news release, you should make a critical assessment of the newsworthiness of the milestone or achievement and determine its most important audience. Corporate management should be comfortable with your judgment and your expectations for the story's use."[8]

The allegiance of the science writers-for-hire belongs to the institution that employs them, even when their work is scrutinized, reviewed, and denatured for bad politics rather than good science. "The first rule in coping with agency editing," warns Borchelt, a member of the board of the National Association of Science Writers, "is never to get personally interested in anything you write. Nine times out of ten you may not recognize it again when it comes out of review."[9]

Rachel Carson was treated to a full dose of "science news" aimed at the "right audience." As I wrote elsewhere in this book, even before *Silent Spring* appeared, editorials and columns by the hundreds had discussed it all over the country. "By late summer," as she told the Women's National Press Club, "the printing presses of the pesticide industry and their trade associations had begun to pour forth a growing stream of pamphlets and booklets to the press and opinion leaders designed to lull the public to sleep from which it had been rudely awakened." Carson remained unfazed, showing the influence of the chemical industry behind the critical reviews and media attacks and the comments of scientists.

That industry never lets up. In 1997, the Center for Public Integrity, headquartered in Washington, D.C., published *How the Chemical Industry Manipulates Science, Bends the Law, and Endangers Your Health.*[10] The authors conducted a three-year investigation during which they found that a substantial number of top EPA officials who worked in toxics and pesticides ended up as employees of chemical companies, their trade associations, and lobbying firms; S. John Byington, former chairman of the Consumer Products Safety Commission, helped the chemical industry launch a campaign to neutralize the regulatory efforts of his old agency; companies manufacturing four common chemicals frequently cited as posing significant health concerns (atrazine, alachlor, formaldehyde, and perchloroethylene) gave free trips to congressmen, EPA personnel; chemical companies employ nearly 90 percent of the nation's "weed scientists"; and the few independent researchers rely heavily on grants from pesticide manufacturers. The chemical industry, they concluded, has overwhelmed the nation's system of safeguarding public health.

Then there is the testimony of Sandra Steingraber, whose book *Living Downstream: An Ecologist Looks at Cancer and the Environment* was well received when it was published in 1997.[11] By mixing personal experience as a cancer survivor, other stories of cancer victims, and a wealth of scientific and historical data, Steingraber succeeded in creating a work that both summarizes and humanizes toxification of the environment. After a string of favorable reviews, she was startled to find her book panned in the *New England Journal of Medicine*—until she discovered that the reviewer, Jerry H. Berke, was not only a physician but also medical director of W. R. Grace & Company, a major chemical manufacturer cited in one of her case histories. After determining that the *Journal* was well aware of Berke's position with Grace, she expressed her disillusionment: "I am more fearful, however, that the actions of the *Journal* are symptomatic of an insidious development: paid industry officials appropriating the media and speaking for the medical research community. When science speaks, whose voice are we hearing these days?"[12]

In my classes I often cited Carson as a model of good science and writing about the environment and could easily do the same with Steingraber. Three graduate students, Sara, Jenny, and Ruth, all academic achievers, were piqued sufficiently to investigate on their own. In 1990 they spent a quarter of independent study working on "Principles of Good Science Writing." As their adviser, I was permitted by them to sit in and listen, perhaps to ask a question, but definitely not to direct or interfere—they were diligent and confident. And this is what they came up with: "After a quarter of studying articles from *Writing about Science,* plus excerpts from a few other sources, we've compiled a list of tips for aspiring science writers. Each is accompanied by excerpts we feel are particularly good (the Do's) or bad (the Don'ts). Page numbers refer to the *Writing about Science* text."

Do's

1. Use simple examples when explaining complex or abstract ideas. Use examples that can be easily visualized, and which appeal to common sense. "An angel whose muscles developed no more power weight for weight than those of an eagle or a pigeon would require a breast projecting for about four feet to house the muscles engaged in working its wings, while to economize in weight, its legs would have to be reduced to mere stilts." (J. B. S. Haldane, "On being the right size," p. 24).

2. Describe the personalities of scientists and struggles they overcame in pursuing important discoveries. Make scientists human. "The first excursion into the physical history of the Earth to result in serious numerical estimates of past time was published in the 1770s by that striking, prolific and courageous figure, Georges Louis Leclerc, Comte de Buffon. Buffon had no hesitations. . . . [He] was less an individual scientist than a committee, and his library was the center for a wide circle of correspondents." (Stephen Toulmin and June Goodfield, "The Earth acquires a history," p. 92).

3. Relate science to common experience. "What can rival a twilit meadow rich with the essence of June and spangled with fireflies? Here is magic, indeed, and the joy of pursuing through grass just touched with early dew a light now here, now there, now gone." (Howard Ensign Evans, "In defense of magic: The story of fireflies," p. 105).

4. Use language in creative and interesting ways. "But we, pale and alone and small in that immensity, hurled back the living stars. Somewhere far off, across bottomless abysses, I felt as though another world was flung more joyfully." (Loren Eiseley, "The star-thrower," p. 192).

5. Use humor where appropriate. "Ethyl alcohol is an organic compound familiar to all and highly valued by most. No doubt the thought that the chemist could make ethyl alcohol from coal, air, and water . . . without the necessity of fruits or grain as a starting point, must have created enticing visions and endowed the chemist with a new kind of reputation as a miracle worker. At any rate, it put organic synthesis on the map." (Isaac Asimov, "Organic Synthesis," p. 40).

6. Define terms likely to be unfamiliar to readers. "The process of swapping bits of chromosome is called *crossing over.* . . . It means that if you got out your microscope and looked at the chromosomes in one of your own sperms (or eggs if you are female) it would be a waste of time trying to identify chromosomes which originally came from your father. . . . Any one chromosome in a sperm would be a patchwork, a mosaic of maternal genes and paternal genes." (Richard Dawkins, "The Selfish Gene," p. 29).

7. Use the active voice wherever possible. "I do not contend that we have put poisonous and biologically potent chemicals indiscriminately into the hands of persons largely or wholly ignorant of their potentials for harm. We have subjected enormous numbers of people to contact with these poisons, without their consent and often without their knowledge." (Rachel Carson, "The obligation to endure," p. 158).

8. Present a clear statement of purpose; tell readers where you're taking them. "It is easy to show that a hare could not be as large as a hippopotamus, or a whale as small as a herring. For every type of animal there is a most convenient size, and a large change in size inevitably carries with it a change of form." (J. B. S. Haldane, "On being the right size," p. 21).

9. Relate historical scientific discoveries to the environment or social climate prevalent at the time of discovery. "The times, however, were dominated by what, in retrospect, we might call the Protein Doctrine. . . . To biologists of the time, proteins seemed all-important, while nucleic acids were a merely somewhat puzzling by-product of life." (Garrett Hardin, "Coding the mechanism," p. 200).

10. Always remember your audience. Choose structure and tone appealing to your particular readers. "A description of nature is what we are concerned with here. From this point of view, then, a

gas, and indeed *all* matter, is a myriad of moving particles."
(Richard P. Feynman, "Physics: 1920 to today," p. 219).

11. Relate your topic to readers' lives; draw broad conclusions.
"Along with the possibility of the extinction of mankind by nuclear
war, the central problem of our age has therefore become the contamination of man's total environment with such substances of in-
credible potential for harm—substances that accumulate in the
tissues of plants and animals and even penetrate the germ cells to
shatter or alter the very material of heredity upon which the shape
of the future depends." (Rachel Carson, "The obligation to endure," p. 154).

12. Vary sentence structure and content. Sprinkle short sentences
among long ones, informal language among fact-packed statements. "In real life, however, even in our worst circumstances we
have always been relatively minor interest of the vast microbial
world. Pathogenicity is not the rule. Indeed, it occurs so infre-
quently and involves such a relatively small number of species, considering the huge population of bacteria on the earth, that it has a
freakish aspect." (Lewis Thomas, "Germs," p. 126). "Since the mid-
1940s over 200 basic chemicals have been created for use in killing
insects, weeds, rodents, and other organisms described in the modern vernacular as 'pests'; and they are sold under several thousand
different brand names. . . . Can anyone believe it is possible to lay
down such a barrage of poisons on the surface of the earth without
making it unfit for all life?" (Rachel Carson, "The obligation to
endure," p. 154).

Don'ts

1. Don't use abstract or confusing examples. "Suppose an event E
occurs to me, and simultaneously a flash of light goes out from me
in all directions. Anything that happens to any body after the light
from the flash has reached it is definitely after the event E in any
system of reckoning time. Any event anywhere which I could have
seen before the event E occurred to me is definitely before the event
E in any system of reckoning time . . ." (Bertrand Russell, "Space-
time," p. 61).

2. Don't let egocentrism interfere with your story. "My doodling of
the [DNA] bases on paper at first got nowhere, regardless of
whether or not I had been to a film. Even the necessity to expunge

"Ecstasy" [a film] from my mind did not lead to passable hydrogen bonds, and I fell asleep hoping that an undergraduate party the next afternoon at Downing would be full of pretty girls." (James Watson, "Finding the secret of life," p. 142).

3. Avoid jargon. "Many forms of life, of which the brachiopod *Lingula* is the best-known example, have demonstrably remained unchanged for enormous periods. . . . Degeneration is a form of specialization in which the majority of the somatic organs are sacrificed for greater efficiency in adaptation to a sedentary or a parasitic life." (Julian Huxley, "Evolutionary progress," pp. 254, 263). "The gram-negative bacteria are the best examples of this. They display lipopolysaccharide endotoxin in their walls, and these macromolecules are read by our tissues as the very worst of bad news. . . . Leukocytes become more actively phagocytic, release lysosomal enzymes, turn sticky, and aggregate together in dense masses, occluding capillaries and shutting off the blood supply." (Lewis Thomas, "Germs," p. 128).

4. Don't include irrelevant or complex diagrams. See Stephen Toulmin and June Goodfield, "The Earth acquires a history," p. 98. Two pages later, the authors state: "Buffon's figures were wrong."

5. Avoid leads that generalize. Don't be afraid to catch readers immediately, with interesting specifics. "If magic be defined as something 'produced by secret forces in nature,' and 'secret' in turn defined as something 'revealed to none or to few' (and these are legitimate definitions), then magic is not likely to be diminished by all the science we can muster." (Howard Ensign Evans, "In defense of magic: The story of fireflies," p. 104).

6. Don't try to jam the spiritual into stuffy "scientific" language, where image, poetry and emotion can carry the magical into words. See Evans example, Don't #5.

7. Avoid too much mysticism. Tell readers what you mean. (Make them work too hard, and you'll lose them.) "Of what man may be I have caught a fugitive glimpse, not among multitudes of men, but along an endless wave-beaten coast at dawn. As always, there is this apparent break, this rift in nature, before the insight comes. The terrible question has to translate itself into an even more terrifying freedom." (Loren Eiseley, "The star thrower," p. 177).[13]

Freelancers Rise Early (or Stay Up Late)

THERE IS NOTHING like your first byline, first paycheck, first book, first or *any* letter from someone afield with words of appreciation for *your* article that helped a good cause. Some of my contemporaries would say the markets are not what they used to be, citing the disappearance of the *Saturday Evening Post, Collier's, True,* and *Holiday,* top-flight magazines, and of major newspapers that have folded, and the decline of others, like the once preeminent *Christian Science Monitor.* But there is good news, too, for a new breed—better yet, breeds—of media is rising all across America to fill the gaps of social concern and critical commentary the mainstream has ignored, the environment notably among them.

I am not even talking about the Internet and the potentials of the new "periodicals" in cyberspace. But the new media in print include more than one hundred alternative newsweeklies, in large and small cities, some with one hundred pages or more, four-color covers, others twenty to twenty-four pages, appealing mostly to sophisticated, upscale young professionals with arts, music, entertainment, and literary journalism. Some are heavy on lifestyle and personal ads, without investigative zeal. Others, however, are outspoken and courageous in coverage of the environment, poverty, racism, women's issues, downtown decay, and criminal justice. They carry long stories, in-depth, and are redefining what is locally newsworthy.

Then there is another genre, focused more directly on the environment. *High Country News,* "A Paper for People Who Care about the West," is the prototype, but there are others, and others coming. I see vitality, excitement, continual improvement, growth, and opportunity in a wide range of periodicals, like *Animals' Agenda, Cascadia Times, Earth First! Journal, Greenpeace, Maine Times, Missoula Independent, Simple Living, Wild Earth,* and more.

Before getting into them in this chapter and the next, let's discuss freelancing as a career. Steve Stuebner, who has survived and thrived as a full-time freelancer since 1991, is right when he says: "It takes an acute news antenna, a ton of energy, disciplined work habits and time-management, smart money management, polished writing, good relationships with editors, persistence, and thick skin."

Like most freelance writers, Stuebner likes getting up each day without having to go to work for someone else, but he warns against trying to jump into freelancing too soon. He had twelve years of reporting—building experience, contacts, and a bank account—and mastering computer equipment and Internet access:

> Even when I worked for newspapers full-time, I always tried to write freelance articles. I wanted to get published in higher-quality publications and advance my career as a writer. So I did have some knowledge of how to write magazine queries, and I did have a few solid relationships with regional publications before I quit the [Boise, Idaho] *Statesman* in October 1991. That helped. But to make a living as a freelancer is a whole different ball game. I had read a book, *How to be a Free-Lance Writer,* by David Martindale, so I knew what I was getting into. I realized quite rapidly that I had to sell lots of stories or I wasn't going to have much cash flow. That meant writing queries and branching out to land a steady stream of assignments from newspapers and magazines on a regular basis.
>
> Now my goals are to keep my hand in the news business and continue to write magazine and newspaper stories. I hope to develop my new relationship with the *New York Times* so we can get more news stories about the West in the nation's most prestigious newspaper. But in the long term, I want to work more on book projects, and, hopefully, publish a work of fiction by the time I'm forty, two years from now."[1]

Writers get into freelance work for different reasons and at different stages of their careers. Most already have held professional writing jobs and established their connections. I recall one friend who was blacklisted by newspapers for his union work with the Newspaper Guild and had no place to go. Another would say, "I was too lazy [or contrary] to hold a regular job." Ted Williams, who is talented, full of ideas, and successful in writing for outdoor magazines, *Audubon,* and other environmental periodicals, started as editor of *Massachusetts Wildlife,* the state fish and game magazine. Richard Manning, whose departure from the *Missoulian* in Montana I cited earlier, tells it this way: "What helped me most in my break from daily journalism was the way I did it. Saying 'no' to the powers is unusual enough to gather some attention, which in turn started my career rolling. The biggest obstacle was in overcoming the need for security and trusting my skills and luck to carry me from meal to meal and rent payment to rent payment. Not that these problems ever solved themselves, but I just finally quit worrying."[2]

Manning is right. You must trust your skills and quit worrying about the bills. Or have a partner with a regular job, or just spend less. Or maybe be so driven by worry that you write more and better. David Helvarg, author of *The War against the Greens,* balances his environmental writing with television production work. That is one way to do it. It is fulfilling, but not always: "Beyond financial constraints, freelancing has its advantages. It's not like being a beat reporter. I can pick my own stories, develop ideas on my own time. Of ten ideas I propose to editors, three will sell; and then I find some of the others showing up written by somebody else. I find it helps to dress up environmental stories, that it's easier to sell one on immigration or political corruption and bring in the environmental connection."[3]

Helvarg's advice in four simple words is, "Don't be gun-shy." He is absolutely right. Pick your target and go for it. "I always found it essential to keep the article ideas flowing," notes George Laycock, who has written fifty books and hundreds of magazine articles, "adding new ideas to the list, sending queries, making occasional trips east to peddle the most promising ones to the most likely markets."[4]

If you want to get published in a particular periodical, say *National Geographic,* study it closely. Read the back issues over a period of a year. You will get an idea of subjects the editors like, the length of an average article, the length of sentences, treatment of quotes and anecdotes, and more. To be sure, you need the subject, something special, that you have researched and care about, and that makes good reading for the particular audience of your target magazine. John Mitchell, who worked for years as a freelancer before accepting a key position at *National Geographic,* offers this counsel: "Most stories are assigned to *Geographic* staffers and established freelancers, but if you want *in* you'll have to show us some very impressive clips (preferably a book) and a winning idea."[5]

T. H. Watkins in discussing the practical prospects of making a living as a freelance environmental journalist (before he left Washington, D.C., in 1997 to be a professor at Montana State University) underscored the point that successful freelance writers have been around for a while:

> Some people can. I can, you can, a few others maybe can eke out a true living as an environmental writer, but they tend to be those, like you and me, who have been around long enough to have developed contacts and friends who will keep them alive. Up until very recent years, I would not have been able to say that of myself, and, even now, if it were not for the work I am able to do for *National Geographic* (and not all that true environmental journalism), I would have to have a day job. And guess who got me writing for *NG?* My old friend and colleague, John G. Mitchell, that's who.
>
> In short, anyone who hopes to live off what he or she gets as an environmental reporter had better rethink that goal, casting around for a working mate or doing other kinds of writing and reporting to supplement the environmental stuff. Maybe later in the career, with a little luck and a lot more help from friends, you can make a go of it.
>
> To the extent you can break in, my advice would be the same as that to any journalist, no matter what specialty may be involved: read absolutely everything on the subject you can find, then unearth another, better way of presenting it, another angle, better research, a legitimate challenge to accepted truth—or find yourself another Love Canal. And, like Winston Churchill, never never never never give up.

I asked Watkins to mention the publications he likes, or sees advancing:

> Magazines that remain at least decent possibilities are *Audubon*, *Sierra* (though declining badly), *Defenders* (still holding true), *Wildlife Conservation*, *National Wildlife* (though high art it ain't), *Orion* (though a good deal more literary than journalistic), *High Country News* (though not a magazine). I confess that I do not like

E magazine all that much; though it does a lot of reporting the writing strikes me as third-rate. Of the non-enviro mags, *Mother Jones* is the only magazine that regularly runs good environmental stuff (that's changed since the 1980s when even the old ladies, *Atlantic* and *Harper's,* published the likes of Ed Abbey). *Outside* is okay, I guess, but the magazine's love affair with gonzo journalism still turns me off—too smartass, generally, to be entirely reliable. *Backpacker,* of course. *Sports Afield* has been running some decent stuff, but I suspect that is a temporary condition. I would include *National Geographic,* with the disclaimer that it is hard as hell to get into, being not very fond of suggestions offered over the transom (though one or another occasionally gets in).

Books are one way a lot of writers are going (though making a living as a book-writer is, if anything, even more difficult than as a magazine journalist, and I can prove it by my own personal statistics).[6]

Those are my personal statistics, too, but writing books is professionally challenging, and rewarding in ways that far transcend the paycheck. It is the chance to spread out the words, to express a viewpoint, and to leave a record.

To illustrate, in 1996 I received a phone call from a friend, Gregory McNamee, an author and editor whom I have quoted elsewhere in this book. He had been consulting a fellow named Chuck Pezeshki, helping shape a manuscript into a publishable book. Pezeshki evidently wanted me to read it, and McNamee asked if I would. Soon after I was in Moscow, Idaho, and met with Pezeshki, a professor of engineering at nearby Washington State University. He brought the manuscript for *A Clearwater River Anthology,* but I would not take it because the type was too small to read without eyestrain. Chuck ran off a better copy and sent it to me with a fervent letter of commitment to his work. In response, I told him I did not think it publishable in its present form, but that it had solid material that would be well served by cutting the manuscript by at least one-third.

In 1997 I received a letter from Keith Peterson, editor at Washington State University Press, advising that *A Clearwater River Anthology* would be published in spring 1998 under a new title, *Last of the Wild:* "Chuck has for years been very involved in environmental concerns on the Clearwater, and this will be his book about his experiences, the experiences of others, and some of the major issues in that region. I know you saw an earlier version of this work. Since that time, we have worked with Chuck on some major revisions. The result, I think, is a much tighter work. This will be Chuck's first book, but we believe it is a very good one, and an important one."[7]

I thought that was right, that Chuck indeed had written a very good book, because he was determined to, and cared enough about the Clearwater country. He persevered, learned from criticism, and achieved his goal. Who can tell what comes next?

Read the big environmental magazines, including *Amicus Journal, Audubon, National Parks, Nature Conservancy, Sierra,* and *National Wildlife;* if you connect as a regular contributor, you will do pretty well. The trouble with them is each has an organization party line, with its own sacred cows and shibboleths. Over the years Les Line, the editor of *Audubon,* developed considerable editorial independence, producing a superlative magazine without censorship, guidelines, or interference from above—at least until 1991, when he was sacked by Peter Berle, then president of National Audubon. In more recent times, Tom Wicker, former *New York Times* political columnist, wrote a piece for *Audubon* criticizing aspects of President Clinton's environmental policies. It was bought, edited, paid for, and scheduled for the March–April 1996 issue, but it was pulled by Berle's successor, Audubon president John Flicker. Wicker told *Times* media columnist Deirdre Carmody the piece "could damage Audubon's future lobbying efforts" and that he did not believe the society should be "involved in every environmental issue that comes along."

Outdoor magazines constitute another type of market. When I was writing for *Field & Stream* and later for *Western Outdoors,* I felt I was in the right spot to strike a few good blows. Many readers were literate, concerned, and responsive, and I had the chance to state a case for those who were not. But those people have been overloaded with articles and advertisements about mechanized, high-tech gadgetry that make it easier to shoot animals and catch fish, degrading the genuine outdoor adventure.

I received my share of critical letters, mostly about politics, but nothing compared to the responses generated by Ted Williams's work. When he was executive editor of *Gray's Sporting Journal* in the 1970s, Williams received letters complaining, "There are too many 'do-gooder' magazines on the market today and few that give you the joy of remembering a good hunt or the one that got away." Or, "Let me enjoy reading about your skillful exploits, trout fishing and other forms of fishing. Leave the politics alone." A letter to the editor in *Fly Rod and Reel,* where Williams is conservation editor, declared: "Mr. Williams has succumbed to the lifestyle and philosophy of his Sierra Club/Wilderness Society brethren. Use of toilet paper is not condoned because it comes from trees. The true believers take group enemas at the beginning of their monthly meetings."[8]

The outdoor magazines appear to go in cycles. *Sports Afield* in the late 1990s seemed much improved, actually publishing articles on why sportsmen should be involved in the environmental movement and a two-fisted column by Susan Zakin. On the other hand, editors at *Outdoor Life* in 1994 helped reelect Congressman Don Young of Alaska by profiling him as a "fearless Washington advocate of the sportsman's life" and "your kind of politician [who] fights the good fight," although Young consistently has been the most virulent antienvironmentalist in the House of Representatives. Then a new team came on board, determined to do better. But no, in mid-1996 the editor and executive editor, Stephen W. Byers and Will Bourne, quit in protest after an executive of Times-Mirror, which owns *Outdoor Life,* pulled an article scheduled for the September issue. The article was critical of bear baiting, in which raw fish or meat is set out to attract black bears. The practice is illegal in some states and subject to referenda in others. Speaking of the outdoors media, "This is the sort of world where no questions have been asked for a long time," said Bourne. "And a bunker mentality has really set in."

But let's look beyond the negative. There are plenty of other periodicals, including the *Utne Reader, In These Times, Mother Earth, Outside,* and *Backpacker,* to name a few of the new breed. Do not overlook established women's magazines, like *McCall's* and *Good Housekeeping,* or *Parents, Modern Maturity, Harper's,* the *Atlantic,* the *Progressive,* and *Popular Science.* There are more kinds of magazines around with pages to fill week after week, month after month, than you can possibly imagine. The following tips will help find the right ones for you.

Study the market. Treat your writing like a business and look for the outlets that will work for you. Browse the magazines on file at the local library, or at any newsstand. Study the eye-catching "cover lines." They tell exactly what ideas the editors think appeal to readers and sell copies. Picture your subject in a cover line. Will it really make it? Is it new, different, timely, exciting? Has somebody written it already? Will it sell magazines? Have you identified the right magazine for it?

Magazine work differs from writing for newspapers. You have more time to research and report, more space in print to expand on your findings. Each magazine is distinct, with its own personality and purpose, but in general it is okay, even desirable, to express a strong point of view, with feeling. The magazine editor expects the writer to show he or she is thinking while working through the piece, and that conclusions derive from thorough detailed research and reporting.

Read *Literary Market Place*. Most libraries have it, though you may want your own copy of this indispensable catalog, providing vital data on thousands of magazines, including the address and phone, fax, and e-mail numbers, names of key personnel, principal subjects of interest, payment policies, and seasonal deadlines. *Writer's Market* is another good one, designed to show how to sell what you write, and is more affordable if you want to own a copy. *Writer's Digest*, a monthly abundant with tips, may also prove helpful. Invest in a copy, or a subscription.

Write directly to the magazine that interests you for its guidelines. Many will respond with data on content, style, length, and timing (that is, how far ahead the magazine works).

Work on your query letters, outlining your articles generally in a page or less. That query letter is your calling card, so highlight the subject as compellingly as you can. Tell your qualifications and experience, enclosing a tear sheet of something you have published.

Most editors understand that a query, or outline, is not the article, but an idea for one. You are free to offer the idea to two or more publications. If two respond favorably, choose one and tell the other, "Sorry, it's been sold, but perhaps we can do something else together." No editor will be upset or hold it against you. It is different when you offer completed manuscripts to magazines. Bad things can happen with multiple submissions, particularly to competing magazines. All the editors will be unhappy, so *do not do it*. On the other hand, with a book manuscript, multiple submissions are perfectly acceptable. Above all, put your best foot forward and avoid mistakes in your query.

Here is a sample query letter, with a few notations to help you:

(1)
Ms. Joan Hamilton
Editor-in-Chief
Sierra
85 Second Street
San Francisco, CA 94105

Dear Ms. Hamilton:

(2, 3)
I would like to write an article for *Sierra* on "How to survive a cougar encounter," based in part on my own personal experience in meeting a cougar eye-to-eye on a wilderness trail.

(4)
The idea first came to me last year after a college classmate and close friend, Henry Kendall, reported on his experience. He was running alone about four miles south of Bellingham when he felt he had company, that he was being stalked. He glimpsed only a fleeting shadow, but he was in the very area where two Bellingham residents had reported seeing a cougar. When Henry said, "I make sure I don't run by myself up there any longer," I felt that could be a good tip in a how-to-survive feature.

Then, one month later, my fiancée, Kay Martin, and I were hiking in Manning Provincial Park, in British Columbia. I was twenty or thirty yards ahead when I came face-to-face with a cougar. Intuitively, I picked up part of a dead tree limb and extended it toward the cougar with both arms, as though preparing to defend myself. The animal quietly withdrew into the woods.

(5)
Since then, I have talked with wildlife management personnel in both Washington and British Columbia, all of whom said I did the right thing. They make the point that sudden movement or flight may trigger an attack. It's best to hold your ground or back away slowly. Speak to the cougar in a firm, calm voice.

(6)
In hiking wilderness trails in the Northwest, California, Colorado, and the Southwest over the past ten years, I have learned the likelihood of even seeing a cougar is extremely rare, and of being attacked by one even rarer. Nevertheless, as development continues to encroach on rural areas, cougar sightings are becoming more common and people are apprehensive. I believe that providing

Sierra readers with sound information would help them *and* the panther.

(7)
I am a graduate student at Western Washington University majoring in biology. I have an undergraduate degree in communications from the University of Wyoming, where I was managing editor of our undergraduate student magazine. I have written articles on wildlife and wilderness for the *Bellingham Herald,* the *Seattle Times,* and the *Casper Tribune,* samples of which I enclose.

(8)
I am prepared to write an article of a thousand words on "How to survive a cougar encounter" for *Sierra* at your usual rates and to send it to you by November 15. I appreciate your consideration and enclose a self-addressed stamped envelope.

(1) Address your inquiry to a real, live editor at the magazine you have singled out. Make sure you have the address right.

(2) Type the query in the form of single-space business letters (double-space between paragraphs).

(3) Get to the point in the first paragraph, so the editor has concise, sharp understanding of the specific idea you are proposing. Think in terms of a title to grab the editor's attention.

(4) Give the best example or examples to support the proposal.

(5) Show that you have consulted, or intend to consult, a voice (or voices) of authority on the subject.

(6) Give the slant that makes it right for this magazine.

(7) Show your qualifications. Enclose two, no more than three, clippings of your articles in print.

(8) The self-addressed stamped envelope (SASE) makes it easier for the editor to respond, though many editors do not expect frequent contributors and established writers to attach SASEs to queries.

⊸

Know your audience. If you are targeting a particular magazine, read and study a number of issues. Generally, editors want fresh ideas fitting those with which their magazines are already identified. Your challenge is to bring fresh appeal to perennial issues. Nevertheless, do not assume the audience knows the subject, or that it knows more than it does. Orient the reader and help him or her to focus on the most important aspect of your case. Write in words, sentences, paragraphs people can understand. If you must use words like *riparian, anadromous,* and *smolt,* explain what they mean. Make your writing timely to the audience. Check the length, and do not exceed it.

Show in your work that you have an opinion. Point of view makes the writer whom readers remember. Show that your point of view comes out of diligent reporting and research, collecting and analyzing data, thoroughly and fairly. Reach independent conclusions so the reader is not left wondering, "What was that all about?'

Make one important point. William Zinsser in *On Writing Well* advises that you leave the reader with one provocative thought. Not two thoughts, nor five—just one. "So decide what point you most want to leave in the reader's mind."[9]

Try to be patient. It is not easy, and we have all been there, awaiting the word, biting fingernails while wondering what is holding it up. The truth is that sometimes the better an idea or manuscript the longer it takes to get a decision. Frequently it will be read by more than one editor, sometimes three or four. Yes, we have all had horror stories. There comes a time to follow up and ask, maybe in four weeks or so. If the word is negative, learn from it and move on.

Develop a specialty, an area of interest you know and care about, so when an editor thinks of that subject he or she will think of you. Having facts, contacts, and experience at your fingertips makes research a lot easier.

A deadline is a deadline. I remember one well-known writer who when asked the secret of his success responded, "I get my stories in on time and they're neatly typed." Those things count. Most deadlines are lenient anyway, and the editor has his or her deadlines, too.

Never be satisfied where you are, no matter where you are. "Start at the top," counseled a professional. "It's as easy to write for a thousand bucks as for a hundred." I am not sure that is true. The better the publication the better your writing and research need to be, and the more effort you need to invest. Maybe it is best to write for smaller markets, until you are good at it, and then work up with effort and study to where you really want to be. While meeting your commitments and paying the bills, spend a little time each day on a long-term project that means something special to you. Do not compromise with quality, particularly not your own. Do not "write down" to anybody; write up to them all.

This idea leads me to mention the *Maine Times*. It carried an excellent piece of environmental journalism, "Maine's Poisoned Wildlife," by Andrew K. Weegar, about dioxin in Maine rivers, cadmium in moose and deer liver, mercury, lead, PCBs, loons, and eagles. But an editorial column by Peter W. Cox in that issue discussed a deeper question:

> To a public nurtured on "infotainment," any serious writing is boring. The vast majority of Americans do not read for intellectual stimulation, with the result that the best-written literary novel is lucky to sell 10,000 copies nationwide. Thrillers, yes. A new Faulkner, forget it.
>
> For years, the daily press tried to dumb down its stories, to make them shorter and less complex. I always felt the result was that they did not gain the non-reader; they simply lost the involved citizen. I always accepted the fact that most people bought a daily paper for the sports scores, the comics and the TV listings. . . .
>
> Should *Maine Times* be difficult for an uninformed person to read? Yes, there is no way around it. But *Maine Times* should also offer that person the opportunity to become truly informed. . . . For me, the worst result would be a "successful" *Maine Times* that is irrelevant to the future of Maine.[10]

My only objection is that even the person who buys a daily paper for sports, comics, and television listings yearns for serious fare. For publications dealing with the environment beyond infotainment, read on.

Coming Opportunity in Alternative Media

THIS ADVERTISEMENT in *High Country News* may have been meant for you:

> Editor/Desktop Publisher, for the Association of Forest Service Employees for Environmental Ethics, in Eugene, Oregon: Duties include producing bi-monthly magazine for resource professionals, including solicitation of articles, editing and desktop publishing using Macintosh PageMaker and PhotoShop programs. Opportunities for other environmental advocacy initiatives consistent with primary magazine production duties. Excellent writing, editing and computer design skills required. Experience with U.S. Forest Service a plus, as is natural resource education and/or experience. Send resume, cover letter, writing samples and references.[1]

This strikes me as an attractive and challenging opportunity. The Forest Service Employees' twenty-page tabloid, *Inner Voice,* is well written and well designed. It gives encouragement and support to public servants struggling uphill in an antiquated bureaucracy. It is good environmental journalism. And if you missed the ad, and the job, there are many like it, and more coming.

Considerable attention is paid to downsizing and disappearance of traditional old periodicals, but that is only the dark side of the coin. The other side is brightened by the emergence and growth of nontraditional new periodicals. I see and receive dozens of them. They are not all professionally done, but plenty of them are, and they are improving steadily. Besides, maybe professionalism, as we have known it, is not necessarily the best standard of judgment.

The alternative city newsweeklies are an important part of the scene, but only one part. Others relate more directly to the environment, like these titles: *Columbiana,* "sharing ideas of how to live here, in the land drained by the Great River of the West, the Columbia River, and its tributaries"; *Simple Living,* the Journal of Voluntary Simplicity, the antithesis to the superconsumerism promoted by the mainstream media, or to quote the headline over one article, "Simple Bliss Costs Fraction of Former Lifestyle"; *Cultural Survival,* "on the rights of indigenous peoples and ethnic minorities"; *American Rivers,* "dedicated to protecting and restoring American rivers"; *HSUS News,* the magazine of the Humane Society; *Wild Earth,* "melding conservation biology and environmental activism"; and *ZPG Reporter,* of Zero Population Growth. I read, or at least scan, many like these every month. Good places to get acquainted with them are the local newsstand, bookstore, co-op, or health-food store.

As a conservationist, I find such publications sources of invaluable data, surpassing almost anything available through the mass media; as a journalist, I respect them for quality and integrity. And all of them need talented writers and editors.

I find it helpful to look and read beyond my own parameters. I pick up the *Earth First! Journal,* subtitled "The *Radical* Environmental Journal," and tend to think it raucous, vulgar, and sometimes poorly edited, yet it carries important environmental news. For example, in the December 1996 issue Judi Bari reported on the state of her lawsuit against the FBI and the Oakland Police Department for their handling, or mishandling, of the 1990 car bombing that nearly killed her. The lawsuit charges the FBI and the Oakland police with civil-rights violations, including false arrest, illegal search and seizure, denial of equal protection of the law, and violation of First Amendment rights. As she wrote: "We claim that they knew perfectly well that we were the victims, not the perpetrators, of the bomb that exploded under my car seat on May 24, 1990, as we were organizing for Earth First! Redwood Summer. Yet they arrested Darryl [Cherney, her companion] and me and conducted a smear campaign against us in the press in order to discredit us as terrorists and neutralize Earth First!"

The public ought to know about such cases, not because of Earth First! but because of law enforcement agencies, of how they protect and/or threaten civil rights, and whatever liaison there may have been between agency personnel and corporate interests in the redwoods. The public ought to know about people like Judi Bari, who devoted all her energies to her cause and died, much too soon, of cancer.

There are good papers in the new alternative media and able people running them. *High Country News,* the most respected regional environmental journal in the country, is a going concern attracting top writers who consider it a privilege to contribute their articles to it. Betsy Marston, the editor, calls it "a presumptuous little paper that attempts to cover ten western states, believing it *is* possible to cover a green beat fairly, yet care passionately about the issues that involve wildlife, public lands, and rural communities."[2] Perhaps the most presumptuous part about it is that advertising is discouraged—subscribers pay for the stories they read, not for refrigerator ads.

In 1995, *High Country News* marked its twenty-fifth anniversary, with fitting tribute to its founder, Tom Bell. A Wyoming native who grew up on horseback on a ranch near Lander, Bell attended the University of Wyoming, studying natural resources and communication. In World War II he became a gunner on a B-24 heavy bomber, only to lose an eye on his thirty-second combat mission. In the years following, however, he saw well enough to lament the natural beauty of his state going downhill and nobody doing anything about it, least of all the media. Bell became active in the Wyoming Wildlife Federation, organized and became the first executive director of the Wyoming Outdoor Council, and began *High Country News* in 1970. He put everything into the paper, including his ranch and bank savings. It was hard going. In 1973 Bell made certain the paper would survive and moved on.

Ed and Betsy Marston came west from New York in 1983, took over *High Country News,* and relocated in Paonia, a small town in western Colorado. They built the magazine to the point where circulation in 1997 was up to twenty thousand and income for the year projected at more than $950,000, most of it from subscribers. The Marstons pay freelance writers more than $100,000 a year, five times more than a decade ago. "We try to give context to issues. Because *High Country News* is run by a non-profit foundation and read by subscribers who care about the West," explains Betsy Marston, "our reporters are free to write long, jump stories, and tackle complicated issues involving federal agencies and grassroots environmental groups."[3]

Another of my favorites, "Environment Hawaii," is the brainchild of

Pat Tummons, who worked as an editorial writer for the *Saint Louis Post-Dispatch* when she came to Hawaii in 1985 on a sabbatical fellowship. She found herself frustrated by the lack of news on environmental issues provided by the Hawaii media and in due course quit her job, moved to Hawaii, and sank her savings to start "Environment Hawaii," a scrappy newsletter determined to keep the system honest.

Tummons's readers are citizen environmentalists; professionals of environmental groups; professionals in botany, biology, and marine science; planners, architects, lawyers, government personnel, and libraries; and relatives and friends. "Environment Hawaii" has made public officials more accountable. Articles on a huge resort proposed for one of the few undeveloped areas of the coast led to further state scrutiny of the project and ultimately to the developer going into receivership before construction. As with all the off-brand publications, her reports have been picked up by the local dailies—it is like doing the spadework and showing them where the stories are.

It has not been easy for Tummons; growth has been slow. After five years she still had less than a thousand circulation. She converted to a nonprofit corporation, which at least allowed her to accept donations and foundation grants. She paid for a half-page ad in the Hawaii Sierra Club bimonthly and got one response. Word of mouth has proved best, but slow. She hands out copies at meetings and hearings, gives samples to interviewees, "an effective (if tedious) way of getting subscribers."

Maybe good and important groundbreaking efforts are meant *not* to be easy. It was not easy for Tom Bell or Pat Tummons, or for Paul Koberstein, who started *Cascadia Times* in April 1995 as a kind of Northwest version of *High Country News*. Paul had worked for the *Portland Oregonian* for twelve years, helping, along with Kathie Durbin, to institute the paper's investigative natural-resources reporting. Their trouble was they took the assignment seriously. Paul was forced out first, and then Kathie quit a year later, celebrating with a message on his voice mail, "It's time to start that newspaper you've been dreaming about."

Paul and his partner, Robin Klein, who runs the business end, started with more courage than cash. Slowly they raised money from donors, foundations, and subscribers, but two years later were still struggling. Issue after issue were written mostly by the old *Oregonian* sidekicks, Koberstein and Durbin.

"The emergence of *USA Today* showed publishers they could make money by designing newspapers around the lowest common denominator. They moved away from investigative in-depth reporting to shorter pieces—factoid journalism," Koberstein told me during one of our sessions in Portland. "Our publication tries to explain how things work. People live here because the Pacific Northwest is a great place, unique for its quality of life, abundance of resources, and beauty of scenery. Readers hold dear those values and are concerned with reckless development of trees and salmon, promise of growth, and want to know more about them in a regional context, not like daily papers which tend to divide things into small segments that work against a broader understanding."[4]

Koberstein makes the point that if mainstream media were truly meeting the mandates of high-quality journalism, the so-called niche publications would not exist. But that is not the way it works. As television has grown, newspapers have declined. Dailies, the best and worst of them, have folded in every city; those remaining struggle to keep up circulation by trying to compete with television, catering to the same low common denominator, rather than striving to ensure a well-informed public. For example, early in 1997 the *Washington Post* canned Colman McCarthy, whose columns had graced its pages and enlightened readers since the 1960s. The management said McCarthy's work had "run its course." In his farewell column, McCarthy asked, "What should be the moral purpose of writing if not to embrace ideals that can help fulfill the one possibility we all yearn for, the peaceable society?"[5] There will not be much more of that talk in the *Washington Post,* or anywhere else.

I am sure at this stage of history that the editorial voices of alternative periodicals, even those strong and profitable, like *Seattle Weekly* and the *Village Voice,* let alone little guys like *High Country News, Missoula Independent,* and *Cascadia Times,* are not terribly important as compared with the traditional daily press. At least not so far. But cyberspace, audiovisual, and desktop publishing all point to dramatic change and more difficult times for large daily newspapers. The field is open for those who dare to provide the public with cutting-edge contents it cannot find in the mainstream media. Living in the twenty-first century will have to be different, for society cannot continue devouring resources without restraint. Where the old media promote consumption and overconsumption of superfluities, the challenge to the new media is to provide information and inspiration on living without consuming, consuming, consuming.

Some of the alternative weeklies are on the way to doing it. They still depend on advertising revenue so they can be distributed free, but at least they define their roles in terms of social conscience. The *Flagpole* in

Athens, Georgia, explains itself this way: "Alternative to what? Alternative to safe journalism that loses its flavor on the bedpost overnight; alternative to the hustle that says bad music is good for a profit; that says your quality of life is not as important as my money; that says art and music and writing and individuals and small business trying to make it on their own initiative are not as important as the corporate vision that everybody must conform to a set standard of efficiency in the name of uniform return to stockholders."

And consider *Cityview* in Des Moines. "Prior to the fall of 1994, Central Iowa's sole news source was the daily *Des Moines Register,* whose Gannett theory of brevity over substance caused it to lose 50,000 readers in the past decade—despite major population growth. In contrast, *Cityview's* circulation increased 10 percent in the last year alone. We don't write down to readers. We give them subjects and people the *Register* won't touch."

Cityview has covered the Iowa Nazi movement. The *Detroit Metro News* in 1994 focused on the rise of armed-citizen militias, when that movement received almost no media attention. The paper reported the Michigan Militia had brigades in sixty-three of the state's eighty-three counties, armed and opposing government. *Westword* in Denver gave continuing coverage to the Justice Department's machinations in shutting down a grand jury investigating environmental crimes at the Rocky Flats nuclear power plant.

The *San Francisco Bay Guardian,* which began in 1966, has grown into one of the largest, best-known alternative newsweeklies in the country with investigative reporting on tough local issues, such as legislation to place the Presidio, the historic military post, under private control, although presumably administered by the National Park Service. Martin Espinoza, after months of tracking the legislation, wrote: "The goal has been to appease and unite the city's most politically connected leaders, even if that means hiding environmental, good-government, and neighborhood criticisms from Congress while giving local business allies and the GOP in Washington everything they want—most importantly privatization of the country's newest national park."[6]

Many of these publications are written and edited by experienced professionals, and their salaries approach professional levels. While in New Mexico in 1996, I interviewed Robert Mayer, editor of the *Santa Fe Reporter.* He himself came west from New York after working for *Newsday* for ten years as an editor and columnist. He told me the *Reporter* pays staff writers about thirty thousand dollars a year, a figure comparable to the

New Mexico dailies, and that the staff includes one twenty-year veteran with *Time* and a highly competent former freelance editor for the *New Yorker.* Cover articles pay freelancers five hundred dollars, really a pittance for the time and effort involved in producing a decent piece, but how many homes can a writer find for his or her creative work?

It comes down to personal choices, such as living simply within your means, or living simply anyway, of what you want to do with your life, the kind of career that will keep you happy, and the compromises you are willing or unwilling to accept. In a sense, the best kind of journalism is local journalism, and being able to practice the craft in the place where you live is a noble thing to do. In the case of Martin Yant, living and working in Columbus, Ohio, in 1991, twenty years of frustration with mainstream journalism caught up with him. In the *IRE Journal* he explained how and why he became editor and publisher of the *Ohio Observer:* "I had seen, or had, too many stories and columns killed, too many headlines changed to play down the content, too many sacred cows protected as well as milked for favors, and too many good journalists who once questioned the process unhappily become part of it. Although my critical columns on the Persian Gulf War had garnered more mail and positive phone calls than I ever had before, they weren't appreciated by management. When I was told to lay off the subject for a while, I did."[7]

After reading his article, I called Yant. He told me how he had written a book about wrongful convictions, called *Presumed Guilty.* That became his field of specialty. He became a private investigator, then published a forty-page magazine, the *Public Eye,* about a case of wrongful conviction in West Virginia. The distributor sold seven thousand copies in less than a week at $2.50 a copy. It was "guerilla journalism"—going into an area and investigating a story the local news media (out of fear, lack of resources, or lethargy) have not touched. So he started the *Ohio Observer,* with outspoken columnists, including the executive directors of the Ohio Environmental Council and Common Cause/Ohio. Martin pays himself a small wage, and the work is all-consuming, but what better way to spend your life than in what you were meant to do?

Alternative television is coming along, too, maybe not yet on a large scale, but stay tuned. In the face of the dominant corporate-conglomerate networks, General Electric/NBC, Disney/ABC, Westinghouse/CBS, and Murdoch/Fox, something new is critically needed. EnviroVideo in Fort Tilden, New York, is one of the nonprofit groups trying to fill the gap, distributing programs through cable, commercial and public television, satellite, and direct sales. Its best videos, so far, are *Three Mile Island Revisited* and *Nukes in Space.* A weekly half-hour interview show hosted by Karl Grossman, *Enviro Close-Up,* is syndicated on cable television.

Another group, which I profile in the next chapter, Green Fire Productions, run by Rolf Meyer and Karen Meyer at Eugene, Oregon, works directly with activist organizations. Each film shows improvement and becomes more useful. *Troubled Waters,* a ten-minute video produced in 1996, was distributed by a network of nonprofit groups and citizens in an effort to raise public awareness of the economic value of protected public forests and to draw national attention to the 1995 salvage-logging rider (which the Republican-led Congress adopted to spur timber cutting on public lands without regard to environmental controls).

Ecology Center Productions, of Missoula, Montana, made *Southbound 1996,* documenting the shift of multinational timber companies from the national forests of the Northwest to mostly private, recovering woodlands of the Southeast. *Green Rolling Hills* in 1995 documents the debate surrounding the proposal to build the country's largest pulp mill in Apple Grove, West Virginia. *The Paper Colony* was aimed at Maine, just before a 1996 voter referendum designed to ban clear-cutting and reduce the total logging in the Maine woods. The referendum did not pass but made a strong show despite heavy industry opposition.

Innovative nontraditional media with a message clearly are here to stay and grow, with challenge and opportunity, a place to begin for beginners, and perhaps also for professionals who have been around the block and are still looking for fulfillment.

CHAPTER 19

Building a Career—Everybody Comes in Somewhere

"Learn to cook, clean, repair cars, or fix computers, to make sure you can pay your bills," wrote Elena Nussbaum one day in class when students wrote essays of counsel to themselves and classmates. Then she added: "Eat a good breakfast and go for it, and don't let the turkeys get you down."

That is sound advice, considering that everybody comes in somewhere. I remember many years ago approaching my friend Evelyn Grant, the managing editor of *Woman's Day,* with the idea of writing a regular column on travel for that magazine. "But," she said, "Miss Tighe [then the editor] likes to assign articles to people who have written articles for her before." Such words make professional writing sound like a closed corporation, but that is not the case at all. It took a while, but in due course I wrote a travel column in every issue of *Woman's Day* for eleven years, while growing into my career in the environment.

People start in different ways to get where they are going. No two stories are the same, although note that the seven able professionals whom I profile below share certain qualities: they do work they enjoy and keep working and learning to do it better. Take a leaf out of their books, of subjects they studied and how they knocked on doors and made their way. One or another, or all of them, can serve in some way as models for you.

Margaret Foster grew up in Seattle, attended college in the East for a while, then returned for serious studies at the University of Washington. She chose a nontraditional program concentrating on comparative history of ideas, exploring intellectual history, literature, and philosophy—the kind that makes parents wonder, "Whatever will she do with that?"

Margaret wondered, too. When she graduated in 1980, she asked herself: "What am I passionate about? What is at the core of me?" She identified two strong attractions: reading books and recreating in the outdoors, the latter which she had been doing in the mountains with her parents since diaper days. Thus, luckily, Margaret began her professional career with two part-time jobs, one as clerk-receptionist at the public library, the other as receptionist-typist at Pacific Search Press, a small publishing house specializing in Northwest natural history. She was learning from the bottom up, but presently along came marriage and she and her husband went off for a year to teach English in Chile.

When they returned, Margaret's husband entered the graduate school of journalism at Northwestern University, and they moved to Chicago. She found a job as editorial assistant at *Yearbook Medical Publishers,* a subsidiary of the Times-Mirror conglomerate specializing in trade textbooks and journals, where she learned research, editing, and a variety of hands-on, not-altogether-romantic production skills of publishing. However, she missed Seattle, and when *Pacific Search* offered a job as junior editor, she took it and her husband followed. In due course, she became senior editor, learning without mentorship, the hard way, from her mistakes, and from proofreaders, those essential, unheralded, seasoned freelancers, and from the queries they posed on manuscripts, galleys, and page proofs. Margaret worked at *Pacific Search* for four years, had a baby, and was pregnant with the second when *Pacific Search* closed shop and the whole staff dissolved.

For a time Foster did freelance editing and book packaging. Her marriage ended, and at times the going was tough. Then, in 1989, she learned that The Mountaineers had an opening for a managing editor and applied. She had already done freelance editing for them, so it made sense to everybody that she come aboard. Now, as editor-in-chief, at The Mountaineer in Seattle, she no longer edits manuscripts, but works on acquisition and development of the Mountaineers line.

The Mountaineers publishing house is the successful, quasi-independent offspring of an old, respectable outdoors organization headquartered in Seattle, whose mission is "to explore, study, preserve, and enjoy the natural beauty of the outdoors." The Mountaineers is a substantial enterprise, publishing natural history and outdoor guides to greater and lesser destinations all over the world.

"With a strong mandate from the club, we now do conservation books for this region, our own backyard," Margaret told me in early 1997. "That's where I feel I can and want to contribute, more than with outdoor, climbing and how-to guidebooks. The importance of stewardship becomes more prominent and I enjoy it."[1]

The personnel at The Mountaineers are mostly women. Margaret has said: "How come? How come, except in New York, you find mostly women in publishing? When we interview, women are willing to take bottom rung for less money, as women have had to, for a long time. Guys are not willing. When men come out of college they want good jobs with salary to match."[2]

Tom Turner had no training in journalism—or science, for that matter. He fell into the trade almost entirely by accident. He graduated (by the skin of his teeth) from the University of California, Berkeley, his hometown, in 1965 with a degree in political science. Then he spent two years in the Peace Corps in Turkey doing "rural community development," which involved learning to play backgammon and drinking tea out of little glasses.

"I liked to write and wrote to lots of people during those two years. The idea of journalism had always been in the back of my head somewhere; I remember thinking that the guy with the best job in the world was Joseph C. Harsch, NBC-TV's correspondent in London. Then the Peace Corps sent around one of its periodic evaluators to visit me in my village. He had gone to the Columbia journalism school in New York and worked for several papers. He talked about the profession; he said that working on a rural weekly was at least as good a way to learn how to write as attending Columbia."[3]

In 1968, soon after he returned from Turkey, David Brower, the legendary, charismatic executive director of the Sierra Club, hired Turner to edit a book of the writings of the mountaineer Norman Clyde. Brower himself was a creative wizard, who had worked at the University of California Press and then designed the beautiful and influential Sierra Club Format books.

Brower had a way of sparking talent in people he liked, or as Turner recalled, "This was a typical Brower stunt: take an enthusiastic kid and put him to work doing a job he'd never done before." Growing up in

Berkeley, Turner already knew Brower and his wife, Anne. He had been with them and others to Glen Canyon and Escalante Canyon, in southern Utah, in 1963. "To see those places and know that they would soon be gone, through oversight, stupidity, greed, ignorance was incredibly painful—and still is. I thought then that if I could find some way to help ensure that such a thing never happen again it would be a pretty good way to spend a life."[4]

Turner put together the Clyde manuscript and became an assistant to Brower at the Sierra Club. In May 1969 Brower was deposed, and Turner was fired a few days later. Then Brower started Friends of the Earth (FOE), and Tom became editor of its periodical, *Not Man Apart,* the title taken from a poem by Robinson Jeffers. As a subscriber, I enjoyed every issue and remember it as loose and lively.

> We started monthly, begging stories and photographs from friends and acquaintances all over, assigning stories to FOE staff in New York and Washington, signing up unpaid columnists here and there, cadging stuff from the daily papers, and having a ball. We reported environmental news, and printed features, opinion, review and commentary, for the benefit of our members. We made no pretense of objectivity (which does not exist) or balance or neutrality. We viewed the world through a certain kind of lens, and made no bones about it. We were out to save the earth, and that meant dispensing facts and arguments as forcefully and widely as possible. While we did not pretend to be objective, we knew we must be fair. Further, we must not exaggerate and we should not ridicule our adversaries. (We slipped now and again. I mean, how can you not ridicule the likes of Dixie Lee Ray [who ran a verbal battle with environmentalists while serving as chairperson of the Atomic Energy Commission and as governor of Washington] and James Watt [secretary of the interior under Ronald Reagan]?)
>
> We had unmatched freedom. No one reviewed copy before it was printed. Occasionally Dave would present something he thought deserved printing, and we almost always went along. We conferred with the lobbyists about legislative stories; indeed, the lobbyists wrote most coverage from D.C.
>
> Lobbyists and fund raisers often observed that we didn't blow FOE's horn loud or often enough. We argued (and Dave was a strong supporter of this view) that we were trying to be a journal of

news, not braggadocio. If you want to be believed, then go slow on the self-congratulation.[5]

Not Man Apart did good work printing stories that others missed. A high spot was publishing a daily at the UN Stockholm Conference in 1972, *Stockholm Conference Eco,* as a source for reporters from all over the world. Then Brower and Friends of the Earth parted. He went on to Earth Island Institute, and Turner in 1986 to the Sierra Club Legal Defense Fund, now known as EarthJustice Legal Defense Fund, where he edits the quarterly newsletter "In Brief," straightforward, with a lot of news in it. On his own time, he has written many articles for *Sierra, Wilderness,* and other magazines.

David Helvarg found his motivation at an early age. His parents had come to this country as refugees from the Ukraine and Nazi Germany, and many of their friends wore the tattoos of concentration-camp survivors. David found it hard, growing up as an American child, to comprehend how the Holocaust could have taken place without the world's knowledge. In 1968, at age seventeen, he went with friends to protest the Vietnam War at the tumultuous Democratic National Convention in Chicago, and then to northern Ireland in the early 1970s.

After graduating from Goddard College in Vermont, Helvarg moved to San Diego, editing the alternative weekly *San Diego Newsline,* then spent five years in Central America as an Associated Press stringer, not only covering wars but also observing the monoculture of coffee *fincas,* DDT-scented cotton fields, crowded barrios, and burned rain forests, and finding all the issues related. In recent years he settled in San Francisco, where he divides his time between writing (for *Audubon,* the *Nation, Smithsonian,* and others) and producing television documentaries for public broadcasting and cable television on the military, politics, health, and the environment.

In 1994, Sierra Club Books published a major work, David Helvarg's *The War against the Greens,* the first in-depth investigation of the anti-environmental "backlash." Through tireless digging and hundreds of interviews, Helvarg showed how the so-called property-rights movement in fact was heavily subsidized by timber, mining, off-road-vehicle corporate interests, and the National Rifle Association. He examined and described violence and intimidation of public employees and private citizens, and the unsavory role of the FBI.

Over the years Helvarg learned to appreciate the media's ability to expose brutal realities that might otherwise remain hidden or distorted. "My key goal remains to produce the best possible investigative works to help inform, broaden and democratize the crucial environmental debates taking place today. The environment is the defining issue of the 21st century. Environmental journalism is not just about science or economics, but is multi-faceted, about how people live and use resources, and distribute wealth."[6]

Karen Anspacher Meyer at the start of her sophomore year at the University of California at San Diego was not sure of her focus and had not declared her major. Then she took an introductory communications course and was intrigued with the question, "How do we come to know what we know?" Courses examining and critiquing the media led somehow to documentary video production. The first time she picked up a video camera and started to create and capture images she knew she had found her place.

When the class was assigned to produce a ten-minute program the students were frantic, but the instructor calmly said, "Pick something you're really interested in, because you're going to work with the subject for a long time." Neither he nor Karen realized how true that would be. She called the local Sierra Club chapter, which encouraged her to do a program on the last free-flowing river in San Diego scheduled to be dammed, which the chapter went on to use in its public-outreach efforts. For the next three years she kept taking documentary courses, culminating in a yearlong independent-study project: coproducing with a fellow student a thirty-minute documentary on the management of Yosemite National Park.

After interning with commercial video producers, Karen knew she wanted to stay in the field but did not want to work at a news station or for a commercial firm. Impressed with the distinctive music of Paul Winter, combining the sounds of wildlife with musical instruments, she sought him out. He advised her to follow her dreams to make the most of life. Consequently, since graduation in 1984, she has worked as an independent video producer and since 1989, the year she and her husband, Rolf Meyer, founded Green Fire Productions, exclusively on environmental issues.

"I can't say the pay is great, but I've made choices in lifestyle that enable me to pursue fulfilling work. It's a tradeoff. I pursue the dream to create electronic media—video, Internet, CD Rom—for environmental and social-change organizations in their media and lobbying efforts. It involves creating the projects, finding funding, and working with the organizations to best utilize the materials. It means finding the stories that motivate people to become active and involved."[7]

In 1994 Green Fire produced *Beyond Borders,* a twenty-two-minute video for the Alliance for the Wild Rockies, examining the largest remaining tracts of native forests in the northern Rockies and how to protect them. In 1996 more than seven thousand copies of *Troubled Waters,* a ten-minute video, were distributed through a network of nonprofit groups to draw national attention to the disastrous effects of the 1995 congressional salvage-logging rider designed to accelerate timber cutting on public lands. That was no small attainment. Karen Anspacher Meyer and Rolf Meyer, and Green Fire, were on the way.

Dan Oko at age twenty-eight in 1997 became editor of the literate, lively, struggling Montana weekly tabloid the *Missoula Independent,* where he had worked for two years, almost the entire life of the paper. Long before coming west, he had started writing with dreams of becoming a novelist or a poet, but when he saw the practicality of getting paid began to look seriously at journalism. Now he was doing it.

Oko grew up in New York City and attended the University of Michigan, studying literature and philosophy. Writing philosophy was excellent practice for learning to write about science. "After all," as he observes, "the complicated issues of biodiversity, evolution and global warming in some ways are little more than elaborate theories, not unlike those handed down by epistemologists and others throughout the ages."[8] Besides, he found that the ability to balance two sides of an argument—a capacity he was forced to hone while performing philosophical exegesis—is close to the thoroughness that makes for the best articles.

Oko came to Seattle, doing odd jobs, including writing theater and book reviews for an offbeat Seattle weekly, the *Stranger.* He had not thought much about science, politics, and nature, but in the course of knocking around Mount Rainier, the Olympics, and the North Cascades became aware of the ecological and political challenges facing the old-growth forests and decided to write about them:

> I didn't have any science background (I only took one biology
> course ever in my life), but soon I had read enough to form what I
> believed were informed opinions. And then I came to Montana and
> soon had a vocabulary of biodiversity and related subjects. I met
> Rick Bass, Doug Peacock, Terry Tempest Williams and other

Western writers, who happily answered my questions about writing and journalism, the role of fiction and art, and the importance of things wild—both real and imagined. At that point, I literally had role models, who provided a glimpse at one of the paths my career might follow, and I made connections which I imagine, as my career develops, might be helpful.[9]

Starting at the *Independent* was as much a hands-on experience as one could hope for, setting Oko to the task of becoming a professional with a commitment to the community and accountability that made him careful to get both sides of the story. Being a free weekly, driven by advertising, takes a dedicated sales staff. The best sales personnel try to show businesspeople the appeal of a readership that cares for the community and its environment; though it is not easy, the *Independent* has continued to grow.

John G. Mitchell from his boyhood in Cincinnati felt a personal link between language and the land. At Yale, majoring in English early in the 1950s, when he thought of himself as a promising writer of fiction, his attempts at a novel or short story were set in the outdoors. After graduation, working as a reporter on small dailies in New Mexico and California, the most satisfying stories he covered, his best work, were about the land: the expansive Navajo Reservation, ghost towns in the San Joaquin valley, damming of rivers in the High Sierra, and Bing Crosby's designs to turn Mineral King valley, high in the Sierra Nevada, into a ski resort. (Crosby failed; so did Disney, and Mineral King, open to development as national-forest land, ultimately was added to Sequoia National Park.)

When he arrived at the *New York Journal–American* as a reporter in 1958, Mitchell found little interest in conservation. For seven years he wrote mostly about cops and robbers, drug dealers, and show-business celebrities. He did, however, manage a five-part series on air pollution, even though his bosses said: "What do you mean, Mitchell? Smoke means jobs!" Still, he received a fan letter from Bob Considine, the star syndicated Hearst columnist, for a reflective article about John James Audubon.

Mitchell did not want to stay at the *Journal-American;* he wanted to write about conservation. One day he called on Charles Callison, the executive vice president of the National Audubon Society, at the society's headquarters in New York, about the possibility of joining the staff of *Audubon.* I remember Callison well as one of the finest conservationists of his time. He was a journalism graduate of the University of Missouri who had worked on newspapers in Kansas and Missouri before joining the staff of the Missouri Conservation Commission where he established the *Missouri Conservationist* and began a full-time career in conservation. But now he dissuaded Mitchell: "You can do more good where you are, inside the mainstream media. We don't need another preacher to the already-converted. Stay outside and preach to the unconverted."

Mitchell followed Callison's advice, but two months before the *Journal-American* folded he moved to *Newsweek* as a writer for the back-of-the-book sections—press, education, religion, and life and leisure. Later he was promoted to science and space editor. But it was *outer* space, not *open* space (though he did manage good shots on the battle to establish Redwoods National Park in California and the nationwide shortage of recreational open space). He was heeding Callison's advice, but was singled out at *Newsweek* as a daisy sniffer and tree hugger who ought to move his office to Central Park.

In the spring of 1967 Mitchell went to California for *Newsweek* to separate fact from opinion in the redwood forests, a storm center of controversy. In a collection of his work, *Dispatches from the Deep Woods*, he recalls:

> It was hard work to detach yourself from opinion in redwood country, those days. Hard, if you cared about wild things as much as you cared about journalistic integrity; hard, if you listened to the assurances of the foresters at Arcata Redwood Company or Georgia-Pacific and then got in a car with Lucille Vinyard or Dave Van de Mark of the Sierra Club and followed a back-country track to the tractor clearcuts the foresters did not want you to see. . . . Somehow I managed the separation [between fact and opinion]. Or perhaps my editors managed it for me, so that—at least on the copydesks of Madison Avenue if not in the boardrooms of Arcata and Georgia-Pacific—a measure of journalistic integrity appeared to survive my experience, even as many of the wild mid-slope redwoods we had passed on the way downstream would survive not at all. Years later, after all the park-making and remaking were legislatively over, what I would remember most vividly of that first time in redwood country was the carnage that could not then dispassionately be described—the rutted skid trails, the slash and the silt in the streambeds, the stumps on the battered slopes. And the slick propaganda. "It takes big equipment to move the heavy logs over steep country," explained Arcata Redwood, then a subsidiary of the

Weyerhaeuser Company, in one of its brochures. "The ground gets scuffed. Like a cornfield just after harvest."[10]

In May 1968, Mitchell left "the media" for the Open Space Action Committee, later the Open Space Institute, headed by Richard H. Pough, which Pough had founded to help protect open lands in the New York area, and had installed as its chief Charles E. Little, a transformed Madison Avenue adman. Little wanted to start a magazine called *Open Space Action* and installed Mitchell as editor. In 1970 when both the Ford and the Rockefeller foundations withdrew support, Mitchell became editor-in-chief of Sierra Club Books. However, within four years he left in protest after Sierra directors replaced Paul Brooks, the venerable retired Houghton Mifflin editor, as chairman of the publications committee, with an English professor without editorial or publishing experience.

Mitchell freelanced for twenty years, including fifteen years as field editor of *Audubon,* writing many assignments for Les Line, the editor, who hired the best talent and produced an outstanding magazine—until a new Audubon president, Peter A. A. Berle, fired Line and replaced him with an editor ordered to fire most of the full-time staff. Field editors Mitchell and George Laycock resigned rather than continue writing for the Berle makeover.

"Whereupon," in the Mitchell saga, "at the tender age of 63, I accept an offer to return to the nine-to-five media as senior assistant editor for the environment at *National Geographic* magazine." Now there's a dream assignment. But Mitchell asks himself:

> Did I make a mistake going against Charlie Callison's advice by forsaking the mainline media? Yes, insofar as financial security is concerned. Had I stayed at *Newsweek,* or come much earlier to *Geographic,* I would have earned twice what I did as a freelance, and piled up a bit of a pension to boot. But I don't believe I made a mistake insofar as advancing the environmental agenda is concerned. I probably did a lot more good tackling complex issues in depth for *Audubon* and *Wilderness* and *Wildlife Conservation*—and doing those stories in a wholly effective yet idiosyncratic way that would never have been tolerated on a magazine such as *Newsweek* or *Geographic.* If I did my work as effectively as I think I did, then at least I helped lend some credibility to the enviro-magazines I

wrote for, because the enviro media was and still is up to its eyeballs in windbags, nature mystics, and nonjournalists.

Mitchell is still not at the end of the line: "I want to write one good book, something with a bit of shelf life. I hope I will find the language to do justice to the land."[11]

Sara Olason Noland already had a degree in zoology from the University of Washington in 1989 when she came to study environmental journalism at Western Washington University. Here she proceeded to earn As in absolutely everything, including editing the student environmental quarterly, the *Planet*. When she graduated, Noland became a technical editor for a large environmental consulting firm in Seattle and proceeded to make the most of it:

> My job didn't seem too promising at first for someone whose passion is environmental writing, but it's actually turned out to be an excellent learning experience, in terms of writing, editing, working with scientists, environmental regulations, government agencies and what they do, and generally how to act professionally in the business world.
>
> My job as a technical editor continues to teach me a lot. Editing is itself a kind of constant criticism, asking questions from "Is this sentence constructed correctly?" to "So, author, what's your point and who cares?" Being able to pose those questions to writers in a way that improves their writing but doesn't feel to them like a personal attack is a useful skill. If you can focus on the issues and not personalities, you'll get a lot further. That's definitely true for editing.[12]

Besides her job, Noland was also doing freelance editing and desktop publishing (some volunteer, some for pay) and as much of her own reading and writing as she could squeeze in before work each day, including a study of environmental and nature poetry. She believes, as I do, that good poetry serves as a direct path to inner truth for both poet and reader, as well as stimulating the use of language in beautiful, original ways.

Noland and her husband, Tom, have both gained experience by doing legwork research for environmental organizations. When she worked for the local land trust, she went to the county assessor's office, planning department, and records office to find information about properties the trust was trying to help landowners conserve. Sometimes landowners themselves were unaware of the details. She gained experience from her collegiate writing, too, plus a folio of impressive work to show wherever she goes, like this article from the *Planet,* which begins:

> I've always believed the nose is the center of the soul. No sense is more primal, more capable of arousing emotion and conjuring memories than that of smell. In wandering the streets and parks of Bellingham, I've found the city's scent palette covers a range of hues. Sometimes, on windy days or after a brisk rain, I breathe deeply the fragrance of evergreens and the scent of newly mowed lawns, and rejoice in the pure air I've found in my two-year residence in Bellingham.
>
> All too often, however, the atmosphere is less than heady. After a few days of stagnant air, the accumulated woodsmoke, aromas from the Georgia-Pacific pulp and paper mill, and car exhaust in some places become choking. The sight of a haze of pollution on the horizon makes me wonder if, with a little less wind and rain to wash away our pollution, Bellingham might slip into the smog of another Los Angeles. Will a visit to the nearby North Cascades ten or twenty years from now find lakes and forests dying from drifting air pollution? Will the city parks and historic buildings we treasure be someday blighted and dissolved under acid rain?[13]

Toward the Green Tomorrow

Environmental journalism helps to see and shape a better society, and a better democracy. Gifford Pinchot, a prime mover in twentieth-century conservation, said there is no reason the American people should not take into their own hands again the full political power that was theirs by right, before the special interests began to nullify the will of the majority. Thus, the challenge is to learn and understand how the system functions, and how to make it responsive.

I have always believed the role of the journalist is to illuminate issues of importance in a manner that enables citizens to participate intelligently in the democratic process. The saying goes that a handful can make a difference. So can one good story.

As a discipline, environmental journalism counteracts feelings that the fate of things is entrenched in the hands of powerful interests in industry and government, that people are powerless to reverse the degradation of natural systems. It is not easy, but trying to make a difference makes a difference in the person who tries. It shows the future to be exciting and worthwhile. It keeps the journalist upbeat, free of cynicism.

That is how it should be, considering the world needs affirmation, hopeful yea-saying. Environmental stories often are perceived as bad news, warnings of impending disaster, but there ought to be room for optimism, too, in what we write. John Burroughs, the naturalist, had the right idea when he wrote: "If we think birds, we shall see birds wherever we go. If we think arrowheads, as Thoreau did, we shall pick up wildflowers in every field." Let's go from there: if we think environment, we shall see a better environment.

Studies of environmental journalism should embrace the concept that we are in this for the long haul, assuming part of the challenge of raising the sights of society above narrow profit-driven economics to broad ethics and compassion, while finding joy and satisfaction in small gains along the way. Students should learn from the long experience of others. They should learn to write with grace, stick to issues, avoid preaching, tolerate other viewpoints, and appreciate that truth and right are never absolutes.

True enough, radical changes may be needed. Extreme proposals can perform important functions. Criticism is valid, not only of self-serving bureaucracies in government and industry, but also of environmental organizations. If they have it coming, let them have it: criticism honestly given keeps institutions honest.

By the same token, if you can break into and make it in the mainstream, more power to you. I hope that more publishers and editors will recognize their environmental coverage is noteworthy not for what it does but for what it fails to do. They need to get on with an infusion of talent and vision—you may be knocking on the door at the right time.

But you may find your opportunity elsewhere. Many important environmental stories appear first in alternative newsweeklies and monthlies treating environmental and social issues. *High Country News* gets most of its income from subscribers and carries minimal advertising, saving space for writers to show their talent in long, in-depth stories. The market is broadening, not narrowing, with room, on all fronts, for new John Muirs and Rachel Carsons.

Wherever you go, always tell the truth, and never be afraid to. (But watch the law, and do not base opinion on facts you cannot prove.) Get it right. Otherwise you have lost credibility, now and in the future.

Use dialogue in your writing. It gives life and breadth. Develop a style meant for the audience—conversational, clear, natural. Tell a story—let it unfold bringing the reader along, a touch of suspense, with conflict, leading to the conclusion. Don't be afraid to name names. Somebody is responsible. Decide who and lay out your case. Give the individual a chance to say whether, and how, he or she will personally work to fix the problem. Keep it human.

Volunteer, show willingness to learn and to pitch in on nitty-gritty chores. When Ted Pankowski was publisher and editor of the Washington Environmental Council's periodical, *ALERT,* he was always on the lookout for people to contribute articles of five hundred to fifteen hundred words on issues of current concern. Some became staff members following the visibility and recognition they had received as volunteer writers. Many sources report the same: that on-the-ground experience gives credibility and insight to writing, and eventually leads to a paying job. Sierra Club chapters, National Audubon chapters, and many other local groups have monthly newsletters and are always open to volunteers.

Never complain. Do not assume sinister motives. When you are turned down, leave with a smile. You never know who is likely to call you back or to ask for another look at your writing. Women for too long have worked for less, but my advice, to male or female, is to start wherever you can for whatever you can get and work up from there. The main point is to get your foot in the door. Sure, there are doors you should pass by, and bosses you do not want to work for, but do not let suspicions and quick assumptions get in your way. Put your best forward, and keep it there.

Failure creates another chance to succeed. There will be those times of rejection, when things go wrong. Do not be defeated by mistakes and criticism—they are part of the game. The challenge is to learn from them and turn them around. Hear the testimony of Ted Williams, one of the finest and best-read outdoor and environmental writers of the 1990s:

> I remember how bummed out I was in 1979 when *Sports Illustrated* rejected a piece they'd assigned me to do on Dickey Lincoln dams [proposed for construction in Maine]. So I sent it to Les Line [editor of *Audubon*], who loved it. And here I am, writing 3,700-word "columns" every month and disproving all the editors who used to tell me that I had to be "objective" and not be "emotional" about the mass destruction of wild, beautiful places. I never obeyed, so Les Line created a special platform just for my kind of unacceptable, emotional environmental advocacy, which is called "Incite." It gets read more than anything else in *Audubon.* Now other magazines ask me to do the same thing. "Let's hear your opinions," they say.[1]

Get an internship or grant. If you are in college, find an internship and earn credits while you learn practical lessons. *High Country News* has run a successful and satisfying internship program for young people who come from all over the country to work for a while in western Colorado. Make a list of publications and organizations that appeal to you. Try them one at a time, from the top, until you connect. Keep your eyes and ears open for grants and scholarships. Many are listed in writers journals and bulletins of colleges and universities. Preparing the grant proposal is always good exercise, and if you do not score at first, rewrite the proposal and try it somewhere else. One choice opportunity for students is offered by the Outdoor Writers Association of America (OWAA). The Fund for Investigative Journalism offers stipends to professionals and students.[2]

If you have problems with grammar or spelling, be assured that many others do, too. Overcome weaknesses with your motivation and help from a friend or tutor. For correct usages, turn to the indispensable *Elements of Style,* by Strunk and White. Take heart from the experience of Jozef Teodor Konrad Nalecz Korzeniowski, who was born in Poland in 1857 and went to sea. He did not learn English until his twenties but in due course became celebrated as Joseph Conrad, the novelist of great tales of the sea.

Keep track of current issues. To write about the environment, you need to know what is going on. Keep in touch with environmental organizations and how issues are handled in the media.

Join writers organizations and read their journals. Those I belong and commend to you include the Society of Environmental Journalists, Investigative Reporters and Editors, the Outdoor Writers Association of America, the American Society of Journalists and Authors, and the Authors Guild.

The Society of Environmental Journalists (SEJ) aims "to advance public understanding of environmental issues by improving the quality, accuracy and visibility of environmental reporting."[3] The organization is influenced largely by mainstream, tradition-bound reporters, but it is good to belong; you will meet people and learn a lot at the annual conventions.

Investigative Reporters and Editors was organized in 1975 and held its first conference the following year.[4] Later that year mobsters in Phoenix bombed the car of founding member Don Bolles, who was working on Arizona's organized-crime network. Instead of scaring off members, the action provoked outrage and the growth of IRE. The organization publishes a bimonthly journal and maintains an archive of ten thousand print and broadcast investigations, many of them submitted to the IRE annual awards contest, conducts training programs in "computer-assisted reporting," holds an important conference annually, and offers scholarships.

The Outdoor Writers Association of America was founded in 1927.[5] "Hook-and-Bullet" activities are the dominant influence, but it keeps trying for greater breadth. It now accepts student members and offers scholarships; the monthly "Outdoors Unlimited" newsletter carries helpful articles on craft improvement and the environment. OWAA annual conventions include worthwhile panels.

The American Society of Journalists and Authors (ASJA) was founded in 1947 and now includes more than one thousand freelance writers of magazine articles, trade books, and other forms of nonfiction writing who meet standards of professional achievement.[6] Join it when you can. Meantime, try to attend one of the ASJA Writers' Conferences held yearly on both coasts. They bring together leading writers, publishers, literary agents, and editors. The conferences are open to professional and aspiring writers.

The Authors Guild has long lobbied in behalf of its six-thousand-plus members for fairer book contracts and more forthright consideration of authors in dealing with advances, royalties, and subsidiary rights.[7] With its sister organization, the Dramatists Guild, it forms the Authors League of America, working on issues of copyright protection, taxation, legislation, and freedom of expression. Get your first book and join!

Renew motivation and avoid burnout by cultivating a sense of humor and taking regular breaks in the outdoors, away from the noise of the world. Give your computer, cell phone, and radio a break, too, by leaving them at home.

In summary, set your sights and standards high. Look for mentors and models who can take you beyond practical pointers, valuable as they may be. The Spring 1998 Authors Guild Bulletin reported how the Authors Guild Foundation presented the 1998 Award for Distinguished Service to the Writing Community to Alfred Kazin, "whom many had considered the finest living critic of American literature until his death June 5, at the age of 83." Kazin was unable to attend the awards dinner in March, but sent a message, in which he recalled how at times in his career he had jumped at the chance of being a good reporter on assignment for publications like *Fortune* and *Atlantic.* But more important: "Being a college teacher (I hate the word professor) in many places here and in Europe was a way of conducting my own education in literature. Above all, I have tried to make the young understand that feeling, not structure or ideas by themselves, is the power that drives all good literature." Cultivate the feeling, and with hard work the ideas and structure will come.

And finally: my life journey has led step-by-step into a community of sacred values, where the gods walk on every road and every road is sacred. Along the way I came to believe that society needs transformation, a viewpoint of human concern to counter injustice and greed. The spiritual ecological dimension of writing with green ink provides a way of life with its own rewards.

Suggested Reading List

AMERICAN SOCIETY OF JOURNALISTS AND AUTHORS. *The Complete Guide to Writing Non-Fiction.* Ed. Glen Evans. New York: HarperCollins, 1990. This guide includes contributions by the society's working members.

BAGDIKIAN, BEN. *The Media Monopoly.* 5th ed. Boston: Beacon Press, 1997.

BROOKS, BRIAN S. *Journalism in the Information Age: A Guide to Computers for Reporters and Editors.* Needham Heights, Mass.: Allyn and Bacon, 1997.

BROOKS, PAUL. *The House of Life: Rachel Carson at Work.* Boston: G. K. Hall, 1972.

CARSON, RACHEL. *Silent Spring.* 25th ed. 1962. Reprint, with a foreword by Paul Brooks. Boston: Houghton Mifflin, 1987.

FLATTAU, EDWARD. *Tracking the Charlatans—An Environmental Columnist's Refutational Handbook for the Propaganda Wars.* Washington, D.C.: Global Horizons, 1998.

FREDETTE, JEAN M., ed. *Handbook of Magazine Article Writing.* Cincinnati: Writer's Digest Books, 1989.

FROME, MICHAEL. *Chronicling the West: Thirty Years of Environmental Writing.* Seattle: Mountaineers Books, 1996.

HELVARG, DAVID. *The War against the Greens: The "Wise-Use" Movement, the New Right, and Anti-Environmental Violence.* San Francisco: Sierra Club Books, 1994.

HOLM, KIRSTEN C., ed. *The Writer's Market—Where and How to Sell What You Write.* Cincinnati: Writer's Digest Books, 1998.

LEE, MARTIN A., and Norman Solomon. *Unreliable Sources: A Guide to Detecting Bias in News Media.* New York: Carol Publishing Group, 1990.

LEVINE, MARK L. *Negotiating a Book Contract: A Guide for Authors, Agents, and Lawyers.* Mount Kisco, N.Y.: Moyer Bell, 1994. This book will help guard against provisions that grant publishers all rights.

LITERARY MARKET PLACE. New York: R. R. Bowker, 1998.

MITCHELL, JOHN G. *Dispatches from the Deep Woods.* Lincoln: University of Nebraska Press, 1991.

SHABECOFF, PHILIP. *A New Name for Peace: International Environmentalism, Sustainable Development, and Democracy.* Hanover, N.H.: University Press of New England, 1996.

STEFFENS, LINCOLN. *The Autobiography of Lincoln Steffens.* New York: Harcourt, Brace & World, 1931; New York: Harvest/HBJ, 1958.

STEGNER, WALLACE. *The Uneasy Chair: A Biography of Bernard DeVoto.* Salt Lake City: Peregrine Smith Books, 1988.

STRUNK, WILLIAM, JR., and E. B. White. *The Elements of Style.* 3d ed. New York: Macmillan, 1979. This classic is never out-of-date. Every writer should read it at least once a year.

WEINBERG, STEVE. *The Reporter's Handbook: An Investigator's Guide to Documents and Techniques.* New York: St. Martin's Press, 1996.

WILLIAMS, TED. *The Insightful Sportsman—Thoughts on Fish, Wildlife and What Ails the Earth.* Camden, Maine: Down East Books, 1996.

ZINSSER, WILLIAM K. *On Writing Well: An Informal Guide to Writing Nonfiction.* New York: Harper & Row, 1985.

PREFACE

1. Bagdikian, interview by author, Berkeley, Calif., September 20, 1988; Laycock, interview by author, Cincinnati, Ohio, January 18, 1998.

2. Elaine Walker, "Sawgrass Mills Expanding Its Mall Horizons," *Miami Herald,* January 15, 1998.

3. Sawgrass Mills, as it happens, is a project of the Ogden Corporation, which opened its first wilderness make-believe at the Ontario Mills megamall forty miles east of Los Angeles, and the second at Arizona Mills mall (Phoenix-Tempe), with others planned at Dallas (Grapevine Mills), Chicago (Gurnee Mills), and more to come. In "The Great Indoors" (*Sierra,* March/April 1998), B. J. Bergman described his visit to Ontario Mills, "where the scenery never changes, the cats live in fishbowls, and admission is just $9.95": "We stroll by a porcupine, a fisher, a badger, and sundry other live specimens, and before we know it we've passed seamlessly out of the wilderness and into 'Naturally Untamed,' which purveys T-shirts, CD-ROMs, and even *Sierra* magazine. In barely an hour we've hiked to five imitation biomes, a full-service restaurant, and a nature-themed gift store—all of it, the brochure reminds us, 'just pawprints away from your favorite Ontario Mills shops.' "

4. Aucoin, *I.R.E.: Investigative Reporters and Editors, the Arizona Project, and the Evolution of American Investigative Journalism* (Evergreen, Ala.: Raging Cajun Books, 1997), 82, 96–97.

5. Wilson, "Chain Papers' Mission: Profits," *Eugene (Oreg.) Register-Guard,* August 3, 1997.

6. Blumberg, *Treasure State Review* (autumn 1997).

7. Sara Olason, *Planet* (spring 1990).

CHAPTER 1

1. Keith Schneider, who replaced Shabecoff, went after government cleanup programs. On August 15, 1991, he wrote a front-page article titled "U.S. Backing Away from Saying Dioxin Is a Deadly Peril." He wrote that the chemical compound dioxin, "once thought to be much more hazardous than chain smoking, is now considered by some experts to be no more risky than spending a week sunbathing." Later, he wrote three of five articles in a *New York Times* series called "What Price Cleanup?" published in spring 1993. The series focused on the cost of government and corporate cleanup programs, echoing paper- and chlorine-industry demand for regulatory "reform." Virtually all research has underscored the dangers of dioxin. In particular, John Graham of the Harvard School of Public Health, whose material Schneider had cited in defense of his claim, said that dioxin's effects on the immune system make it "more dangerous than we thought."

Schneider, and others, stirred the wrath of Robert H. Boyle, who wrote in "Garbage Time—Latest Threat to the Environment: Misinformation That Flows through the Mainstream Media": "Also in the *Times* series, Schneider wrote, 'There is no acid rain in South Carolina.' That is false. The federal government has been measuring the acidity of rain in South Carolina for almost 10 years, and the latest data available, for 1991, show the state's precipitation to be 10 times more acidic than unpolluted rain. In addition, Schneider stated that 'winds generally blow anything in South Carolina's air out to sea, not to nearby states.' False again. Forty-three percent of the sulphur dioxide, the main precursor of acid rain, emitted in South Carolina lands in other states."

In an article titled "Greens vs. Congress: A Play-by-Play," published in *Amicus Journal*, quarterly of the Natural Resources Defense Council (fall 1996): 24–29, Shabecoff wrote: "Before and for a considerable period after the November [1994] elections, not only did most of the media fail to grasp the extent and significance of the gathering anti-environmental storm, but the coverage of some reporters for major news organs in effect abetted it. In the two to three years before the 104th Congress took office, John Stoessel of ABC television and Keith Schneider of the *New York Times* paved the way for the onslaught, intentionally or not, with coverage implying that the health risks from toxic substances had been exaggerated. During the first months of the new Congress, Gregg Easterbrook of *Newsweek* came out with a book *[A Moment on Earth]* carrying a 'Don't worry, be happy' message that environmental problems would soon be solved."

2. FAIR was organized in 1986. Jeff Cohen, founder and executive director, explains its mission: "FAIR is the media watch group that challenges the narrowing range of news and views presented by the corporate-owned media. We educate the public about who owns the media. We've worked hard to let the average American know that GE owns NBC. But we don't just educate; we also agitate. FAIR and its members fight so that public interest voices—peace spokespersons, consumer advocates, environmentalists, social justice advocates—get access to the media" ("A Call to Media Activism," in *Unreliable Sources: A Guide to Detecting Bias in News Media*, by Martin A. Lee and Norman Solomon, 340–58).

3. Jim Gordon, "Clean-Up Job," *EXTRA!* (September–October 1996).

4. "Shaking Off Man's Taint," *New York Times*, June 9, 1996; "Life's Hubbub," *New York Times*, June 10, 1996.

5. Gordon, "Clean-Up Job."

6. "Years After a Plant Closed," *New York Times*, June 10, 1996.

7. The conference was held in Bellingham, Wash., on October 15–16, 1993. It was convened on the campus of Western Washington University and was attended by 130 representatives of federal, state, and local agencies, print and broadcast media, northwestern industries, environmental organizations, and instructors and students in journalism and environmental studies. Bill Dietrich, a

science reporter for the *Seattle Times,* declared: "Most reporters at the *Times* are consumption reporters: We advise what foods to eat, gadgets to get, businesses to buy stocks in, fads to conform to. Two-thirds of the newspaper is devoted to advertising urging people to consume. A periodic lonely environmental story is regarded by some as a dire threat to American civilization."

8. "Survey: Owl Set-Asides," *Bellingham (Wash.) Herald,* May 20, 1990. F. Bryant Furlow, a student in the evaluation and ecology program in the biology department at the University of New Mexico, reported on his study "Newspaper Coverage of Biological Subissues in the Spotted Owl Debate, 1989–1993" in the *Journal of Environmental Education* (26:1). He researched computer archives for twenty-seven U.S. dailies (including major papers in the Northwest and others across the country from Anchorage to Washington and Miami) and analyzed 128 articles. "Have newspapers used this debate as an opportunity to better inform their audiences?" asked Furlow, explaining that his primary goal was to determine the degree to which "pertinent biological subissues and ecological concepts were conveyed to readers in articles addressing the larger environmental issue of the spotted-owl debate." For example, a subissue: "The northern spotted owl nests and forages in ancient forests (more than 200 years old), where structural habitat (especially dead trees, or snags, that provide cavities in which pairs nest) and optimal prey base are available. . . . Its preferred prey, the northern flying squirrel, depends nutritionally upon truffles and other fungi associated with ancient forests' moist microclimates. Because the flying squirrel is twice as abundant in old forest as in young forest, . . . a foraging owl requires much more territory in heavily logged and second-growth forest landscapes than in the ancient forest habitat to which it is adapted. Thus, logging increases the territorial requirements of individual owls while reducing forest acreage available to meet that increased need."

And an example of relevant ecological concepts: "Coverage of nontimber ecosystem services to humankind (e.g., clean water, game species habitat, fisheries, wild food, medicinal compounds found in plants) remind the public that forests are more than trees, and that exploitation of timber to the exclusion of other goods and services is an inefficient use of these publicly owned ecosystems. Heavy logging and road building on steep slopes in spotted owl habitat degrades stream water quality, smothers salmonid eggs with eroded silt, and is incompatible with other forest services for humans. . . ."

Furlow concluded the newspaper reporting he reviewed was conceptually shallow: "Complex issues such as the decline of a species require more than a polarized and superficial 'jobs versus environment' style of reporting. Informed consideration of environmental issues requires a basic comprehension of factors that the media provided minimally in the articles I analyzed for this study."

9. Hayes, letter to the author, August 10, 1996.

10. Jim Fisher, editorial writer and columnist of the *Lewiston (Idaho) Morning Tribune,* takes exception, writing in a letter to the author, August 9, 1996: "I

think of a paper like the *Lewiston Tribune,* which pursues neutral reporting (I dislike the misleading term 'objectivity') and vigorous editorial comment but still makes space available for all its writers, and any other employees to comment on any issue in a personal front-page column called Up Front. To date, no comeuppance has been delivered to anyone who has taken that opportunity."

11. Day, *Intermountain Observer.*

12. Shenk, "The Fame Game," *U.S. News and World Report* (October 6, 1997).

13. *Columbia Journalism Review* (March–April 1980).

14. Robert W. Snyder, "Virgins, Vamps and the Tabloid Mentality: A Prosecutor Contends That When Rape Makes News, the Press Offers Titillation, Not Education," *Media Studies Journal* (winter 1998).

15. Sax, interview by author, San Francisco, October 1988.

16. Sholly, with Steven M. Newman, *Guardians of Yellowstone* (New York: William Morrow, 1991), 239. In mid-September, surrounded by smoke on all sides but north, Sholly wondered if there would be enough time to evacuate Mammoth and Gardiner if the winds suddenly picked up. "And what kind of stories and pictures would those hundreds of journalists who had rushed here from Old Faithful be sending out next to the world? So far their accounts had been largely slanted to the dramatic, inaccurate about the extent of damage to the park, and nearly always simplistic and devoid of scientific data. The Associated Press, whose news items were repeated daily by thousands of newspapers and radio stations, had said most of the park was blackened. It, like the rest, never mentioned that over half of the vegetation in each burn area was not burned, or that five of the major fires had started outside the park, even though those points were made right on their reporters' fire map handouts each morning" (243–44).

And even after it was over, Sholly noted: "For months reporters continued to call to try to get the 'scoop' on whose head was going to the chopping block. The reporters didn't want to hear about ecology, but about politics and possible scandal. It was as if they couldn't bring themselves to believe that wildfires were mostly nature's doing, not some administrator's" (259).

17. Papers presented by Conrad Smith to International Communications Association, San Francisco, May 1989; Visual Communications Conference, June 26, 1989; Association for Education in Journalism and Mass Communication, Washington, D.C., August 1, 1989.

Sean D. Cassidy, a professor at Lewis-Clark State College in Idaho, earned a Ph.D. in telecommunications and film in 1992 at the University of Oregon based on his studies of the news media's presentation of information about Greenpeace. In the concluding chapter of his dissertation, Cassidy wrote: "Certain patterns governing the construction of stories about Greenpeace and nuclear-weapons testing were remarkably consistent between 1970 and 1990. The major patterns evident in the coverage of almost every antinuclear campaign included the following:

1. Emphasis on the event over the issue.

2. Little historical content given on the issue or event.

3. Omission of information on the health and environmental effects of nuclear testing.

4. Heavy preference given to statements by Government officials over those issued by Greenpeace representatives.

5. News media refusal to recognize the impact nuclear tests had on the people of the South Pacific."

Cassidy analyzed the difference in news coverage of Greenpeace protests against nuclear-weapons testing and protests against whale hunting. On one hand, the media loved the dramatic visuals of confrontation Greenpeace brought to stories of whaling, and clamored for more. On the other hand, Cassidy noted: "Obviously the threat of nuclear annihilation is of far greater importance than the extinction of whales, if for no other reason than a nuclear war would very likely kill off the whales as well as humankind. However, the different treatment the two issues received is about something more than the relative importance of a story. It is about the way news media process dissent. Despite journalists' claims of being objective observers of the events that make the news, the evidence collected here suggested the media's predisposition toward an issue is shaped by ideological assumptions, and these assumptions have a major impact on how stories related to that issue are framed in the news."

18. *Architecture Memphis* (March–April 1970).

19. "The Power of the Press Has a Price" is the title of an article in the July–August 1997 issue of *EXTRA!* written by Lawrence Roley, professor of communications at Marquette University, which identified advertisers, not government, as the principal news censors of the United States. He quoted Sandra Duerr, former president of the Society of American Business Editors and Writers (and business editor of the *Louisville Courier Journal*) as declaring: "Business journalists have always struggled against advertiser pressures, but our members are telling us it's getting worse." Roley himself surveyed 241 members of Investigative Reporters and Editors employed at commercial television stations, asking about "advertiser muscling of their news operations and their stations' responses to these pressures." Most respondents reported that advertisers had either tried to influence the contents or tried to kill news stories, or had threatened to withdraw advertising because of stories they did not like; most also confirmed pressure on news people from within the stations to please the advertisers.

20. Knecht, *Wall Street Journal,* April 30, 1997; *Wall Street Journal,* June 21, 1997.

21. Bagdikian, *The Media Monopoly,* ix.

22. See Robert W. McChesney, "The Global Media Giants," *Extra!* (November–December 1997), based on Robert W. McChesney and Edward S.

Herman, *The Global Media: The New Missionaries of Corporate Capitalism* (Washington, D.C.: Cassell, 1997).

Chapter 2

1. *BATS* (spring 1992).

2. Grizzly bears, wolves, and coyotes are particular species suffering from historic misunderstandings. J. Frank Dobie explains it simply and directly in *The Voice of the Coyote* (Lincoln: University of Nebraska, 1961): " 'I was wrathy to kill a bear,' David Crockett said, and that is essentially all one learns from the mightiest of frontier bear-hunters—except that he killed a hundred and five in one season and immediately thereafter got elected to the Tennessee legislature on his reputation. . . . The majority of country dwellers in western America today would consider it necessary to apologize for not killing a coyote they happened to see doing something unusual. This traditional killer attitude is a part of the traditional exploitation of the land" (x–xi).

The late J. Frank Dobie, one of the foremost writers of the American Southwest and longtime professor of English at the University of Texas, was among those who sparked a change in public attitude toward "unwanted wildlife," leading ultimately to more enlightened policies in our own time, including the successful reintroduction of wolves into Yellowstone National Park and (in 1997) proposed reintroduction of wolves into Olympic National Park. The 1989 film *The Bear* recounts the symbolic story of an enormous grizzly relentlessly pursued by a hunter. In their ultimate confrontation, the bear holds the upper hand but allows his prey to live and leave, with a new sense of human-wildlife balance.

3. In a letter published in the April 1967 issue of *American Forests*, Mrs. William W. Deupree, a leader of Citizens to Preserve Overton Park, wrote of her disappointment in the role of the local media: "Here is the saddest tale of all—the two papers are both Scripps-Howard but I think they stand behind the Downtown Association for fear of losing the advertising of 100 large firms. Mr. Meeman [Edward Meeman, editor emeritus of the *Press Scimitar*] saw this and stood by and grieved. We conservationists cannot even get a letter printed, and the news has been slanted to make the public think they can do nothing— that it is all settled. . . . If they had assigned one reporter to uncover the terrible greed that is sacrificing this park it would win an award anywhere on earth!"

4. John B. Oakes, "Adirondack SOS," *New York Times*, October 29, 1988; Cuomo, letter to the editor, *New York Times*, November 17, 1988.

5. Simons, *New York Times*, December 23, 1988.

6. Behm, Rown, and Marchionne, *Milwaukee Journal*, September 19–26, 1993.

7. See Andrew Scott, ed., *101 Computer-Assisted Stories from the IRE Morgue* (Columbia, Mo.: Investigative Reporters and Editors, 1993.) Many stories described in the book were entries in an IRE-sponsored awards competition; others came from files of the Institute of Computer-Assisted Reporting at the School of Journalism, University of Missouri.

CHAPTER 3

1. Muir, *Atlantic Monthly* (January 1898).

2. Carson, in a letter to a close friend, cited by Paul Brooks on the concluding page of *Speaking for Nature: How Literary Naturalists from Henry Thoreau to Rachel Carson Have Shaped America* (San Francisco: Sierra Club Books, 1983). Carson, after her statement that she could never be happy again in nature if she did not try to save it, continued: "But now I can believe that I have at least helped a little. It would be unrealistic to believe one book could bring a complete change." And then Brooks chose for himself the last word: "It may have been unrealistic, but history has proved it true."

3. Brooks, *The Pursuit of Wilderness* (Boston: Houghton Mifflin, 1971), 3–4.

4. *Bellingham (Wash.) Herald,* September 26, 1996.

5. Ibid.

6. William Strunk Jr., and E. B. White, *The Elements of Style,* 23. White cited this paragraph in the introduction in tribute to his mentor, William Strunk Jr., adding: "There you have a short, valuable essay on the nature and beauty of brevity—sixty-three words that could change the world." The same could be said for this little book of less than one hundred pages.

7. Gray, "Environmental Photography: A Tool for Advocacy," *Planet* (winter 1991): 8–10. In defining what he called "the essence of environmental photography," Gray referred to the work of his mentor: "Pat O'Hara's success as a master of the natural image has allowed him enough professional freedom to pursue two book projects that were truly labors of his love for the natural world. . . . The first, *Washington Wilderness: The Unfinished Work,* was instrumental in passage of the Washington Wilderness Act of 1984. *Washington's Wild Rivers: The Unfinished Work,* published last year [1990], aims to increase awareness of how the Wild and Scenic Rivers Act works; namely, what the act permits while still keeping the state's rivers free-flowing. Both books combine beautiful photographs of potentially threatened wildlands with descriptive prose, a common approach in environmental photography. As everyone familiar with *National Geographic* knows, the combining of word and image almost always produces a whole greater than the sum of its parts."

CHAPTER 4

1. Strunk and White, *Elements of Style,* 66–67.

2. Wallace Stegner, *The Uneasy Chair: A Biography of Bernard DeVoto,* 379–80.

3. *The Nation Looks at Its Resources,* Report of the Mid-Century Conference on Resources for the Future, December 2, 3, 4, 1953 (Washington, D.C.: Resources for the Future, 1954), 365–66.

4. Stegner, *The Uneasy Chair,* 314, 315.

5. Tarbell, *All in the Day's Work* (New York: Macmillan, 1939), 399.

6. Meeman, speech to the North American Wildlife Conference, 1965.

7. Oakes, interview by author, Washington, D.C., April 20, 1992.

8. Oakes, interview by author, New York, N.Y., June 10, 1992.

9. Evans, keynote address, Northwest Media and the Environment, Bellingham, Wash., October 15, 1993.

10. Egan, "In Battle over Public Lands, Ranchers Push Public Aside," *New York Times,* July 21, 1995.

11. Statement presented as part of a panel discussion at the conference Media and the Environment: Passion, Politics and Empowerment, conducted by the Association for Education in Journalism and Mass Communication, Reno, Nev., April 9, 1994.

12. Manning, *Northern Lights* (January 1990). In *Last Stand: Logging, Journalism, and the Case for Humility* (Salt Lake City: Peregrine Smith Books, 1991), Manning wrote that the editors called him in to offer a different beat. So he quit. He offered to stay a while, but the editor ordered checks cut and in an hour he was out the door (166–67).

13. Statement presented as part of a panel discussion at the conference Media and the Environment: Passion, Politics and Empowerment, conducted by the Association for Education in Journalism and Mass Communication, Reno, Nev., April 9, 1994.

14. After leaving the *Times,* Shabecoff initiated and became publisher of Greenwire, a daily environmental news service disseminated by fax, and an author. His first book, *A New Name for Peace,* was published by the University Press of New England in 1996.

15. Rose felt that he and his work were treated so badly that one day he walked out of the newspaper office with a colleague, the religious editor, and around the block and never went back to the office. Personal interview with the author at Yosemite National Park, September 1995.

16. Long, letter to the author, June 14, 1997.

17. Watkins, letter to the author, October 12, 1997.

18. Andrew Patner, *I. F. Stone: A Portrait* (New York: Pantheon Books, 1988), 161. See audiotape of Stone at the National Press Club, March 24, 1988. Patner's book includes the following from Stone: "Independence is always important in any society to combat the establishment mind. I have more stuff in print than any journalist of my time. And really, I think this stuff has made a contribution to the literature of American journalism. And I don't think many people have written that well. These big establishment figures—not that I'm against them, but I think my stuff is going to last longer than they can . . ." (162).

CHAPTER 5

1. Thomas Merton, *Raids on the Unspeakable* (New York: New Directions, 1964), 67. Father Merton was not in a cheerful mood when he wrote this beautiful yet disturbing Christmas meditation, which continues: "The primordial blessing, 'increase and multiply,' has suddenly become a hemorrhage of terror. We are numbered in billions, and massed together, marshaled, numbered,

marched here and there, taxed, drilled, armed, worked to the point of insensibility, dazed by information, drugged by entertainment, surfeited with everything, nauseated with the human race and with ourselves, nauseated with life. As the end approaches, there is no room for nature. The cities crowd it off the face of the earth" (70).

2. Stone, "Notes on Closing, but Not in Farewell," *I. F. Stone's Weekly* (December 14, 1971).

3. Hagood, "Hunters' Privilege—State Wildlife Agencies Cling to the Past," *HSUS News* (fall 1996).

4. Bloom, *The Closing of the American Mind* (New York: Simon & Schuster, 1987). In *Killing the Spirit: Higher Education in America* (New York: Viking Penguin, 1990), Page Smith notes: "In many universities, faculty members make no bones about the fact that students are the enemy. It is students who take up precious time that might otherwise be devoted to research. I have heard colleagues boast of having infrequent office hours at awkward times to avoid having contact with students outside the classroom. . . . 'Research' is a word without soul or substance, as broad as the ocean and as shallow as a pond. It covers a multitude of academic sins and conceals a poverty of spirit and a barrenness of intellect beyond calculating" (6–7).

5. Rogers, *On Becoming a Person: A Therapist's View of Psychotherapy* (Boston: Houghton Mifflin, 1961), 13.

6. *The Jungle,* by Upton Sinclair, first published in 1906, is a protest novel, an exposure of intolerable working and living conditions in the city of Chicago at the turn of the century. *The Jungle* conveyed information about the food the country was eating, the modern work process, how the city functioned, with its complex mesh of graft and corruption, and the poverty and degradation of its slums. Sinclair challenged powerful private interests and explosive issues: the Rockefellers and the coal industry in *King Coal* (1917), the Teapot Dome scandal and the oil industry in *Oil!* (1927), and the Sacco-Vanzetti case in *Boston* (1928).

Chapter 6

1. Burroughs wrote to his friend Myron Benton about comparison with Thoreau: "There is really little or no resemblance between us. . . . Thoreau's aim is mainly ethical. . . . my own aim, so far as I have any, is entirely artistic. . . . I will not preach one word" (cited in Brooks, *Speaking for Nature,* 11–12).

2. Burroughs, *The Summit of the Years* (Boston: Houghton Mifflin, 1913), 2–4.

3. *John Muir Summering in the Sierra,* ed. Robert Engberg, a collection of articles written by Muir for the *San Francisco Daily Evening Bulletin* in the years 1874–1875 (Madison: University of Wisconsin Press, 1984), xiii.

4. From remarks at the conference Northwest Media and the Environment, Bellingham, Wash., October 15–16, 1993.

5. From remarks at the Sierra Club Biennial Wilderness Conference, San

Francisco, April 7–9, 1967; see proceedings published as *Wilderness and the Quality of Life*, ed. Maxine E. McCloskey and James P. Gilligan (San Francisco: Sierra Club Books, 1969), 89.

At the 1967 conference the Sierra Club presented the John Muir Award to Sigurd Olson "in recognition of the excellence of his writing and leadership in conservation that we believe will truly make a difference a hundred years from now in the face of this land and in the mind of man."

6. Brooks, *The Pursuit of Wilderness,* 210. Besides editing the works of others, Brooks wrote magazine articles about endangered wilderness in the North Cascades, Alaska, Everglades, and East Africa, and the following books: *Roadless Area, The Pursuit of Wilderness, The House of Life: Rachel Carson at Work,* and *Speaking for Nature.* He served on the board of the Sierra Club.

7. Brooks, *The House of Life,* 5; Carson, *Silent Spring,* xiii.

8. Douglas, *The Everglades: River of Grass* (St. Simons Island, Ga.: Mockingbird Books, 1989), 300.

9. Kevin Proescholdt, Rip Rapson, and Miron L. Heinselman, *Troubled Waters* (St. Cloud, Minn.: North Star Press of St. Cloud, 1995), 120.

10. Abbey, *One Life,* 271. Dave Foreman, one of the founders of the militant Earth First! movement and a loyal Abbey ally, in *Confessions of an Eco-Warrior* (New York: Crown, 1991), pays this tribute: "Ed Abbey was the Mudhead Kachina of the conservation movement, perhaps of the whole goddamn social change movement in this country. . . . And thereby doing sacred work" (174).

Chapter 7

1. Brooks, *World of Washington Irving* (Cleveland, N.Y.: World Publishing, 1946), 68–69, 250–51. See Hans Huth, *Nature and the Americans* (Lincoln: University of Nebraska, 1972). "Like two giants, [James Fenimore] Cooper and Bryant opened the path for the early nineteenth-century approach to nature. . . . When Bryant died in 1878, [George W.] Curtis said of him: 'whoever saw Bryant saw America' " (35–36).

2. Whitman, *The Complete Poetry and Prose of Walt Whitman* (1948), 115.

3. James B. Trefethen, *Crusade for Wildlife* (Harrisburg, Pa.: Stackpole, 1961), 325–27.

4. Steffens, *The Autobiography of Lincoln Steffens,* 549.

5. Ibid., 786.

6. Brant, *Saturday Evening Post,* June 26, 1926.

7. Brant, *Adventures in Conservation,* ed. Ruth Brant Davis and Robin Brant Lodewick (Flagstaff, Ariz.: Northland, 1988), 15.

8. Ibid., 17.

9. Ibid., 74.

10. A letter to the author written May 12, 1972, shows Brant still going strong

at eighty-seven. He had just written half a dozen senators and congressmen, including the following text: "To my personal knowledge the triangular tie-up of the Forest Service, the American Forestry Association and the timber industry runs back at least to 1930, and I don't know how much further. In 1930 I testified at a supposedly impartial public hearing (unofficial) in Washington, D.C. on proposed additions to Yellowstone National Park, including part of the Jackson Hole area and Grand Tetons, now in the Grand Teton National Park. To my astonishment I found that this meeting was managed and rigged against the additions by Ovid Butler, editor of *American Forests* and formerly of the Forest Service."

Brant went on to describe the close liaison between the AFA and the West Coast Lumbermen's Association and the National Lumber Manufacturers Association. "Ovid Butler," he wrote, "served as undercover propaganda agent both of the timber interests and the Forest Service, while taking strong conservation stands on innocuous subjects."

11. Stegner, *The Uneasy Chair*, 321.

12. Ibid., 378.

13. See Steve Neal, ed., *They Never Go Back to Pocatello: The Selected Essays of Richard Neuberger* (Portland: Oregon Historical Society Press, 1988).

14. Meeman, *The Editorial We* (Memphis: Memphis State University Printing Services, 1976), 72.

15. Ibid., xvii.

16. Ibid., 129–34. This section of Meeman's autobiography begins: "I have two vantage points to observe what needs to be done and can be done in the field of conservation of nature and the recreation that grows out of such conservation. The first vantage point is the place where I live, Forest Farm, where I have learned what being close to nature can mean. The second is my job, that of the editor of a daily newspaper, in the midst of human affairs. At both vantage points, the opportunities for observation and activity growing out of that observation are unlimited, and I experience the embarrassment of riches."

17. Ibid., 131.

18. Oakes, "Conservation," *New York Times,* March 4, 1951.

19. *New York Times,* January 1, 1977.

20. *New York Times,* December 31, 1980; July 29, 1981; January 19, 1983; September 16, 1985; October 29, 1988.

21. Henry David, *Saturday Review* (August 31, 1963).

22. Hennessy, *Catholic Worker* (October–November 1997).

23. Robert Ellsberg, ed., *Dorothy Day: Selected Writings* (Maryknoll, N.Y.: Orbis, 1992), 87–95.

24. Ibid., xxxix.

25. Day, *Crossing the Line* (Baltimore: Fortkamp Publishing, 1991), 222–23.

CHAPTER 8

1. My fellow "dictation boys"—who took articles on the telephone from reporters on assignment at various bureaus around Washington—included Edwin Newman, later prominent on NBC-TV; William Umstead, who became managing editor of the *New York Daily News;* and Eugene Rachlis, a magazine and book editor.

2. Frome, *Washington Post,* June 2–June 6, 1946.

3. DeVoto, "Let's Close the National Parks," *Harper's* (October 1953).

4. The first was *Better Vacations for Your Money,* a Doubleday Book Club selection in 1959 and 1960. The second was *Washington: A Modern Guide to the Nation's Capital,* published in 1960. Other titles in this period included *Parade Turnpike Guide* (1957, 1958); *Parade Family Vacation Guide* (1960); *Kodak Guide to America's National Parks* (1969); and *Kodak Guide to Colonial America* (1970).

5. Samuel S. Vaughan, my editor at Doubleday, wrote to me on April 19, 1960: "One thing occurs to me having to do with your development as a writer: I hope you are reading carefully such works as will inspire you to the writing of beautiful and precise description. You are going to need all your lyrical resources when it comes to the national forests. What with writing for *Parade* and other publications fairly short on space, you have probably been urged to keep your style down to bare bones. This makes good, quick reading, but I think you can let yourself go a little bit more in book form."

6. Udall and Stansbury, Los Angeles Times Syndicate, August 7–8, 1971.

7. *Living Wilderness* (autumn 1971): 21–40.

8. Soucie, letter to Towell, April 22, 1971; Towell, letter to Soucie, April 26, 1971; Towell, letter to Edmiston, August 11, 1971, all included in ibid.

9. "A Voice in the Wilderness," *Time* (November 4, 1974): 56.

CHAPTER 9

1. Noland, letter to the author, January 15, 1998.

2. Frome, "A Writer Finds Hope," *High Country News* (April 2, 1984).

CHAPTER 10

1. Frome, *Whose Woods These Are* (Garden City, N.Y.: Doubleday, 1962; Boulder, Colo.: Westview, 1984), 106.

2. Frome, "America the Beautiful" *Changing Times* (November 1962).

3. Frome, "Predators, Prejudice, and Politics," *Field & Stream* (December 1967).

4. Frome, "Vindication of the Craigheads," in *Chronicling the West: Thirty Years of Environmental Writing* (Seattle: The Mountaineers, 1996), 140–43.

5. Frome, "We Are Loving Our National Parks to Death," *Sohioan* (spring 1972); Frome, "Ungreening the National Parks," *Travel Agent* (October 1981). An

early piece was the main editorial in the *Saturday Evening Post* of April 11, 1959, titled "Beer Halls at Gettysburg? Our National Shrines Need Protection!" The opening two paragraphs read: "The commercial invasion of Gettysburg and other Civil War battlefields demonstrates the need of a firm new policy regarding privately owned land within our national shrines. Without such a policy we shall witness the spread of residential subdivisions, automobile graveyards and beer halls in the midst of cherished historic areas. The traditional practice of buying one acre when 100 acres are threatened, and of depending on land donations from the states and wealthy public-spirited citizens, isn't good enough."

6. Frome, "Parks in Peril . . . Critical Problems Facing America's Wilderness," *Washington Post*, April 12, 1981; Frome, "Close Yellowstone!" *Chicago Tribune*, March 8, 1992.

7. Morris, letter to the author, January 9, 1975.

CHAPTER 11
1. Steinberg, "Do-It-Yourself Deathscape: The Unnatural History of Natural Disaster in South Florida," *Environmental History* (October 1997).

2. Ibid.; *Miami Herald*, July 28, 1936; *Miami Daily News*, November 5, 1935.

CHAPTER 12
1. Watkins, letter to the author, April 14, 1997.

2. Jefferson, letter to Randolph, December 26, 1808.

CHAPTER 13
1. Welcome, *Albuquerque Tribune*, November 15–17, 1993.

2. Carson, *Silent Spring*, 1.

3. Shabecoff, letter to the author, September 24, 1996.

4. McNamee, letter to the author, August 16, 1996.

5. McNamee, "Grass That Ate Sonora—Buffelgrass Changes the Face of the Desert," *Tucson Weekly*, April 18, 1996.

6. Shabecoff, letter to the author, September 24, 1996.

7. Selcraig, "The Filthy West," *High Country News* (September 16, 1996), 1, 5–9.

8. Ibid., 8.

9. Ibid., 8, 9.

10. Frome, "Neon Signs," *Parade* (December 14, 1958).

11. These four articles appeared in *Changing Times*, in November 1962, September 1963, July 1972, and October 1976, respectively.

12. Besides his work on air quality, Guthrie was active in the Izaak Walton League in South Florida, which rallied with other groups to defend Biscayne Bay against a proposed oil refinery on the mainland and a subdivision on the off-

shore keys. Public concern led to establishment of Biscayne National Monument in 1968 and the significantly enlarged Biscayne National Park in 1980.

13. Shabecoff, letter to the author, September 24, 1996.

Chapter 14

1. Udall, interview by author, Tucson, Ariz., 1987.

2. Helvarg, interview by author, Bellingham, Wash., November 1996.

3. Helvarg, *The War against the Greens*, 127.

4. Write the Reporters Committee for Freedom of the Press, 1101 Wilson Boulevard, Suite 1910, Arlington, VA 22209, for a copy of the booklet "How to Use the Federal FOI Act."

5. Frome, *Strangers in High Places* (Knoxville: University of Tennessee Press, 1994), 283.

6. Huxley College of Environmental Studies, a division of Western Washington University, conducted a two-day conference called Northwest Media and the Environment, October 15–16, 1993, on the campus at Bellingham, Wash.

7. Frome, "Poison Coverup in Tennessee," *Field & Stream* (January 1970), reprinted in Frome, *Conscience of a Conservationist: Selected Essays* (Knoxville: University of Tennessee Press, 1989), 60–69.

8. Cited in Frome, "Blowing the Whistle," *Center Magazine* (November–December 1978): 50–58.

9. Frome, *Promised Land* (Knoxville: University of Tennessee Press, 1994), 223.

10. Shabecoff, letter to the author, September 24, 1996.

Chapter 15

1. Manning, letter to the author, December 10, 1996.

2. Townsend, "Wired for Action," *Greenpeace Quarterly* (summer 1997).

3. Mander, *The Case against the Global Economy* (San Francisco: Sierra Club Books, 1996). See also Mander's other books, *In the Absence of the Sacred* (San Francisco: Sierra Club Books, 1992) and *Four Arguments for the Elimination of Television* (New York: William Morrow, 1978).

Chapter 16

1. Manning, letter to the author, December 10, 1996.

2. Stuebner, letter to the author, November 19, 1996.

3. Shabecoff, letter to the author, September 24, 1996.

4. Adolph Murie, *A Naturalist in Alaska* (New York: American Museum of Natural History, 1963), xii. Olaus Murie's foreword continues: "Our civilization is now going through a severe strain. We are trying to find our way, those of us who are concerned with it. And to do so, it behooves us to get serenity in order to think and get back to fundamentals for a clearer view into the future. I believe

such writing as this gives a view of truth combined with avenues of natural beauty, as a help toward a richer life."

5. "The Politics of Preserving Biodiversity," address by Peter H. Raven, at the plenary session of the forty-first annual meeting of the American Institute of Biological Sciences, Richmond, Va., August 5, 1990, published in *BioScience* (November 1990): 769–74.

6. Palca, "AAAS Observer," November 3, 1989.

7. Deborah Blum and Mary Knudson, eds., *Field Guide* (Oxford University Press, 1997), 227.

8. Ibid., 251–52.

9. Ibid., 231.

10. Dan Fagin and Marianne Lavelle, *How the Chemical Industry Manipulates Science* (Washington, D.C.: Birch Lane Press, 1997).

11. Sandra Steingraber, *Living Downstream: An Ecologist Looks at Cancer and the Environment.* Reading, Mass.: Addison Wesley Longman, 1997.

12. See Sandra Steingraber, "Trashed by the Company Doctor," in *SEJournal* (Society of Environmental Journalists), Winter 1998.

13. Sara Olason, Jenny Flynn, and Ruth Noellgen, "Principles of Good Science Writing."

CHAPTER 17

1. Stuebner, letter to the author, November 19, 1996.

2. Manning, letter to the author, December 10, 1996.

3. Helvarg, interview by author, Bellingham, Wash., September 12, 1996.

4. Laycock, letter to the author, January 30, 1998.

5. Mitchell, letter to the author, January 22, 1998.

6. Watkins, letter to the author, March 17, 1997.

7. Peterson, letter to the author, July 3, 1997.

8. Letter to the editor, *Fly Rod and Reel* (July 1996).

9. Zinsser, *On Writing Well,* 62–63.

10. Cox, *Maine Times,* July 15, 1994.

CHAPTER 18

1. *High Country News,* June 10, 1996.

2. Marston, letter to the author, January 10, 1996.

3. Ibid.

4. Koberstein, interview by author, Portland, Oreg., May 10, 1996.

5. McCarthy, *Washington Post,* January 7, 1997.

6. Espinoza, *San Francisco Bay Guardian,* June 28, 1995.

7. Yant, *IRE Journal* (March–April 1996).

Chapter 19

1. Foster, interview by author, Seattle, Wash., March 9, 1997.
2. Ibid.
3. Turner, letter to the author, April 20, 1996.
4. Ibid.
5. Ibid.
6. Helvarg, interview by author, Bellingham, Wash., September 12, 1996.
7. Meyer, interview by author, Lewiston, Idaho, April 20, 1995.
8. Oko, letter to the author, January 7, 1997.
9. Ibid.
10. Mitchell, "Unfinished Redwood," in *Dispatches from the Deep Woods,* 148–49.
11. Mitchell, interview by author, Missoula, Mont., April 20, 1997; Mitchell, letter to the author, May 8, 1997.
12. Noland, letter to the author, January 12, 1998.
13. Noland, *Planet* (spring 1990).

Chapter 20

1. Williams, letter to the author, July 7, 1996.
2. Contact the Outdoor Writers Association of America at 2017 Cato Avenue, Suite 101, State College, PA 16801, or call them at (814) 234–1011. Contact the Fund for Investigative Journalism at 1755 Massachusetts Avenue NW, Washington, D.C. 20036, or call them at (202) 464–1844.
3. Society of Environmental Journalists, P.O. Box 27280, Philadelphia, PA 19118; (215) 247-9712. See Karl Grossman, "Saving the Earth Isn't Their Job: Rachel Carson Wouldn't Recognize Many 'Environmental Journalists' Today," *EXTRA!* (January–February 1997), in which he says: "Much of the SEJ, a group now consisting of more than 1,000 journalists who cover environmental issues, has a problem with investigative journalism—or anything else that could be labeled 'advocacy.' Later in the day [at a 1996 conference to consider the organization's future direction], Noel Grove, the incoming editor of the group's quarterly publication, *SEJ Journal,* asked the assemblage whether they thought it · would be a good idea for the publication to go from being printed on 30 percent to 100 percent recycled paper. 'That would be advocacy!' came a chorus in reply."

The May–June 1997 issue of *EXTRA!* published a letter responding to Grossman from Jim Detjen, founding president of the SEJ, which included: "I agree wholeheartedly with Karl's view about the importance of investigative journalism. But I don't believe that SEJ should 'advocate' any specific stand on an environmental issue. SEJ has grown in importance and stature because the organization is seen by most as an independent organization that does not espouse any particular point of view on any environmental issues."

4. Investigative Reporters and Editors, Inc., 100 Neff Hall, School of Journalism, University of Missouri, Columbia, MO 65211; (573) 882-2042.

5. In 1991 when Defenders of Wildlife tried to initiate dialogue by joining the Outdoor Writers Association of America, a large element of the association felt that Defenders must be antihunting and moved to expel it. Defenders voluntarily withdrew. "All we had in mind was an occasional exchange of views," read the farewell letter. "Yours for diversity, biological and otherwise, M. Rupert Cutler, President." Joel Vance, who had just finished his term as OWAA president, wrote: "For shame! We've run off a group that wanted to communicate with us . . . and we call ourselves communicators? We're just a bunch of hypocrites who can't stand a contrary view."

6. American Society of Journalists and Authors, 1501 Broadway, Suite 302, New York, NY 10036; (212) 997-0947.

7. Authors Guild, Inc., 330 West Forty-second Street, New York, NY 10036; (212) 563-5904.

Du Pont, 80
Dubois, Mark, 119, 120
Duerr, Sandra, 179
Durbin, Kathie, 30, 31, 34, 35, 39, 40, 150

E, 139
eagles, 74, 75, 90, 108, 126, 146
Earth Day, 4, 38, 84
Earth First!, 148
Earth First! Journal, 136, 148
Earth Island Institute, 14, 159
EarthJustice Legal Defense Fund, 159
East/West Network, 80
Easterbrook, Gregg, 176
Eastern Airlines, 107, 108
"Easy Chair," 59, 60
Ecological Perspectives, 23
Ecology Center Productions, 154
Edge of the Sea, The, 46
Edge, Rosalie, 57, 58
Edison, Thomas A., 44
Editorial We, The, 61
Edmiston, Beulah, 78
Egan, Timothy, 29
Ehrlich, Paul, 94, 128
Einstein, Albert, 126
Eiseley, Loren, 131, 134
Eisenhower, Dwight D., 25, 60, 96, 111
Elements of Style, The, 22, 24, 170, 181
Ellsworth Bill, 25
Elsevier, Reed, 12
Emergency Conservation Committee, 57–59
Emerson, Ralph Waldo, 35, 37, 94
Endangered Species Act, 18
Engberg, Robert, 43
Enviro Close-Up, 154
EnviroLink, 122
"Environment Hawaii," 149, 150
Environmental Action, 79
Environmental Protection Agency, U.S., 17, 104–106, 130
EnviroVideo, 153
Escalante Canyon, 158
Espinoza, Martin, 152
Esquire, 60
Eugene (Oregon) *Register-Guard*, xi, xii
Evans, Dan, 4, 27, 28

Evans, Howard Ensign, 131, 134
Everglades, x, xi, 48, 49
Everglades National Park, 48
Everglades: River of Grass, The, 48
EXTRA!, 2, 3
Exxon, 8, 79

Fairness and Accuracy in Reporting, 2, 176
Fairstein, Linda, 7
Family Circle, 15
Faulkner, William, 35, 146
Federal Bureau of Investigation, 32, 148, 159
Federal Bureau of Land Management, 29
Feynman, Richard P., 133
Field & Stream, 54, 55, 74, 75, 78–81, 89, 92, 93, 115, 117, 140
Field Guide for Science Writers, A, 128, 129
Final Jeopardy, 7
Fish and Wildilfe Service, U.S., 46, 104, 116, 117
Fisher, Jim, 177, 178
Flagpole, 151, 152
Fletcher, Alice Cunning, 35, 36
Flicker, John, 140
Fly Rod and Reel, 141
Ford, Gerald, 75
Ford, Henry, 44
Ford Motor Co., xi, 12
Foreman, Dave, 184
Forest and Stream, 54
Forest Service, U.S., 5, 25, 58, 75–77, 114, 117, 147, 185. *See also*, national forests
forestry, 4, 30, 36, 37, 39, 55, 76, 94, 117; and monoculture, 116, 159
formaldehyde, 130
Fortune, 171
Foster, Margaret, 155–157
Fradkin, Philip, 29
Frank, Barney, 22
Fraser Bill, 49
Fraser, Don, 49
Free Willy, 14
Free Willy Foundation, 14
Freedom of Information Act, 103, 114, 117, 188

National Academy of Science, 47
National Agricultural Chemical Association, 48
National Association of Science Writers, 129
National Audubon Society, 5, 54, 108, 140, 162, 164, 169
National Communicable Disease Center, 117
National Council on State Parks, 62
national forests, 31, 58, 59, 73, 75, 154, 162. *See also* U.S. Forest Service
National Geographic, 137–39, 164
National Institute for Computer-Assisted Reporting (NICAR), 123
National Park Service, 62, 73, 91, 152
National Parks, 90, 140
national parks, 48, 59, 73, 79, 86, 91, 92, 107, 111: attacked, 18; discovered, 72; hunting in eliminated, 54; privatization of, 152; transfer of suggested, 58
National Parks Advisory Board, 72
National Parks and Conservation Association, 48, 49, 91
National Pest Control Association, 117
National Press Club, 32, 123
National Public Radio, 128
National Rifle Association, 159
National Wilderness Preservation System, 62
National Wildlife, 138, 140
National Wildlife Federation, 117
national wildlife refuges, 18
Native Neighborhoods, 122
Naturalist in Alaska, A, 127
Nature and the Americans, 184
Nature Conservancy, 140
Navajo Reservation, 162
Naval Petroleum Reserve, Tupman, Calif., 106
Nazi movement, 152
NBC (National Broadcasting Corp.), 9, 153, 157
Negri, Sharon, 119, 120
Nelson, Gaylord, 73
NetAction, 123
"NetAction Notes," 123
Neuberger, Richard L., 59–61, 73, 185

Never Cry Wolf (film), 11, 12
New England Journal of Medicine, 130
New Masses, 97
New Melones Dam, 119
New Name for Peace, A, 182
New Republic, 97
"New Sage," 84
New York Commercial Advertiser, 44, 55, 56
New York Evening Post, 52, 53, 55
New York Journal-American, 162, 163
New York Times, 2, 3, 6, 16, 17, 27, 29, 31, 46, 60, 62, 63, 66, 72, 104, 105, 114, 122, 136, 140, 175, 176
New Yorker, 47, 153
Newman, Edwin, 186
Newman, Steven M., 178
News Corporation, 13
Newsday, 152
Newsweek, 95, 163, 164
newsweeklies, alternative, 151, 152
Niagara (NY) *Gazette*, 63
Niemann Fellowship, 60
Night Comes to the Cumberlands, 64
Noland, Sara Olason, 45, 46, 83, 165, 166
Noranda, 7, 8
North Carolina Wildlife Resources Commission, 89
Northeast Regional Pest Coordinators, 117
Northwest Media and the Environment, conference, 4, 28, 115
Not Man Apart, 158, 159
nuclear weapons, 66, 67, 122, 178, 179
Nukes in Space, 154
Nukewatch, 67
Nussbaum, Elena, 155

O'Hara, Pat, 181
O'Neill, Roger, 9
Oakes, John B., 27–29, 62, 63, 72
Oakland (Calif.) Police Department, 148
"Objectivity," 40
Odum, Eugene, 128
Ogden Corporation, 175
Ohio Environmental Council, 153
Ohio Observer, 153
Oil!, 183